RICA Reading Instruction Competence Assessment

Teacher Certification Exam

By Sharon Wynne, M.S
Southern Connecticut State University

"And, while there's no reason yet to panic, I think it's only prudent that we make preparations to panic."

XAMonline, Inc.

Boston

To obtain permission(s) to use the material from this work for any purpose including workshops or seminars, please submit a written request to:

XAMonline, Inc.
21 Orient Ave.
Melrose, MA 02176
Toll Free 1-800-509-4128
Email: info@xamonline.com
Web www.xamonline.com
Fax: 1-781-662-9268

Library of Congress Cataloging-in-Publication Data

Wynne, Sharon A.
    Reading Instruction Competence Assessment:
    Teacher Certification / Sharon A. Wynne. 2nd ed. ISBN 978-1-58197-595-6
    1. Reading Instruction Competence Assessment.   2. Study Guides.
    3. RICA   4. Teachers' Certification & Licensure.   5. Careers

Disclaimer:

The opinions expressed in this publication are the sole works of XAMonline and were created independently from the National Education Association, Educational Testing Service, or any State Department of Education, National Evaluation Systems or other testing affiliates.

Between the time of publication and printing, state specific standards as well as testing formats and website information may change that is not included in part or in whole within this product. Sample test questions are developed by XAMonline and reflect similar content as on real tests; however, they are not former tests. XAMonline assembles content that aligns with state standards but makes no claims nor guarantees teacher candidates a passing score. Numerical scores are determined by testing companies such as NES or ETS and then are compared with individual state standards. A passing score varies from state to state.

Printed in the United States of America   œ-1

RICA: Reading Instruction Competence Assessment
ISBN: 978-1-58197-595-6

Table of Contents

About the Test

The RICA consists of two separate assessments: the RICA Written Examination and the RICA Video Performance Assessment. Both the Written Examination and the Video Performance Assessment are based on the RICA Content Specifications. A passing score on either assessment represents successful completion of the RICA requirement. A passing score must be used to apply for California certification within five years of the test date or submission deadline on which the score was earned.

RICA Written Examination: The RICA Written Examination consists of two sections that, together, permit a broad and deep assessment of the candidate's knowledge about effective reading instruction in the four RICA domains and the candidate's ability to apply that knowledge.

The multiple-choice section of the RICA Written Examination includes 70 multiple-choice questions.

The constructed-response section of the RICA Written Examination requires the candidate to write essays, as described below.

- o Focused Educational Problems and Instructional Tasks (4 essays, each covering one domain).

- o Case Study (1 essay).

RICA Video Performance Assessment: The RICA Video Performance Assessment offers candidates the option of an evaluation based on actual classroom performance rather than a written examination. Candidates who choose the Video Performance Assessment create and submit videotapes of themselves teaching reading.

The RICA Video Performance Assessment requires the candidate to prepare three Video Packets.

For one Video Packet, the candidate must demonstrate whole-class instruction; for another, small-group instruction; and for the third, individual instruction. One Video Packet should demonstrate competencies in RICA Domains I and II, one should demonstrate competencies in RICA Domains I and III, and one should demonstrate competencies in RICA Domains I and IV.

- • For all additional information on submissions, test dates and program details visit the RICA website at: **http://www.rica.nesinc.com**

Great Study and Testing Tips!

What to study in order to prepare for the subject assessments is the focus of this study guide but equally important is *how* you study.

You can increase your chances of truly mastering the information by taking some simple but effective steps.

Study Tips:

1. Some foods aid the learning process. Foods such as milk, nuts, seeds, rice, and oats help your study efforts by releasing natural memory enhancers called CCKs (cholecystokinin) composed of tryptophan, choline, and phenylalanine. All of these chemicals enhance the neurotransmitters associated with memory. Before studying, try a light, protein-rich meal of eggs, turkey, and fish. All of these foods release the memory-enhancing chemicals. The better the connections, the more you comprehend.

Likewise, before you take a test, stick to a light snack of energy boosting and relaxing foods. A glass of milk, a piece of fruit, or some peanuts all release various memory-boosting chemicals and help you to relax and focus on the subject at hand.

2. Learn to take great notes. A by-product of our modern culture is that we have grown accustomed to getting our information in short doses (i.e. TV news sound bites or *USA Today*-style newspaper articles.)

Consequently, we've subconsciously trained ourselves to assimilate information better in neat little packages. If you scrawl notes all over the paper, you fragment the flow of the information. Strive for clarity. Newspapers use a standard format to achieve clarity. Your notes can be much clearer through use of proper formatting. A very effective format is called the Cornell Method.

- Take a sheet of loose-leaf lined notebook paper and draw a line all the way down the paper about 1-2" from the left-hand edge.

- Draw another line across the width of the paper about 1-2" up from the bottom. Repeat this process on the reverse side of the page.

Look at the highly effective result. You have ample room for notes, a left-hand margin for special emphasis items or inserting supplementary data from the textbook, a large area at the bottom for a brief summary, and a little rectangular space for just about anything you want.

3. Get the concept, and then the details. Too often we focus on the details and don't gather an understanding of the concept. However, if you simply memorize only dates, places, or names, you may well miss the whole point of the subject.

A key way to understand things is to put them in your own words. If you are working from a textbook, automatically summarize each paragraph in your mind. If you are outlining text, don't simply copy the author's words.

Rephrase them in your own words. You remember your own thoughts and words much better than someone else's, and you subconsciously tend to associate the important details to the core concepts.

4. Ask Why. Pull apart written material paragraph by paragraph and don't forget the captions under the illustrations.

Example: If the heading is "Stream Erosion," flip it around to read "Why do streams erode?" Then answer the questions.

If you train your mind to think in a series of questions and answers, not only will you learn more but you will also lessen the test anxiety because you are used to answering questions.

5. Read for reinforcement and future needs. Even if you only have 10 minutes, put your notes or a book in your hand. Your mind is similar to a computer; you have to input data in order to have it processed. *By reading, you are creating the neural connections for future retrieval.* The more times you read something, the more you reinforce the learning of ideas.

Even if you don't fully understand something on the first pass, *your mind stores much of the material for later recall.*

6. Relax to learn so go into exile. Our bodies respond to an inner clock called biorhythms. Burning the midnight oil works well for some people, but not everyone.

If possible, set aside a particular place to study that is free of distractions. Shut off the television, cell phone, and pager and exile your friends and family during your study period.

If you really are bothered by silence, try background music. Light classical music at a low volume has been shown to aid in concentration.

Music that evokes pleasant emotions without lyrics are highly suggested. Try just about anything by Mozart. It relaxes you.

7. <u>Use arrows, not highlighters</u>. At best, it's difficult to read a page full of yellow, pink, blue, and green streaks.

Try staring at a neon sign for a while and you'll soon see my point; the horde of colors obscures the message.

A quick note: a brief dash of color, an underline, and an arrow pointing to a particular passage are much clearer than a horde of highlighted words.

8. <u>Budget your study time</u>. Although you shouldn't ignore any of the material, *allocate your available study time in the same ratio that topics may appear on the test.*

Testing Tips:

1. <u>Get smart, play dumb</u>. Don't read anything into the question. Don't assume that the test writer is looking for something other than what is asked. Stick to the question as written and don't read extra things into it.

2. <u>Read the question and all the choices *twice* before answering the question</u>. You may miss something by not carefully reading and then rereading both the question and the answers.

If you really don't have a clue as to the right answer, leave it blank on the first time through. Go on to the other questions as they may provide a clue on how to answer the skipped questions.

If later on, you still can't answer the skipped ones . . . *Guess.* The only penalty for guessing is that you *might* get it wrong. Only one thing is certain; if you don't put anything down, you will get it wrong!

3. <u>Turn the question into a statement</u>. Look at the way the questions are worded. The syntax of the question usually provides a clue. Does it seem more familiar as a statement rather than as a question? Does it sound strange?

By turning a question into a statement, you may be able to spot if an answer sounds right, and it may also trigger memories of material you have read.

4. <u>Look for hidden clues</u>. It's actually very difficult to compose multiple-foil (choice) questions without giving away part of the answer in the options presented.

In most multiple-choice questions you can often readily eliminate one or two of the potential answers. This leaves you with only two real possibilities and automatically your odds go to fifty-fifty for very little work.

5. <u>Trust your instincts</u>. For every fact that you have read, you subconsciously retain something of that knowledge. On questions that you aren't certain about, go with your basic instincts. **Your first impression on how to answer a question is usually correct.**

6. <u>Mark your answers directly on the test booklet</u>. Don't bother trying to fill in the optical scan sheet on the first pass through the test.
Just be very careful not to mismark your answers when you eventually transcribe them to the scan sheet.

7. <u>Watch the clock</u>! You have a set amount of time to answer the questions. Don't get bogged down trying to answer a single question at the expense of 10 questions you can more readily answer.

Foundations of Reading

"Any child, who doesn't learn how to read early and well, will not easily master other skills and knowledge and is unlikely to ever flourish in school or in life." "Reading is Rocket Science," American Federation of Teachers

"If our teaching of reading is to be an art, we need to draw from all we know, think and believe in order to create something beautiful."
Lucy Calkins

This guide was developed to serve the needs of test takers on the Pre-K-6 level who are preparing for the Foundations of Reading certification test. The quotes which introduce this work point to the crucial nature and significance of effective teaching of reading for our children and our nation's future.

The competencies and skills shared in this guide are also intended to support the educator new to reading certification in ongoing teaching and learning in reading. Therefore, sample strategies, web resources, student trade books, picture book citations, and explanations of ready-to-use practices are included.

This guide had a specified page limit and is designed for immediate use. The web resources and bibliographies provided will allow the reader to keep up with new research or investigate a particular strategy, referenced theorist, or term in a deeper, more detailed fashion. In addition, in the Appendix is a dictionary of words and terms essential to your knowledge base as a reading teacher. Yet another study guide, a directory of key reading theorists, is included for your use as well.

My hope is that this study guide will merit placement in your home or on your classroom professional library shelf for use as you begin your teaching career. Enjoy and share with your colleagues and parents as we work together to nurture lifelong readers and writers.

Please let XAMonline know how you are able to use this guide to help you in your teacher certification experience and in your ongoing or future teaching and learning.

DOMAIN I. **PLANNING AND ORGANIZING READING INSTRUCTION BASED ON ONGOING ASSESSMENT**

COMPETENCY 1.0 **CONDUCTING ONGOING ASSESSMENT OF READING DEVELOPMENT**

Skill 1.1 Principles of assessment

Assessment is the practice of collecting information about children's progress, and evaluation is the process of judging the children's responses to determine how well they are achieving particular goals or demonstrating reading skills.

Assessment and evaluation are intricately connected in the literacy classroom. Assessment is necessary because teachers need ways to determine what students are learning and how they are progressing. In addition, assessment can be a tool which can also help students take ownership of their own learning and become partners in their ongoing development as readers and writers. In this day of public accountability, clear, definite and reliable assessment creates confidence in public education. There are two broad categories of assessment.

Formal assessment is composed of standardized tests and procedures carried out under circumscribed conditions. Formal assessments include state tests, standardized achievement tests, NAEP tests, and the like. **Informal assessment** uses observations and other non-standardized procedures to compile anecdotal and observation data/evidence of children's progress. It includes but is not limited to checklists, observations, and performance tasks.

To be effective, assessment should have the following characteristics:

1. It should be an ongoing process with the teacher making informal or formal assessments on an ongoing basis. The assessment should be a natural part of the instruction and not intrusive.

2. The most effective assessment is integrated into ongoing instruction. Throughout the teaching and learning day, the children's written, spoken and reading contributions to the class or lack thereof need to and can be continually noted.

3. Assessment should reflect the children's actual reading and writing experiences. The children should be able to show that they can read and explain or react to a similar literary or expository work.

4. Assessment needs to be a collaborative and reflective process. Teachers can learn from what the children reveal about their own individual assessments. Children, even as early as grade two, should be supported by their teacher to ask themselves questions continually and routinely to assess their reading. They might ask: "Am I understanding what the author wanted to say?" "What can I do to improve my reading?" "How can I use what I have read to learn more about this topic?" Teachers need to be informed by their own professional observation *and* by children's comments as teachers assess and customize instruction for children.

5. Quality assessment is multidimensional and may include but not be limited to samples of writings, student retellings, running records, anecdotal teacher observations, self-evaluations, and records of independent reading. From this multidimensional data, the teacher can derive a consistent level of performance and design additional instruction that will enhance the child's reading performance.

6. Assessment must take into account children's ages and ethnic/cultural patterns of learning.

7. Assessment should help teach children from their strengths, not their weaknesses. Find out what reading behaviors children demonstrate well and then design instruction to support those behaviors.

Assessment should be part of children's learning process and not done *to* them, but rather done *with* them.

Formal Assessment

Criterion-referenced are tests where the children are measured against criteria or guidelines which are uniform for all the test takers. Therefore by definition, no special questions, formats or considerations are made for the test taker who is either from a different linguistic/cultural background or is already identified as a struggling reader/writer. On a criterion-referenced test, a child test taker can possibly score 100% because the child may have actually been exposed to all of the concepts taught and mastered them. A child's score on such a test would indicate which concepts have already been taught and what needs additional review or support to master.

Two criterion-referenced tests that are commonly used to assess children's reading achievement are the Diagnostic Indicators of Basic Early Literacy Skills (DIBELS) and the Stanford Achievement Test. DIBELS measures progress in literacy from kindergarten to grade three. It can be downloaded from the Internet free at dibels.uoregon.edu. The Stanford is designed to measure individual children's achievement in key school subjects. Subtests covering various reading skills are part of this test. Both DIBELS and the Stanford Achievement Test are group-administered.

Degrees of Reading Power (DRP)—This test is targeted to assess how well children understand the meaning of written text in real life situations. This test is supposed to measure the process of children's reading, not the products of reading such as identifying the main idea and author's purpose.

CTPIII—This is a criterion-referenced test which measures verbal and quantitative ability in grades 3-12. It is targeted to help differentiate among the most capable students, i.e., those who rank above the 80th percentile on other standardized tests. This is a test that emphasizes higher order thinking skills and process-related reading comprehension questions.

Norm-referenced tests measure children against one another. Scores on this test are reported in percentiles. Each percentile indicates the percent of the testing population whose scores were lower than or the same as a particular child's score. Percentile is defined as a score on a scale of 100 showing the percentage of a distribution that is equal to it or below it. This type of state standardized norm-referenced test is being used in most districts today in response to the No Child Left Behind Act. While this type of test does not help track the individual reader's progress in ongoing reading development, it does permit comparisons across groups.

There are many more standardized norm-referenced tests to assess children's reading than there are criterion-referenced. In these norm-referenced tests, scores are based on how well a child does compared to others, usually on the local, state and national level. If the norming groups on the tests are reflective of the children being tested (e.g. same spread of minority, low income, gifted students), the results are more trustworthy.

One of the best known norm-referenced tests is the Iowa Test of Basic Skills. It assesses student achievement in various school subjects and has several subtests in reading. Other examples of norm-referenced tests used around the country are the Metropolitan Achievement Tests, the Terra Nova-2, and the Stanford Diagnostic Reading Test-4. These are all group tests. An individual test that reading specialists use with students is the Woodcock Reading Mastery Test.

Concepts of Validity, Reliability, and Bias in Testing

Validity is how well a test measures what it is supposed to measure. Teacher-made tests are therefore not generally extremely valid although they may be an appropriate measure for the validity of the concept the teacher wants to assess for children's achievement.

Reliability is the consistency of the test. This is measured by whether the test will indicate the same score for the child who takes it more than once.

Bias in testing occurs when the information within the test or the information required to respond to a multiple choice question or constructed response (essay question on the test) is information that is not available to some test takers who come from a different cultural, ethnic, linguistic, or socio-economic background than do the majority of the test takers. Since they have not had the same prior linguistic, social, or cultural experiences that the majority of test takers have had, these test takers are at a disadvantage in taking the test and, no matter what their actual mastery of the material taught by the teacher, can not address the "biased" questions. Generally other "non-biased" questions are given to them and eventually the biased questions are removed from the examination.

To clarify what might be abstract to the reader about bias, let's consider an example. On a recent reading test in my school system, the grade four reading comprehension multiple choice asked questions about the well known fairy tale of the Gingerbread Boy. These questions were simple and accessible for most of the children in the class. But two children who were recent new arrivals from the Dominican Republic had learned English there. They were reading on grade four level, but in their Dominican grade school, the story of the Gingerbread Boy was not a major one. Therefore a question about this story on the standardized reading test did demonstrate examiner bias and was not fair to these test takers.

Informal Assessments

A running record of children's oral reading progress in the early grades K-3 is a pivotal informal assessment. It supports the teacher in deciding whether a book is matched to the child's stage of reading development. In addition this assessment allows the teacher to analyze a child's miscues to see which cueing systems and strategies the child uses and to determine which other systems the child might use more effectively. Finally the running record offers a graphic account of a child's oral reading.

Generally, a teacher should maintain an annotated class notebook with pages set aside for all the children or individual notebooks for each child. One of the benefits of using running records as an informal assessment is that they can be used with any text and can serve as a tool for teaching, rather than an instrument to report on children's status in class.

Another good point about using running records is that they can be taken repeatedly and frequently by the teacher, so that the educator can truly observe a pattern of errors. This in turn provides the educator with sufficient information to analyze the child's reading over time. As any mathematician or scientist knows, the more samples of a process you gather over time, the more likely the teacher is to get an accurate picture of the child's reading needs.

Using the notations which Marie Clay developed and shared in her *An Observation Study of Early Literacy Achievement*, Sharon Taberski details in her book, *On Solid Ground*, how to keep a running record of children's reading. She writes in the child's miscue on the top line of her running record above the text word. Indeed she records all of the child's miscue attempts on the line above the text word. Sharon advises the teacher to make all the miscue notations as the child reads, since this allows the teacher to get additional information about how and why the child makes miscue choices. Additionally, the teacher should note self corrections (coded SC) when the child is monitoring his/her own reading, crosschecks information, and uses additional information.

As part of the informal assessment of primary grade reading, it is important to record the child's word insertions, omissions, requests for help, and attempts to get the word. In informal assessment the rate of accuracy can be estimated by dividing the child's errors by the total words read.

Results of a running record assessment can be used to select the best setting for the child's reading. If a child reads from 95%-100% correct, the child is ready for independent reading. If the child reads from 92% to 97% right, the child is ready for guided reading. Below 92% the child needs a read-aloud or shared reading activity. Note that these percentages are slightly different from those one would use to match books to readers.

One of the increasingly popular and meaningful forms of informal assessment is the compilation of the literacy portfolio. What is particularly compelling about this type of informal portfolio is that artists, television directors, authors, architects and photographers use portfolios in their careers and jobs. This is a most authentic format for documenting children's literacy growth over time. The portfolio is not only a significant professional informal assessment tool for the teacher but also a vehicle and format for the child readers to take ownership of their individual progress over time. It models a way of compiling one's reading and writing products as a lifelong learner, which is the ultimate goal of reading instruction.

Portfolios can include the following categories of materials:

Work Samples include children's story maps, webs, K-W-L charts, pictures, illustrations, storyboards, and writings about the stories which they have read.

Records of independent Reading and Writing include the children's journals, notebooks or logs of books read with the names of the authors, titles of the books, date completed, and pieces related to books completed or in progress.

Checklists and Surveys include checklists designed by the teacher for reading development, writing development, ownership checklists, and general interest surveys.

Self Evaluation Forms are the children's own evaluations of their reading and writing process framed in their own words. They can be simple templates with starting sentences such as: "I am really proud of the way I …

I feel one of my strengths as a reader is _____

To improve the way I read aloud I need to _____

To improve my reading I should _____

Generally at the beginning of a child's portfolio in grade 3 or above there is a letter to the reader explaining the work that will be found in the portfolio; from fourth grade level up, children write a brief reflection detailing their feelings and judgments about their growth as readers and writers.

When teachers are maintaining the portfolios for mandated school administrative review, district review, or even for their own research, they often prepare portfolio summary sheets. These provide identifying data on the children and then a timeline of the teachers' review of the portfolio contents plus professional comments on the extent to which the portfolio documents are satisfactory and reflect ongoing growth in reading.

Portfolios can be used beneficially for child/teacher and of course parent/teacher conversations to review the child's progress, discuss areas of strength, set future goals, make plans for future learning activities and evaluate what should remain in the portfolio and what needs to be cleared out for new materials.

Rubrics are quantifiable scales in assessment. Holistic scoring involves assessing a child's ability to construct meaning through writing. It uses a scale called a rubric which can range from 0 to 4.

0: This indicates the piece can not be scored. It does not respond to the topic or is illegible.

1: The writing does respond to the topic but does not cover it accurately.

2: This piece of writing does respond to the topic but lacks sufficient details or elaboration.

3: This piece fulfills the purpose of the writing assignment and has sufficient development (which refers to details, examples, and elaboration of ideas).

4: This response has the most details, best organization, and presents a well expressed reaction to the original writer's piece.

Miscue Analysis is a procedure that allows the teacher a look at the reading process. By definition, the miscue is an oral response different from the text being read. Sometimes miscues are also called unexpected responses or errors. By studying a student's miscues from an oral reading sample, the teacher can determine which cues and strategies the student is correctly using or not using in constructing meaning. Of course, the teacher can customize instruction to meet the needs of this particular student.

Informal Reading Inventories (IRI) are a series of samples of texts prearranged in stages of increasing difficulty. Listening to children read through these inventories, the teacher can pinpoint their skill level and the additional concepts they need to work on.

Group Versus Individual Reading Assessments

In assessment, tests are used for different purposes. They have different dimensions or characteristics whether they are given individually or in a group and whether they are standardized or teacher-made. The chart below shows the relationships of these elements.

	Standardized	**Teacher-made**
Individual	*Characteristics* • is uniformly administered *Uses* • is best for younger children • helps with placement for special services	*Characteristics* • has more flexibility *Uses* • assists teaching decisions • used for diagnostic purposes
Group	*Characteristics* • is uniformly administered • is time efficient *Uses* • permits comparisons across groups • used for policy decisions by administrators	*Characteristics* • has high face validity • is time efficient *Uses* • informs teach-reteach & enrichment decisions • documents students' learning

Skill 1.2   Assessing reading levels

Determining Students' Independent, Instructional, and Frustration Reading Levels

Instructional reading is generally judged to be at the 95 percent accuracy level, although researcher and educator Sharon Taberski places it between 92 and 97 percent. Taberski tries to enhance the independent reading levels by making sure that readers on the instructional reading levels read a variety of genres and have a range of available and interesting books within a particular genre to read.

Taberski's availability for reading conferences helps her both assess first hand her children's frustration levels and model ongoing teacher/reader book conversations by scheduling child-initiated reading conferences when she personally replenishes their book bags.

To allay children's frustration levels in their reading and to foster their independent reading, the teacher should personally take time out to hear them read aloud and to check for fluency and expression. Children's frustration level can be immeasurably lessened if they are explicitly told by the teacher after they have read aloud that they need to read without pointing and that they should try chunking words into phrases which mimic their natural speech.

Awareness of Text Leveling

The classroom library in the context of the balanced literacy approach to reading instruction is focused on leveled books. These are books which have been leveled with the support of Fountas and Pinnell's Guided Reading: *Good First Teaching for All Children* and *Matching Books to Readers: Using Leveled Reading in Guided Reading,* K-3.

The books which are leveled according to the designations in these reference books need to be stored in bins or crates with front covers facing out. This makes them much easier for the children to identify. In that way the children can go through the appropriate levels and find those books that they are particularly interested in which are also at the right level for them to read. These are books which the children can read with the right degree of reading accuracy. When young children can see the cover of a book, they are more likely to flip through the book until they can independently identify an appealing book. Then they will read a little bit of the book to see if it's "just right."

"Just right" leveled books—those that children can read on their own—need to be available for them to read during independent reading. The goal is for the more fluent readers to select books on their own. Ultimately the use of leveled books helps the children and the teacher decide which books are appropriate.

Levels are indicated at the right upper corners by blue, yellow, red, and green dot stickers which parallel emergent, early, transitional, and fluent reading stages. They are then kept in containers with other "blue," "yellow," "red," and "green" books.

Another list used to match children with "just right" books includes the Reading Recovery level list. Ultimately, the teacher has to individualize whatever leveling is used in the library to address the individual child's needs.

Techniques for Assessing Particular Reading Skills

Sharon Taberski recommends that the teacher build in one-on-one time for supporting individual children to consider what makes sense, sounds right, and matches the letters.

She has noted that emergent and early readers tend to focus on meaning without adequate attention to graphophonic cues. She suggests using the following prompts for children who are having problems with graphophonic cues:

Does what you said match the letters?

If the word were what you said ___, what would it have to start with?

Look carefully at the first letters. Then look at the middle letters. Then look at the last letters. What could it be?

If it were _____, what would it end with?

Oral retellings can be used to test comprehension. Children who are retelling a story to be tested for comprehension should be told that that is the purpose when they sit down with the teacher.

When you let the children start the retelling on their own, you can see whether the children need prompts to retell the story. Many times more experienced readers summarize what they have read. This summary usually flows out along with the characters, the problem of the story, and other details.

Other signs that children understand what they are reading when they give an oral retelling include their use of illustrations to support the retelling, references to the exact text in the retelling, emotional reaction to the text, making connections between the text and other stories or experiences they the readers have had, and giving information about the text without your asking for it.

Awareness of the Challenges and Supports in a Text

Illustrations can be key supports for emergent and early readers. You should not only use wordless stories (books which tell their narratives through pictures alone) but also make targeted use of Big Books for read-alouds so that young children become habituated to the use of illustrations as an important component for constructing meaning. You should model for the child how to reference an illustration for help in identifying a word in the text the child does not recognize. Of course, children can also go on a picture walk with you as part of a mini-lesson or guided reading and anticipate the story (narrative) using the pictures alone to construct meaning.

Decodability: Use literature which contains examples of letter sound correspondences you wish to teach. First, read the literature with the children or read it aloud to them. Then take a specific example from the text and have the children reread it as you point out the letter-sound correspondence to the children. Then ask the children to go through the now familiar literature to find other letter-sound correspondences. Once the children have correctly made the letter-sound correspondences, have them share similar correspondences they find in other works of literature.

Cooper (2004) suggests that children can become word detectives so that they can independently and fluently decode on their own. Children should learn the following word detective routines so that they can function as an independent fluent reader who can decode words on their own. First the children should read to the end of a sentence. Then the children should search for word parts which they know. Children child should also try to decode the word from the letter sounds. As a last resort, they should ask for help or look up the word in the dictionary.

Assessment of the Reading Development of Individual Students

For young readers who are from ELL backgrounds, even if they have been born in the United States, the use of pictures validates their story authoring and story telling skills and provides them with access and equity to the literary discussion and book talk of their native English speaking peers. These children can also demonstrate their storytelling abilities by drawing sequels or prequels to the story detailed in the illustrations alone. They might even be given the opportunity to share the story aloud in their native language or to comment on the illustrations in their native language.

Since many stories today are recorded in two or even three languages at once, discussing story events or analyzing pictures in a different native language is a beneficial practice which can be accomplished in the 21st century marketplace.

Use of pictures and illustrations can also help the K-3 educator assess the capabilities of children who are struggling readers if the children's learning strength is spatial. Through targeted questions about how the pictures would change if different plot twists occurred or how the child might transform the story through changing the illustrations, the teacher can begin to assess struggling reader's deficits and strengths.

Children from ELL backgrounds can benefit from listening to a recorded version of a particular story which they can read along with the tape. This gives them another opportunity to "hear" the story correctly pronounced and presented and to begin to internalize its language structures. In the absence of taped versions of some key stories or texts, teachers themselves may want to make sound recordings.

Highly proficient readers can also be involved in creating these literature recordings for use with ELL peers or younger peers. This of course develops oral language proficiency and also introduces these skilled readers into the intricacies of supporting ELL reading instruction. When they actually see their tapes being used by children, they will be tremendously gratified.

Skill 1.3   Using and communicating assessment results

Adjustment of Reading Instruction
Based on Ongoing Assessment

The running records taken of children help teachers learn about the cueing systems that children use. Based on the pattern of miscues gathered from several successive reading records, you will adjust the students' reading instruction. When you carefully review a given student's substitutions and self corrections, certain patterns begin to surface. Children may use visual cues as they read and add meaning to self correct. To the alert teacher, the reliance on visual miscues indicates that the readers are not making sense of what they are reading. This means that the teacher needs to identify what cueing system the children are using when they read the "just right" books. Children who use meaning and structure but not visual/graphophonic cues need to be reminded and facilitated to understand the importance of getting and reconstructing the author's message. They have to be able to share the author's story, not their own.

Not only can and should you use the material in the children's ongoing assessment notebook to adjust the current instruction but the material also serves to document the children's growth as successful readers over time. In addition, if the same concerns surface over the use of a particular cueing system or high frequency word, you can adjust the class wall chart and even devote a whole class lesson to the particular element.

You need to document any assessment of students and keep samples so that the parents and other teachers can understand what you mean. Communicating the findings of assessment does not have to wait for parent-teacher interviews or the report card. Teachers should report to parents on a regular basis, such as in monthly notes, telephone calls, arranged meetings, or even simple chats.

Guidance and speech counselors should communicate the results of assessments to teachers and parents as soon as possible after the testing is complete. In many districts this is called a debriefing and takes the form of an arranged meeting. In this meeting the counselor discusses the findings and suggests way to meet the needs of the child.

Quite often the only communication between the school and parents takes the form of end–of-term reports and parent-teacher interviews. Parents are sometimes reluctant to come to the school because they feel that the teachers are more knowledgeable than they are. To ensure effective literacy communication between the school and parents, teachers and reading specialists can employ different techniques:

- Holding a curriculum night during the first two weeks of school. At this time the teacher can explain how the children will be taught and what textbooks and materials will be used.
- Having an open door policy where parents can feel free to come into the classroom and observe what is happening.
- Telephoning or emailing the parents on a regular basis. Parents dread getting a call from the teacher because it usually means that their children have been in trouble or are experiencing problems in school. When you make these phone calls to report progress, parents become an ally in helping their children at home.
- Providing notes to parents in the child's agenda are also helpful in keeping parents informed about how to help at home and about how well their children are doing.
- Inviting parents or members of the community into the classroom to help with literacy centers gives those outside the school a chance to experience what is happening in the classroom. This could be listening to children read, helping them revise and edit writing, or even helping them choose books to take home.

COMPETENCY 2.0   PLANNING, ORGANIZING, AND MANAGING READING INSTRUCTION

Skill 2.1   Factors involved in planning reading instruction

**Significant Theories,
Approaches, Practices and Programs**

Decoding

In the late 1960s and the 1970s, many reading specialists, most prominently Fries (1962), believed that successful decoding resulted in reading comprehension. This meant that if children could sound out the words, they would then automatically be able to comprehend the words. Many teachers of reading and many reading texts still subscribe to this theory.

Asking Questions

Another theory or approach to the teaching of reading that gained currency in the late sixties and the early seventies was the importance of asking inferential and critical thinking questions of the reader which would challenge and engage the children in the text. This approach to reading went beyond the literal level of what was stated in the text to an inferential level of using text clues to make predictions and to a critical level of involving the child in evaluating the text. While asking engaging and thought-provoking questions is still viewed as part of the teaching of reading, it is only viewed currently as a component of the teaching of reading.

Comprehension Skills

As various reading theories, practices, and approaches percolated during the 1970s and 1980s, many educators and researchers in the field came to believe that the teacher of reading had to teach a set of discrete "Comprehension Skills" (Otto et al, 1977). Therefore the reading teacher became the teacher of each individual comprehension skill. Children in such classrooms came away with main idea, sequence, cause and effect, and other concepts that were supposed to make them better comprehenders. However, did it make them lifelong readers?

Transactional Approach

During the late 1970s and early 1980s, researchers in the field of education, psychology, and linguistics began to examine how the reader comprehends. Among them was Louise Rosenblatt who posited that reading is a transaction between the reader and the text. It is Rosenblatt (1978) who explained successful reading as the reader constructing a meaning from the text that reflected both the reader and the text. She described two general purposes for reading: *efferent* and *aesthetic*. Efferent reading is looking for and remembering information to use functionally. Examples would be filling out a job application, reading a story in preparation for a test, or reading a newspaper article to find out who won the state basketball championship. Aesthetic reading is done to connect one's own life to the text, to be swept away by the beauty of a poem, or to respond emotionally to a book such as *Bridge to Terabithia*.

These differing purposes call for somewhat different reading strategies: one might skim the newspaper article for basketball information but read a poem closely ten times and create mental images of different passages. Lastly, when children are asked to read all fiction efferently (What's the setting? What's the main conflict in the plot? There will be a test on this on Thursday!), it can thwart a child's joy in the written word and work against the student's desire to be a lifelong reader.

Bottom-up, Top-down, Interactional Theories of Reading

Bottom-up theories of reading assume that children learn from part-to-whole starting with the smallest segments possible. Instruction begins with a strong phonics approach, learning letter-sound relationships and often using basal readers or **decodable books**. Decodable books are vocabulary-controlled using language from word families with high predictability. Thus we get sentences like "Nan has a tan fan." Reading is seen as skills-based, and the skills are taught one at a time.

Top-down theories of reading suggest that reading begins with the reader's knowledge, not the print. Children are seen as having a drive to construct meaning. This stance views reading as moving from the whole to the parts. An early top-down theory was the **whole word** approach. Children memorized high-frequency words to assist them in reading the Dick and Jane books of the 30s. Then teachers helped children discover letter-sound correspondences in what they read. A more recent top-down theory is the **whole language** approach. This approach was influenced by research on how young children learned language. It was thought that children could learn to read as naturally as they learned to talk. Children were surrounded by print in their classrooms, using quality literature often printed in Big Books and were viewed as writers from the start. Hence journals were kept by kindergarten children. Advocates of whole language viewed the "skill'em, drill'em, and kill'em" approach based on bottom-up theories as a deadly dull introduction to the world of reading.

Interactive theories of reading combine the strengths of both bottom-up and top-down approaches. Teachers need to be able to teach decoding, vocabulary, and comprehension skills to support children's drive for meaning and desire for a stimulating exchange with high-quality literary texts from their earliest days in school. Strategies include shared, guided, and independent reading, Big Books, reading and writing workshops, and the like. Today this approach is called the **balanced literacy approach**, considered to be a synthesis of the best from bottom-up and top-down methods.

Skill 2.2 Organizing and managing reading instruction

Strategies for Planning, Organizing, Managing, and Differentiating Reading Instruction

The physical set up of your classroom is exceedingly important to support the effective development of all children. Here is one such example.

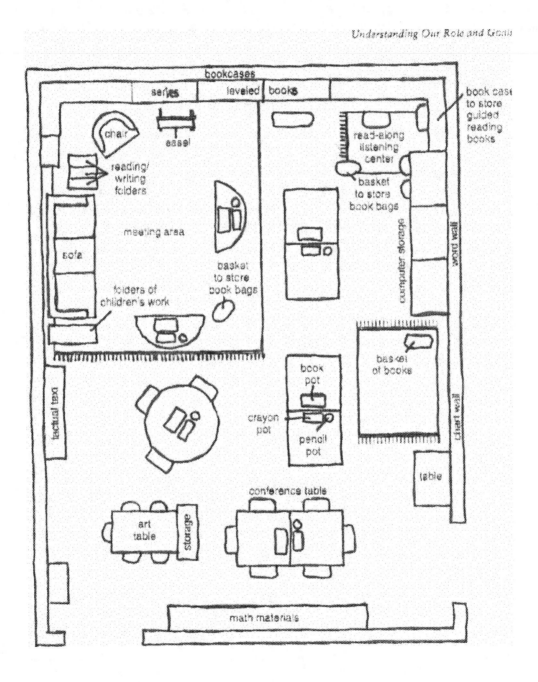

The homey look of the classroom belies its deliberate design as a space where children can experience, practice, share, and learn. Some teachers have done away with the large desk and use smaller tables instead. Sharon Taberski advocates adjusting the height of the table legs so that young children K-3 can use the tables as writing spaces and sit on the floor. Taberski gives each of her children a personal 12"x 9"x 2" tray on which they place their home possessions, books, homework, folder, and the like. This is kept in a small storage unit near the coat closet during the day.

Children put their completed homework in a wire basket and notes from parents or the office in a second wire basket. Supplies such as pencils, markers, crayons, scissors, and erasers are not brought from home but rather are available for all in the class from "community" containers at the center of each of the children's tables.

All the children's reading, writing, and individual math folders are stored together in plastic bins in the meeting area. Every child has an individual book bag which is kept in one of two large wicker baskets set in different areas of the room.

This storing of materials away from children decreases their "fiddling with" their belongings during class, makes the room look much neater, and frees the children to focus on their learning experiences rather than where their belongings are at any given time of day.

As you can see on the accompanying diagram the 10'x10' meeting area is the center of classroom learning. This is where the whole class is gathered at the beginning of the reading and the writing workshop and for sharing sessions. It is also the demonstration and modeling center for both the teacher and for children.

Generally, the presenter sits on the adult chair (in some balanced literacy classrooms, this is a rocking chair) near the easel with the chart. Generally, this chair and the easel are strategically positioned so that the teacher can see the door and any visitors or urgent messages from the office. Rearranging furniture during the day takes away from instruction time and is disruptive. Have a designated comfortable section of the room that can be a gathering place for a literacy community and then organize the rest of the classroom activities around that center.

The conference table which is at the back of the room (see diagram) is another key piece of classroom space furniture. It is the place where the four or five children and the teacher confer, wait, and do their work. Having children come to a set conference table rather than the teacher's going to them (although some teachers do advocate going to the children) saves time for Taberski. It serves to keep her and the children on task.

Taberski keeps two separate trays of supplies: a small magnetic board, letters, chalkboard, chalk, sentence strips, index cards, and blank books for her demonstrations during her conferences. She believes that teachers should store materials close to where they are used, so the teacher does not have to take time from the child to get up and get the materials.

The Classroom Library

On the tables, Taberski generally has book crates with books that are not leveled. Children choose from these books during the first independent reading session of her day which is from 8:40-9:00. During the second reading session from 9:30-10:20 the children select books from the leveled reading bins which are stored on the bookcase shelves.

Beyond the leveled books, which have already been discussed, Taberski also maintains a non-leveled, non-fiction library which includes dictionaries, atlases, almanacs, and informational books related to the themes, projects, and investigations that the children will undertake throughout the year.

Beyond the leveled books and non-fiction books in the classroom, Taberski and other balanced literacy advocates generally include at least 10-15 Big Books which they routinely use to engage children with the text.

Since Guided Reading with groups of six children is a major part of the balanced literacy approach, Taberski and other disciplined and dedicated teacher educators "bundle" up six copies of selected books so that they can distribute them to their guided reading groups whenever they choose to do them. Taberski models the concept of a home library collection for the children by keeping books which she particularly likes in a bookcase behind her chair. She sometimes places "her" books on the easel so that they can be shared by the children and returned to her.

Wall Works

Much of creating a family atmosphere lies in the use of the room walls to document the children's learning experiences, skills work, and readings.

Generally at least one wall in a reading classroom is the Chart Wall. Charts with various spelling patterns discussed in class can be posted. If a child later has issues or concerns with that particular pattern, the child should be directed to review the chart.

One of the centerpieces of the K-2 classroom is the High Frequency Word Chart. This is a growing list of commonly used words which the teacher tapes under the appropriate beginning letter according to the children's directions. At the end of each month, the newest high frequency words go into the children's folders and become part of their spelling words. Therefore reading, writing, and spelling are all intricately connected.

Supplies for children K-3 and beyond can include:
- A red plastic double pocket reading folder
- A blue plastic double pocket reading folder
- A four-sectioned pressed board spelling/poetry folder
- A 4" x 6" assessment notebook for reading
- A 4" x 6" assessment notebook for writing
- A reading response notebook (loose-leaf, 60 pages)
- A handwriting notebook

The Reading Folder contains the assessment notebooks, the reading response notebooks, a Weekly Reading Log, and the strategy sheets the child may be using that particular week.

The Assessment Notebook is a key evaluative tool and a recording document for the conscientious balanced literacy specialist. The teacher uses the notebook to record the child's running record, the retellings of stories shared by the child, and summarizing talks about leveled books read. Within the assessment books, the teacher also has notes about the child's progress, the strategies the child has learned to use well, the books the child has read, and those strategies the child still needs to practice. These assessment notebooks must be kept accessible so that the teacher can use them to confer with the child, parents, and administrator as needed.

The reading response notebook becomes a compilation of reading strategy sheets and children's writings and art in response to literature.

The Weekly Reading Log allows the children to maintain for themselves the titles of books they have read and to write a bit about the narrative, style, and genre of that given book.

Book Bag

These are 10" x 12" heavy duty freezer bags which keep 3-10 books a child is "working on" during free time. The teacher generally matches the children to the books and changes these books as needed by the children.

Writing Folders

Children keep several pieces of writing in their folders at a time. Within the writing folder are also a handwriting notebook and a beginning word book as well. The Spelling/Poetry Folder helps children focus on the sequence of letters in words and learn more how words work.

The balanced literacy advocates have a definite schedule for the teaching of reading and writing workshop from which they generally do not deviate. A sample follows.

8:40-9:00   First Independent Reading/Word Study Group

9:00-9:30   Whole Group Session in the meeting area
Read Aloud, Shared Reading, or Shared Writing

9:30-10:30   Reading Workshop
Reading Conferences or Guided Reading
Second Independent Reading
Reading Share 10:20-10:30

10:30-10:40 Writing Mini Lesson or Writing Share

10:40-11:20 Writing Workshop Writing Conferences, Guided Writing, Modeled Writing, Independent Writing
Writing Share 11:10-11:20

Literacy and Literacy Learning

To be literate in the 21st century means more than being able to read and write. To live well and happily in today's society, an individual has to be able to read, and not only newspapers and books but also emails, blogs, cell phone directions, and the like. A "disconnect" has evolved between the isolated reading comprehension skills the schools were teaching and the literacy skills including listening and speaking that are crucial for employment and personal and academic success. Thornburg (1992, 2003) has also noted that technology capacities and the ability to communicate online are now integral parts of our sense of literacy.

Cooper (2004) views literacy as reading, writing, thinking, listening, viewing, and discussing. These are not viewed as separate activities or components of instruction but rather as developing and being nurtured simultaneously and interactively. Children learn these abilities by engaging in authentic explorations, readings, projects, and experiences.

Just as in learning how to ride a bike, the learner goes through various approximations before learning how to actually ride the bike so too does the reader with the scaffold (support) of the teacher go through various approximations before developing independent literacy skills and capacities.

Emergent Literacy is the concept that young children are emerging into reading and writing with no real beginning or ending point. Children are introduced into the word of print as soon as their parents read board books to them at the age of one or two. When children scribble write or use invented spelling during the preschool years, they reveal themselves as detectives of the written word, having watched parents and teachers make lists, write thank-you notes, or leave messages. This view of the reader assumes that all children have a drive to make meaning in print and will begin doing it almost on their own if surrounded by a print-rich environment.

Reading Readiness is an approach which is antithetical to emergent literacy in that it assumes that all children must have mastered a sequence of reading skills *before* they can begin to read. This approach stands in contrast to emergent literacy.

Language Acquisition is continuous and never-ending. From the perspective of this theory and research, all children come to school with a language base which the school must build on. As a consequence of the connection between oral language and reading, schools build literacy experiences around the language the children bring to the school.

Instructional Reading Strategies for Promoting the Development of Particular Reading Skills

Phonemic awareness can be developed through using leveled books that deal with rhyming words and segmenting phonemes into words. Children can also work with word or letter strips to continue the poems from the books and create their own "sequels" to the phoneme-filled story. They can also create an in-style rhyming story using some of the same phonemes from the leveled story they have heard.

Word Identification—Selective Cue Stage. Sometimes children are not yet aware of the conventions of print and labeling in their own environments. The teacher or an aide may go on a label adventure and support children in recognizing or affixing labels to parts of the classroom, halls, and school building. A neighborhood walk with a digital or hand held camera may be required to help children identify uses and functions of print in society. A classroom photo essay or bulletin board could be the outgrowth of such an activity.

Sight Vocabulary. Beginning readers may enjoy outdoing Dolch (1936), who compiled the best known sight vocabulary word list. They can create their own class version of this list with illustrations and even some comments about why they have nominated certain words for the list.

Uses of Large Group, Small Group, and Individualized Reading Instruction

The framework for organizing the balanced literacy classroom is referred to as the one book-whole class mode. What this means is that everyone in the class has experiences with the same book. Everyone in the class discusses the literature. The teacher starts by activating prior knowledge and developing the context or background for the piece of literature. Some of the children within the class may have less prior knowledge or context with which to frame the book. The teacher should preview the book or develop key concepts to provide a stronger base for what the class will read together.

Some children will have to work with a paraprofessional or with a reading tutor before the class studies the book. Different modes of reading are accommodated within the class, by the books being read as a read-aloud, as part of shared reading or as guided reading. Student reader choices can also include cooperative reading, reading with a partner, or independent reading.

Following the reading, the children respond to it which can be done through a literature circle and/or the whole class or in writing.

Strategies for Selecting and Using Meaningful Reading Materials at Appropriate Levels of Difficulty

Matching young children with "just right" books fosters their independent reading, no matter how young they are. The teacher needs an extensive classroom library. Books that emergent readers and early readers can be matched with should have fairly large print and appropriate spacing, so that the reader can easily see where word begins and ends. There should be only a few words on each page so that the young reader can focus on all important concerns of top-to bottom, left-to-right, directionality and the one-to-one match of word to print.

Illustrations for young children should support the meaning of the text and language patterns, and predictable text structures should make these texts appealing to young readers. Most important of all, the content of the story should relate to the children's interests and experiences as the teacher knows them.

Only after all these considerations have been addressed can the teacher select "just right" books from an already leveled bin or list. In a similar fashion, when the teacher is selecting books for transitional and fluent readers, the following ideas should be considered:

- The book should take at least two sittings to read, so children can get used to reading longer books. The fluent and transitional reader needs to deal with more complex characters and more intricate plotting.
- Look for books that set the stage for plot development with a compelling beginning. Age appropriateness of the concepts, plot and themes is important so that the child will sustain interest in the book.
- Look for book features such as a list of chapters to help children navigate through the book.

Series books are wonderful to introduce at this point in the children's development.

Creation of an Environment that Promotes Love of Reading

You can promote the love of reading by creating warm and comfortable environments. For example, the meeting area and the reading chair (sometimes a rocking chair) with throw pillows around it promote a love of reading. Beyond that, some classrooms have adopted an author's hat, decorated with the pictures of famous authors and book characters which children wear when they read from their own works.

Many classrooms also have children's storyboards, artwork, story maps, pop-up books, and "in the style of" writing inspired by specific authors. Some teachers buy calendars for the daily schedule which celebrate children's authors or types of literature. Children are also encouraged to bring in public library books and special books from their home libraries. You can model this habit of sharing beautiful books and inviting stories from their home libraries.

In addition, news stories about children's authors, series books, television versions of books, theatrical film versions of books, stuffed toy book character decorations and other memorabilia related to books can be used to decorate the room.

Various chain book stores including Barnes and Nobles and Borders give out free book marks and promotional display materials related to children's books. Place these around the room for children to use as they read independently or in their guided groups. They might even use these artistic models to inspire their own book themed artifacts.

Uses of Instructional Technology to Promote Reading Development

One of the most interesting ways in which the web complements the Reading and Writing Workshop is the proliferation of author-specific websites. If used judiciously, these web resources allow authors to come into the classroom and enable children to write, question, discuss, and share their literacy experiences with the authors themselves. Children can also readily become part of a distanced community of peers who are also reading works by a given author.

For instance, children who have been introduced to the work of Faith Ringgold, the author of *Tar Beach*, can easily visit her online site, www.faithringgold.com. Here they will not only find extensive biographic data on Ringgold, but they will also be able to learn a song inspired by her main character Cassie. They can illustrate a new story Ringgold has put up on the website and see if any of the questions they may have generated in their shared or independent reading of her books has already been answered in the "frequently asked questions" section of her web resource. A few of the author websites respond online to individual children's questions.

There are even some reader response web resources such as the spaghetti review web site where young readers can post their response to different books they are reading. For example, see http://www.book-club-review.com/view.php?cid=1

DOMAIN II.   **DEVELOPING PHONOLOGICAL AND OTHER LINGUISTIC PROCESSES RELATED TO READING**

COMPETENCY 3.0   PHONEMIC AWARENESS

Skill 3.1   Assessing phonemic awareness

Phonemic Awareness

"The two best predictors of early reading success are alphabetic recognition and phonemic awareness."—Marilyn Jager Adams

"In order to benefit from formal reading instruction, children must have a certain level of phonemic awareness . . . phonemic awareness is both a prerequisite for and a consequence of learning to read."—Hallie Kay Yopp

Phonemic awareness is a specific skill within the broader category of phonological awareness. Probably developing fairly late, it is the knowledge that words are comprised of individual phonemes that can be blended.

Theorist Marilyn Jager Adams who researches early reading has outlined five basic types of phonemic awareness tasks.

Task 1: The ability to hear rhymes and alliteration.
    For example, the children would listen to a poem, rhyming picture book, or song and identify the rhyming words heard which the teacher might then record or list on chart.

Task 2: The ability to do oddity tasks (recognize the member of a set that is different [odd] among the group).
    For example, the children would look at the pictures of grass, a garden and a rose, answering, "Which one starts with a different sound?"

Task 3: The ability to orally blend words and split syllables.
    For example, the children can say the first sound of a word and then the rest of the word and put it together as a single word.

Task 4: The ability to orally segment word.
    For example, the ability to count sounds. The child would be asked to count or clap the sounds in "hamburger."

Task 5: The ability to do phonics manipulation tasks.
    For example, replace the "r" sound in rose with a "p" sound.

Phonological awareness means the ability of the reader to recognize the sounds or phonemes of spoken language. This recognition includes how these sounds can be blended together, segmented (divided up), and manipulated (switched around). This awareness eventually leads to phonics, a method for decoding language by unlocking letter-sound or grapheme-phoneme relationships.

Assessment of Phonological Awareness

Teachers can maintain ongoing logs and rubrics for assessment throughout the year of phonemic awareness for individual children. Such assessments would identify particular stated reading behaviors or performance standards, the date of observation of the child's behavior (in this context-phonemic activity or exercise), and comments.

The rubric or legend for assessing these behaviors might include the following descriptors:
- Demonstrates or exhibits reading behavior consistently,
- Makes progress/strides toward this reading behavior, and
- Has not yet demonstrated or exhibited this behavior.

Depending on the particular phonemic task the teacher models, the performance task might include:
- Saying rhyming words in response to an oral prompt
- Segmenting a word spoken by the teacher into its beginning, middle and ending sounds
- Counting correctly the number of syllables in a spoken word

Phonological awareness involves the recognition that spoken words are composed of a set of smaller units such as onsets and rimes, syllables, and sounds.

These skills can be assessed by having the child listen as you say two words. Then ask the child to decide if these two words are the same word repeated twice or two different words. When making this assessment using two different words, make certain that they only differ by only one phoneme, such as /d/ and /g/. Children can be assessed on words which are not real words that are familiar to them. Words used can be make-believe words.

Skill 3.2   The role of phonemic awareness

The Role of Phonological Awareness in Reading Development

Phonemic awareness is a specific type of phonological awareness which focuses on the ability to distinguish, manipulate, and blend specific sounds or phonemes within an individual word. Think of phonological awareness as an umbrella and phonemic awareness as a specific spoke under this umbrella.

Children who have problems with phonics generally have not acquired or been exposed to phonemic awareness activities at home or in preschool-2. This includes extensive songs, rhymes and read-alouds.

Points to Ponder
- Phonological awareness is auditory.
- It does not involve print.
- It begins before children have learned letter-sound relationships.
- It is the basis for the successful teaching of phonics and spelling.
- It can and must be taught and nurtured.
- It precedes and must be in place before the alphabetic principle can be taught.

Consideration for ELL Students

Given the demographics of our country with its influx of new Americans, the likelihood is that you will be teaching at least some children who are from a non-native English speaking background. Therefore, as a conscientious educator, you should understand the special factors involved in supporting children's second language literacy development.

Not all English phonemes are present in various ELL native languages; for example, the sound of /th/ does not appear in Spanish. Some native language phonemes conflict with English phonemes.

It is recommended that all teachers of reading and particularly those who are working with ELL students use meaningful, student-centered, and culturally customized activities. These activities may include language games, word walls, and poems. Some of these activities might, if possible, be initiated in the child's first language and then reiterated in English.

Struggling Readers

"Students who cannot read by age 9 are unlikely to become fluent readers and have a greater tendency to drop out."—Beth Antunez

Among the causes of reading difficulties for some children (and adults) are auditory trauma or ear infections that affect their ability to hear speech. Such children need one-on-one support with articulation and perception of different sounds. When a child says a word such as "parrot" incorrectly, repeat it back as a question with the correct pronunciation. If the child "gets" the sound correctly after your question, all is well. Extra support was needed. If the child still has difficulty with pronunciation after repeated instances, then consult with a speech therapist or audiologist. Early identification of medical conditions that affect hearing is crucial to reading development.

Skill 3.3   Developing phonemic awareness

Development of phonological skills for most children begins during the pre-K years. Indeed by the age of five, a child who has been exposed to fingerplays and poetry can recognize a rhyme. Such a child can demonstrate phonological awareness by filling in the missing rhyming word in a familiar rhyme or rhymed picture book. The procedure of filling in a missing word is called the cloze procedure. It can be used in oral or print literacy activities.

You teach phonological awareness by directly pointing out the sounds made by letters singly (as in /b/) or in combination (as in /bl/), and to recognize individual sounds in words.

Phonological awareness skills include but are not limited to the following:
- Rhyming and syllabification
- Blending sounds into words—such as pic-tur-bo-k
- Identifying beginning or initial phonemes and ending or final phonemes in short, one-syllable words
- Breaking words down into sounds, which is also called "segmenting" words
- Removing initial sounds, and substituting others. An example is /bat/ minus the /b/ with an /m/ substituted becomes /mat/.

Instructional Methods

Since the ability to distinguish between individual sounds, or phonemes, within words is a prerequisite to association of sounds with letters and manipulating sounds to blend words—a fancy way of saying "reading"—the teaching of phonemic awareness is crucial to emergent literacy (early childhood K-2 reading instruction). Children need a strong background in phonemic awareness in order for phonics instruction (sound–spelling relationship-printed materials) to be effective.

Instructional methods that may be effective for teaching phonemic awareness can include:

- Clapping syllables in words
- Distinguishing between a word and a sound
- Using visual cues and movements to help children understand when the speaker goes from one sound to another
- Incorporating oral segmentation activities which focus on easily distinguished syllables rather than sounds
- Singing familiar songs (e.g. "Happy Birthday," "Knick Knack Paddy Wack") and replacing key words those of a different ending

- Dealing children a deck of picture cards and having them sound out the words for the pictures on their cards or calling for a picture by asking for its first and last sound

Other activities could revolve around games and books.

1. In auditory games, children recognize and manipulate the sounds of words, separate or segment the sounds of words, take out sounds, blend sounds, add in new sounds, or take apart sounds to recombine them in new formations.

2. In a snap game, the teacher says two words. The children snap their fingers if the two words share a sound, which might be at the beginning, or end of the word. Children hear initial phonemes most easily, followed by final ones. Medial or middle sounds are most difficult for young children to discriminate. You see this in their oral responses as well as in their invented spelling. Silence occurs if the words share no sounds. Children love this simple game, and it also helps with classroom management.

3. Language games model for children identification of rhyming words. These games help inspire children to create their own rhymes.

4. Read books that rhyme such as *Sheep in a Jeep* by Nancy Shaw or *The Fox on a Box* by Barbara Gregorich.

5. Share books with children that use alliteration (words that begin with the same sound) such as *Avalanche, A to Z*.

Blending Letter Sounds

Prompts for Graphophonic Cues

> You said (the child's incorrect attempt). Does that match the letters you see?
> If it were the word you just said, (the child's incorrect attempt), what would it have to start with?
>
> If it were the word you just said (the child's incorrect attempt), what would it have to end with?
>
> Look at the first letter/s. Look at the middle letter/s. . . the last letter. What could it be?
>
> If you were writing (the child's incorrect attempt), what letter would you write first? What letters would go in the middle? What letters would go last?

A good strategy to use in working with individual children is to have them explain how they finally correctly identified a word that was troubling them. If prompted and habituated through one-on-one teacher/tutoring conversations, they can be quite clear about what they did to "get" the word.

If the children are already writing their own stories, the teacher might say to them: "You know when you write your own stories you would never write any story which did not make sense. You wouldn't, and probably this writer didn't either. If you read something that does make sense, but doesn't match the letters, then it's probably not what the author wrote. This is the author's story, not yours right now, so go back to the word and see if you can find out the author's story. Later on, you might write your own story."

Letter Sound Correspondence and Beginning Decoding

Use this procedure for letter-sound investigations that support beginning decoding.

First, focus on a particular letter/s which you want the child to investigate. It is good to choose one from a shared text which the children are familiar with. Make certain your directions to the children are clear and either focus them on looking for a specific letter or listening for sounds.

Next, begin a list of words that meet the task given to the children. Use chart paper to list the words that the children identify. This list can be continued into the next week as long as the children's focus is maintained on the list. This can be easily done by challenging the children with identifying a specific number of letters or sounds and "daring" them as a class team to go beyond those words or sounds.

Third, continue to add to the list. Focus the children at the beginning of the day on the goal of their individually adding to the list. Give them an adhesive note (sticky pad sheet) on which they can individually write down the words they find. Then they can attach their newly found words with their names on them to the chart. This provides the children with a sense of ownership and pride in their letter-sounding abilities. During shared reading, discuss the children's proposed additions and have the group decide if these meet the directed category. If all the children agree that they do meet the category, include the words on the chart.

Fourth, do a word sort from all the words generated and have the children put the words into categories that demonstrate similarities and differences. They can be prompted to see if the letter appeared at the beginning of the word or in the end of the word. They might also be prompted to see that one sound could have two different letter representations. The children can then "box" the word differences and similarities by drawing colors established in a chart key.

Finally, before the children go off to read, ask them to look for new words in the texts which they can now recognize because of the letter sound relationships on their chart. During shared reading, make certain that they have time to share these words they were able to decode because of their explorations.

COMPETENCY 4.0   CONCEPTS ABOUT PRINT

Skill 4.1   Assessing concepts about print

Assessment throughout the Year
of Graphophonemic Awareness

As a reading teacher, you will want to maintain individual records of children's reading behaviors demonstrating alphabetic principle/graphophonemic awareness.

The following performance standards should be part of a record template form for each child in grades K-1 and beyond as needed (depending on ELL or special needs):

- Match all consonant and short vowel sounds.
- Read one's own name.
- Read one syllable words and high frequency words.
- Demonstrate ability to read and understand that as letters in words change, so do the sounds.
- Generate the sounds from all letters including consonant blends and long vowel patterns. Blend those different sounds into recognizable words.
- Read common sight words.
- Read common word families.
- Recognize and use knowledge of spelling patterns when reading: run/running, hop/hopping

You can use the following template "Reading Progress" to record student progress for each child in grades K-1 and beyond as needed (depending on ELL or special needs):

Any record kept of an individual child's progress should include each date of observation and some legend or rubric detailing the level of performance, standard acquisition, or mastery.

Reading Progress

Skill Area	Mastered	Making Progress	Not Yet	Comments
Matches all consonant and short vowel sounds				
Reads one's own name				
Reads one syllable words and high frequency words				
Demonstrates ability to read and understand that as letters in words change, so do the sounds				
Generates the sounds from all letters including consonant blends and long vowel patterns. Blend those different sounds into recognizable words				
Reads common sight words				
Reads common word families				
Recognizes and uses knowledge of spelling patterns when reading: run/running, hop/hopping				

Skill 4.2 Concepts about print

The alphabetic principle is sometimes called graphophonemic awareness. This term means that written words are composed of letter (graphemes) which represent the sounds (phonemes) of written words.

Development of the Understanding that Print Carries Meaning

This understanding is demonstrated every day in the elementary classroom as the teacher holds up a selected book to read aloud to the class. The teacher explicitly and deliberately talks aloud about how to hold the book, focuses the class on looking at its cover, points to where to start reading, and indicates the direction to begin, left to right.

When writing the morning message on the board, the teacher reminds the children that the message begins in the upper left hand corner at the top of the board to be followed by additional activities and a schedule for the rest of the day.

When the teacher invites children to make posters of a single letter such as *b* and list items in the classroom, their home, or outside which start with that letter, the children are concretely demonstrating that print carries meaning.

Reading Progress

Skill Area	Mastered	Making Progress	Not Yet	Comments
Matches all consonant and short vowel sounds				
Reads one's own name				
Reads one syllable words and high frequency words				
Demonstrates ability to read and understand that as letters in words change, so do the sounds				
Generates the sounds from all letters including consonant blends and long vowel patterns. Blend those different sounds into recognizable words				
Reads common sight words				
Reads common word families				
Recognizes and uses knowledge of spelling patterns when reading: run/running, hop/hopping				

The Role of Environmental Print in Developing Print Awareness

An environmental print book, which contains collaged symbols of their favorite lunch or breakfast foods, can be created by the children. The children cut and clip symbols from the packaging of these foods and then place them in alphabetical order in their class-made book. Magazines and catalogues are another source of environmental print that is accessible with ads for child centered products. Supermarket circulars and coupons from the newspaper are also excellent for engaging children in using environmental print as reading, especially when combined with dramatic play centers or prop boxes.

What is particularly effective in using environmental print is that it immediately invites the child from ELL background into print awareness through the familiarity of commercial logos and packaging symbols used.

Development of Book Handling Skills

Understanding the value and importance of the concepts of print for beginning readers developed out of the work of Marie Clay in New Zealand. Assessment of these skills typically occurs in kindergarten and into first grade as necessary. The following skills are part of the assessment process:

- **Print carries a message** – The students can demonstrate this skill even if unable to read the text by pretending to read. This may be demonstrated even if the child does not demonstrate any of the other concepts.
- **Book organization** – Students demonstrate an understanding of the organization of books by being able to identify the title, cover, author, left to right progression, top to bottom order, and one-to-one correspondence. Students may learn these skills individually as they become more familiar with books.
- **Print consistencies** – This is the understanding that text is made up of letters, which then form words, which then are combined to form sentences. As beginning readers makes these connections, they will next develop the concept of capital letters at the beginning and basic punctuation marks.
- **Letter identification** - The final stage of the concepts of print assessment involves the identification of both upper- and lower- case letters. More advanced students may begin to recognize some of the most common spelling patterns in beginning texts.

In other activities, have the children identify the front cover, back cover, and title page of a specific book. You can model storytelling with the book held so that the audience can see the illustrations shown to them. Then have children demonstrate the skills for their peers.

Have children search through the class libraries for special features on the fronts or backs of books as they help return the books to their bins. Have the children display and talk about the special symbols they have found.

Review with the children, in an age and grade appropriate format, additional parts of the book as appropriate during mini lessons and read alouds. These additional parts of the book can include title pages, dedication page, table of contents, copyright date, and glossary.

Strategies for Promoting
an Understanding of the Directionality of Print

To become proficient readers, young students need to develop a complete understanding that all print is read from left to right and top to bottom. Modeling is one of the most important strategies a teacher can use to develop this understanding in children. The use of big books, poems, and charts are strategies teachers can use in both large and small group instruction. Simple questions can engage the students to pay closer attention to these skills (i.e. "We are going to read this passage. Where should I put my pointer to start reading?").

Directionality of print should also be taught during the writing process. In language experience stories, interactive writing, and Kidwriting©, the teacher can incorporate explicit modeling and instruction in these skills. Sometimes it may be necessary to provide children with a dot at the top left corner of the paper in order to provide a visual reminder of where to begin.

Techniques for Promoting the Ability
to Track Print in Connected Texts

You should model directionality and one-to-one word matching by pointing to words, while using a big book, pocket chart, or poem written out on a chart. As you repeatedly lead the children in this reading, they can follow along and eventually track the print and make one-to-one matches on the connected text independently. They can also practice by using a pointer (all children love to use the pointer so then pleasure becomes associated with the reading) or their fingers to follow the words. Children happily volunteer to be the point person. Even before Vanna White, the joy of "signifying letters" existed and has tremendous appeal for children.

Copy a brief, familiar rhyme (perhaps from a favorite book or song) and post it in the room at the children's eye level, so the children can independently walk around and read it.

Copy a brief or familiar rhyme or poem on individual word cards. Then challenge the children in small groups or independently to reassemble and display them on a pocket chart.

As children "play" with constructing and reconstructing this pocket chart, they will develop an awareness of directionality, one on one matching of print to spoken words, spacing, and punctuation.

Model interactive emergent writing with the class. While you may be noting the weather, deliberately ask the children to suggest where the first word in that report should go, top or bottom of the board? Will the first letter be upper case or lower case? What goes at the end of the sentence?

Create with the children sing-song repetitions/rules for using capitals, periods, commas, etc. Encourage the children to begin reciting these sing-songs as soon as they identify specific concepts of print in connected texts.

Model for children how, when pointing at words, they can start at the top and move from left to right. Tell the children that if there are more words to the sentence they are reading under the first line of print, they must go back to the left and under the previous line. Young children enjoy practicing this kinesthetic "return sweep." You might want to teach them to identify the need to do this by saying "Don't fall asleep at the page" or "Time to get to the 'return sweep' stage!" Post this saying and encourage them to singsong as they joyously take ownership of their reading.

Have even beginning readers "read" through the text to find letters they recognize in the story and then share some of the text that includes these specific letters to whet their appetite for reading.

Skill 4.3   Letter recognition

Strategies for Promoting
Letter Knowledge and Letter Formation

Engage the children in a Tale Trail game. Use a story they have already heard or read. Ask the children to circle certain letters and then reread the story, sharing the letters they have circled.

Give the children lots of opportunities to do letter sorts. Pass out word cards which have the targeted letter on them. Ask the children to come up and display their answers to questions like these about the letter, say *R*.

- *R* as the first letter—*r*ose, *r*ise, *r*an,
- *R* as the last letter—ca*r*, sta*r*, fa*r*,
- *R* with a t after it--sta*r*t, hea*r*t, pa*r*t, sma*r*t
- *R*, two r's in the middle of a word—ca*rr*y, so*rr*y, sta*rr*y

Play "What's in a Name?" Select a student's name "William." Write it on a sentence strip. Have the children count the number of letters in the name and how many of them appear twice. Allow them to talk about which letter is upper case and which letters are lower case. Have the students chant the name. Then rewrite the name on another sentence strip. Have the strip cut into separate letters and see if some one from the class can put the name back correctly.

As you read a book with or to children, ask that they show you specific letters or lower case or upper case letters. Read the text first and encourage as many children to come up and identify the letters as possible. Use a big book and have felt and sandpaper letters available for display as well. If grade, age, and developmentally appropriate, have children then write the letter they identified themselves or, even more fun, construct it using pipe cleaners, play dough or coded colored markers (different colors for upper and lower case letters).

Play "letter leap" with the children and have them look carefully at the room to identify labeled items that begin with a specific letter by "leaping" over to them and placing a large lettered placard next to them. Children who are advanced in letter formation can then be challenged to "leap" through the classroom when called upon to literally "letter" unlabeled objects.

Use of Reading and Writing Strategies
for Teaching Letter-Sound Correspondence

Provide children with a sample of a single letter book (or create one from environmental sources, newspapers, coupons, circulars, magazines, or your own text ideas). Make sure that your already published or created sample includes a printed version of the letter in both upper and lower case forms. Make certain that each page contains a picture of something that starts with that specific letter and also has the word for the picture. The book you select or create should be a predictable one so that when the picture is identified, the word can be read.

Once the children have been provided with your sample and have listened to it being read, challenge them to each make a one letter book. Often it is best to focus on familiar consonants for the single letter book or the first letter of the child's first name. Using the first letter of the child's first name invites the child to develop a book which tells about him or her and the words that he or she finds. This is an excellent way to have the reading and writing workshop enhance the teaching of the alphabetic principle.

Encourage children to be active writers and readers by finding words for their book on the classroom word wall, in alphabet books in the special alphabet book bin, and in grade and age appropriate pictionaries, (dictionaries for younger children which are filled with pictures).

Of course, the richest resource within the reading and writing workshop classroom for teaching and fostering the alphabetic principle lies in the use of alphabet books as anchor books for inspiring students writing. While young children in grades K-1 will do better with the one letter book authoring activity, children in grades 2 and beyond can truly be inspired and motivated by alphabet books to enhance their own reading, writing, and alphabetic skills. Furthermore, use of these books which are produced in a variety of formats to enhance social studies, science and mathematical themes, provide an opportunity for even young children to create a meaningful product that authenticates their content study as it enhances alphabetic skills and, of course, print awareness

An annotated bibliography of selected alphabet books has been provided in the bibliography section of this guide. It was limited by space considerations, but the teacher can with no expense and with much pleasure catch up on the latest titles and identify those most appropriate for the grade taught by visiting a bookstore. Hold the print book in hand and then consider selecting an alphabet book that has a particularly inviting concept, art style, or adaptable format within the children's capacity to use as a model.

For instance, Tina Hoban uses actual color photographs of letters in her *26 Letters and 99 Cents.* Children may want to make clay letters or create letter sculptures that develop their own alphabet book similar to Hoban's. If nutrition is the science topic, children might want to examine Ehlert's very accessible *Eating the Alphabet: Fruits and Vegetables from A to Z.* This, combined with an examination of the fruits and vegetables in a local store (perhaps a pleasant walk from the school and a quick break from the routine), can yield a wonderful alphabet book on fruits and vegetables which can also include those fruits and vegetables eaten in various cultures (i.e. mangos, plantains, pomegranates, and the like).

The alphabet book can also offer the class a chance to work collaboratively using a template page created by the teacher. Completion of this collaborative work can be shared with peers in another class and parents and be kept in the classroom library as a model for the following year's class with their recognition and acceptance of the authors!

Development of Alphabetic Knowledge in Individual Students

Researchers Laura M. Justice and Helen K. Ezell (2002) evaluated alphabetic knowledge and print awareness in pre-school children from low income households. In their post-tests, children who had participated in shared reading sessions that emphasized a print focus outperformed their control group peers (other Head Start children) on three measures of print awareness: words in print, print recognition, and alphabetic knowledge.

Other researchers including Chaney (1994) have demonstrated a statistically significant and inverse relationship between household income and children's performance on measures of print awareness and the alphabetic principle.

Lonigan (1999) found that substantial group differences existed on a variety of pre literacy tasks administered to 85 preschool children from lower and middle income households. The researchers looked at environmental print, print and book reading conventions, and alphabet knowledge. Results showed that preschool children from middle income households showed significantly higher levels of skill across all print awareness tasks in comparison with preschoolers from low income households.

Obviously this data highlights the importance of extensive alphabetic knowledge activities and print awareness opportunities for some children from low income households in grades K-1 and even beyond if necessary.

Two other studies undertaken by Ezell and Justice (2000) suggested that structuring adult-child shared book reading interactions to include an explicit print awareness and alphabetic principle focus resulted in a substantial increase in children's verbal interactions with print.

This work highlights the importance of not only classroom and preschool emphasis on print awareness and alphabetic principle routines but also the need for teachers to reach out to parents and to model for them these shared reading experiences so that family life can parallel the classroom experiences. Many schools currently have parent volunteers and reading buddy programs. Training these volunteers, particularly in high need, low economic income status communities, is certainly warranted.

David J. Chard and Jean Osborn (1999) have reflected on the guidelines necessary for teachers to use in selecting supplemental phonics and word-recognition materials for addressing students with learning disabilities. They note that an important way to help children with reading disabilities figure out the system underlying the printed word is leading them to understand the alphabetic principle.

Children with learning disabilities (LD) in particular benefit from organized instruction that centers on letters, sounds, and the relations between sounds and letters. They also benefit from word-recognition patterns instruction that offers practice with word families that share similar letter patterns.

Children who are LD also benefit from opportunities to apply what they are learning to the reading and re-reading of stories and other texts. Such texts contain a high portion of words which reflect the letters, sounds, and spelling patterns the children are learning.

For special-needs children, a beginning reading program should include the following elements of alphabetic knowledge instruction:

1. A variety of alphabetic knowledge activities in which the children learn to identify and name both upper and lower case letters.
2. Games, songs, and other activities that help children to learn to name the letters quickly.
3. Writing activities that encourage children to practice the letters which they are writing.
4. A sensible sequence of letter introduction that can be adjusted to the needs of the children.

COMPETENCY 5.0 SYSTEMATIC, EXPLICIT PHONICS AND OTHER WORD IDENTIFICATION STRATEGIES

Skill 5.1 Assessing phonics and other word identification strategies

Role of Phonics in Developing Automatic Word Recognition, Decoding, and Reading Comprehension

To decode means to change communication signals into messages. Reading comprehension requires that the reader learn the code within which a message is written and be able to decode it to get the message.

Although effective reading comprehension requires identifying words automatically (Adams, 1990, Perfetti, 1985), children do not have to be able to identify every single word or know the exact meaning of the every word in a text to understand it. Indeed, Nagy (1988) says that, children can read a work with a high level of comprehension even if they do not fully know as many as 15 percent of the words within a given text.

Children develop the ability to decode and recognize words automatically. They then can extend their ability to decode to multi-syllabic words.

J. David Cooper (2004) and other advocates of the Balanced Literacy Approach, feel that children become literate, effective communicators and able to comprehend, by learning phonics and other aspects of word identification through the use of engaging reading texts. Engaging text, as defined by the balanced literacy group, are those texts which contain highly predictable elements of rhyme, sound patterns, and plot. Researchers, such as Chall (1983) and Flesch (1981), support a phonics-centered foundation before the use of engaging reading texts. This is at the crux of the phonics versus whole language/ balanced literacy/ integrated language arts, teaching of reading controversy.

As a teacher, you should be familiar with both sides of this controversy as well as the work of theorists who attempt to reconcile these two perspectives, such as Kenneth Goodman (1994). There are powerful arguments on both sides of this controversy, and each approach works wonderfully with some students and does not succeed with others.

As far as the examinations go, all that is asked of you is the ability to demonstrate that you are familiar with these varied perspectives. If asked on a constructed response question, you need to be able to show that you can talk about teaching some aspect of reading using strategies from one or the other or a combination of both approaches.

This guide is designed to provide you with numerous strategies representing both approaches.

As a working teacher you can choose from the strategies and approaches which work best for the children concerned, depending on the perspective of your school administration and the needs of the particular children you serve.

Skill 5.2   Explicit phonics instruction

Sequence of Phonics Skills

- Letter Naming
  - Lower Case Letters
  - Upper Case Letters
- Letter Sounds
  - Continuous Sounds
  - Stop Sounds
  - Both Consonant and Vowel Sounds
- Short Vowels in CVC Words
- Short Vowels with Digraphs and Trigraphs (/tch/
- Short Vowels and Consonant Blends
- Long Vowels
- Variant Vowels and Diphthongs
- R- and L- Controlled Vowels
- Multisyllabic Words

Using Phonics to Decode Words in Connected Text

Identifying New Words: Some strategies to share with children during conferences or as part of shared reading include the following prompts:

- Look at the beginning letter/s. What sound do you hear?
- Stop to think about the text or story. What word with this beginning letter would make sense here?
- Look at the book's illustrations. Do they provide you with help in figuring out the new word?
- Think of what word would make sense, sound right, and match the letters that you see. Start the sentence over, making your mouth ready to say that word.
- Skip the word, read to the end of the sentence, and then come back to the word. How does what you've read help you with the word?
- Listen to whether what you are reading makes sense and matches the letters (asking the child to self-monitor). If it doesn't make sense, see if you can correct it on your own.
- Look for spelling patterns you know from the spelling pattern wall.
- Look for smaller words you might know within the larger word.
- Read on a little, and then return to the part that confused you.

Explicit and Implicit Strategies for Teaching Phonics

Uta Frith has identified three phases which describe the progression of children's phonic learning from ages four through eight. These are:

Logographic Phase

Children recognize whole words that have significance for them such as their own names or the names of stores they frequent or products that their parents buy. Examples are McDonald's, SuperValu, and the like. Strategies which nurture development in this phase include explicit labeling of classroom objects, components, furniture, and materials and showing the children's names in print as often as possible. Toward the end of this phase children start to notice initial letters in words and the sounds that they represent.

Analytic Phase

During this phase the children begin to make associations between the spelling patterns in the words they know and new words they encounter. Children in this phase of reading development are able to generalize that "hat" and "cat" are going to be read in a similar manner because they recognize that the /at/ portions of the words are the same. This is helpful with word families and can be transferred to encoding words through many activities. Some teachers add word families or family houses to their word walls around the room. In this way, students can begin to make these generalizations more rapidly. As the students find more complex words that fall into the family/house, they add them.

Orthographic Phase

In this phase, children recognize words almost automatically. They can rapidly identify an increasing number of words. Students are able to apply many different strategies in a seamless manner to help them decode unknown words. This may include phonics, structural analysis, syntax, semantics, and contextual clues. Students at this level are fluent readers with good prosody. They are reading to make the shift from learning to read to reading to learn–a critical shift for children.

To best support these phases and the development of emergent and early readers, teachers should focus on elements of phonics learning which help children analyze words for their letters, spelling patterns, and structural components. The children need to be involved in activities in which they use what they know about words to learn new ones.

The teacher builds on what the children know to introduce new spelling patterns, vowel combinations, and short and long vowel investigations. The teacher must do this and be aware that these will be reintroduced again and again as needed.

Keep in mind that children's learning of phonics and other key components of reading is not linear but rather falls back to review and then flows forward to build new understandings.

Listed below are suggested activities to support phonics instruction to address the needs of these three phases of phonics.

These activities have specifically been provided in detail so you can study and use them in the sample constructed response questions which have been provided at the end of the guide. Since the role of phonics in promoting reading development is so crucial, it is highly likely that a constructed response question on the certification test will focus on the use of such strategies. Therefore it is a good idea for the certification candidate to study them closely. As a bonus, the detail with which these strategies are set forth also makes them readily useful with classes the teacher is currently teaching.

Sorting Words: This activity allows children to focus closely on the specific features of words and to begin to understand the basic elements of letter sound relationships. Start with one syllable (monosyllabic) words. Have the children group them by their length, common letters, sound, and/or spelling pattern.

Prepare for the activity by writing ten to fifteen words on oak tag strips and place them randomly on the sentence strip holder. These words should come from a book previously shared in the classroom or a language experience chart. Next, begin to sort out the words with the children, perhaps by where a particular letter appears in a word. While the children sort the place of a particular letter in a given word, they should also be coached (or facilitated) by the teacher to recognize that sometimes a letter in the middle of the word can still be the last sound that we hear and that some letters at the end of a word are silent (such as "e").

Encourage children to make their own categories for word sorts and to share their own discoveries as they do the word sorts. The children's discoveries should be recorded and posted in the rooms with their names so they have ownership of their phonics learning.

Letter Holder Making Words: Use a 2" x 3" piece of foam board to make a letter holder. On the front of the board, attach 16 library pockets –one for each letter from A to P. Use the back of the board to attach another 10 pockets for the rest of the alphabet.

Write the letter name on each pocket and use clear bookbinding tape to secure each row of cards with clear tape. Make twelve cards for each letter. On the front of each 2"x 6" strip, make a capital letter and on its back write that letter in lower case. Write consonants in black marker and vowels in red marker.

Through use of this letter holder, children can experience how letters can be rearranged, added, or removed to make new words. They can use these cards also to focus on letter sequences and to support them in recognizing spelling patterns in words.

The words you choose to use for this activity can be selected from Patricia Cunningham and Dorothy P. Hall's *Making Words* (1994). Select a word that is called the "secret word." Build up toward the creation of that word through a focus on the smaller words within it. Words should be chosen which reflect the spelling patterns being studied by the class.

You can create letter holders for the children by folding up the bottom third of a used manila file folder and taping the ends to form a shallow pocket. Give them letter cards which are made of 2"x 6" oak tag. For example, if the secret word is "bicycle," the children would be given the separate letter cards which would make up that word. The children keep the letters on the floor in front of them and only place them in the holder when they are actually making a word.

Making words should begin with making two-letter words and then progress as the individual child is ready to make larger words. The teacher provides the two letters to the child. After the instruction, the children select the correct letters and make the word in their folder. The teacher then writes the word down and the children check their letter holder word against it. The teacher goes around checking through and reviewing the letter holders to see which children are "getting it" and then continues to build up words with more letters if the children are ready.

Word Splits: Through working with compound words, children can actually experience bigger words that are often made up of smaller words. By working with five to ten compound words on oak tag cards, children can analyze letter-sound relationships and meaning.

Before children meet in a group, write five to ten words on oak tag cards and arrange them on the sentence strip holder. After the children have read the words, cut each of the words into its two smaller words and randomly arrange them on the sentence strip holder. Allow the children to take turns randomly, arranging the small words back into the original compound words. Also, encourage them to form new compound words. For example, if one of two original compound words is "rainbow" and the other is "dropping," the children should be able to come with "raindrop." The new words the children come up with should be written on blank oak tag cards with the names of the children who came up with them attached. In this way the children can add to their growing bank of new words and have ownership in the words that they have added.

Development of Phonics Skills with Individual Students

Children who are raised in homes where English is not the first language and/or where standard English is not spoken may have difficulty with hearing the difference between similar sounding words like "send" and "sent." Any child who is not in a home, day care, or preschool environment where English phonology operates may have difficulty perceiving and demonstrating the differences between English language phonemes. If children can not hear the difference between words that "sound the same" like "grow" and "glow," they will be confused when these words appear in a print context. This confusion will of course, sadly, impact their comprehension.

In *On Solid Ground* (2000), researcher and educator Sharon Taberski said that it is much harder for children from ELL backgrounds and children from homes where other English dialects are spoken to use syntactic cues to attempt to self-correct.

These children, through no fault of their own, do not have sufficient experience hearing Standard English spoken to use this cueing system as they read. The teacher should sensitively guide them through by modeling the use of syntactic and semantic cues.

There are many different strategies to help children who are struggling with their phonics skill development. A beginning step is to identify the area of difficulty within phonics. A simple assessment to help determine the exact area of difficulty is the CORE Phonics Survey which can be downloaded free. Once the area of deficit has been identified, small group instruction can be developed around these areas to increase specific skills.

When working on specific phonics skills, try to use decodable texts. There are numerous publishers who have available a variety of different skills and texts for use within the classroom. If students continue to struggle, it may be necessary to use a more specific systematic and explicit phonics program. Some examples of these include: Wilson Reading, Early Intervention Reading, and Open Court.

Considerations for teaching phonological processing to ELL children include recognition by the teacher that what works for the English language speaking child from an English language speaking family does not necessarily work in other languages.

All phonological instruction programs must be tailored to the children's learning backgrounds. Rhymes and alliteration introduced to ELL children should be read or shared with them in their first language, if at all possible. Research recommends that ELL children learn to read initially in their first language as well.

Further, ELL learners should speak English before being taught to read English. Research supports that oral language development lays the foundation for phonological awareness.

Highly proficient readers can be paired as buddy tutors for ELL or special needs classroom members or to assist the resource room teacher during their reading time. They can use the CVC Game developed by Jacki Montierth to support their peers and can even modify the game to meet the needs of classroom peers. Of course, this also offers the highly proficient reader the opportunity to do a service learning project, while still in elementary school. It also introduces the learner to another dimension of reading, the role of the reader as trainer and recruiter of other peers into the circle of readers and writers.

If the highly proficient readers are so motivated or if their teachers so desire, the peer tutors can also maintain an ongoing reading progress journal for their tutees. This will be a wonderful way to realize the goals of the reading and writing workshop.

Skill 5.3   Developing fluency

Fluency is the ability to read a text quickly and accurately. In silent reading, readers can recognize words automatically and they fully comprehend what they read. If comprehension is not immediate, these readers can use context clues to grasp the meaning of the sentence or paragraph. When reading aloud, fluent readers display confidence and read effortlessly and with expression (prosody). Readers that are not fluent read slowly, often one word at a time. By focusing on reading accurately, meaning is lost.

Fluency is an important skill because it helps readers develop from word recognition to comprehension. When readers don't have to spend time focusing on reading individual words, they can group words together to form ideas, which leads to comprehension. Not only can they grasp the main idea of the text, but they can make connections between the text and their prior knowledge and events in their own lives.

Fluency is a skill that is developed over time with repeated practice, exposure to literature, and opportunities to read for various purposes. Early readers read words rather than phrases and sentences and the act of reading often appears to be laborious rather than enjoyable. In order to become fluent, readers have to decode the letters and words. Eventually this leads to comprehension of ideas. Fluency changes over time as readers are exposed to more difficult texts. The most fluent readers at one level may read slowly when they are first introduced to a more difficult text because they need time for comprehension.

Fluency requires more than just a repertoire of recognizable words, however; expression is also part of fluency. To read fluently with expression means that the reader must be able to break the text into meaningful phrases and clauses.

Some techniques to use when teaching students to read fluently include:
- repeated reading of the same text
- oral reading practice using audiotapes
- provide models of what fluent reading looks and sounds like
- read to students
- choral reading
- partner reading
- Readers' Theatre

Automaticity

Automaticity is not the same as fluency. This is the fast and effortless recognition of words that only comes through repeated practice. Automaticity refers to accurate reading of words. It does not refer to reading with expression or reading with comprehension. It deals with word recognition only. It is necessary for fluency, but it is not the only factor that determines whether a student can read fluently.

Skill 5.4   Word identification strategies

Identification of Common Morphemes, Prefixes, and Suffixes

This aspect of vocabulary development is to help children look for structural elements within words which they can use independently to help them determine meaning.

Some teachers choose to directly teach structural analysis. In particular, those who teach by following the phonics-centered approach for reading do this. Other teachers, who follow the balanced literacy approach, introduce the structural components as part of mini lessons that are focused on the students' reading and writing.

Structural analysis of words as defined by J. David Cooper (2004) involves the study of significant word parts. This analysis can help the child with pronunciation and constructing meaning.

The term list below is generally recognized as the key structural analysis components.

Root Word is a word from which another word is developed. The second word can be said to have its "root" in the first, such as *vis, to see,* in visor or vision.

This structural component can be illustrated by a tree with roots to display the meaning for children. Children may also want to literally construct root words using cardboard trees to create word family models.

Prefixes are beginning units of meaning which can be added (the vocabulary word for this type of structural adding is "affixed") to a base word or root word. They can not stand alone. They are also sometimes known as "bound morphemes" meaning that they can not stand alone as a base word. Examples are *re-, un-,* and *mis-*.

Suffixes are ending units of meaning which can be "affixed" or added on to the ends of root or base words. Suffixes transform the original meanings of base and root words. Like prefixes, they are also known as "bound morphemes," because they can not stand alone as words. Examples are *-less, -ful*, and *-tion.*

Compound Words occur when two or more base words are connected to form a new word. The meaning of the new word is in some way connected with that of the base word. Examples are *firefighter, newspaper*, and *pigtail.*

Inflectional Endings are types of suffixes that impart a new meaning to the base or root word. These endings in particular change the gender, number, tense, or form of the base or root words. Just like other suffixes, these are also termed "bound morphemes." Examples are *–s* or *-ed.*

Base Words are stand-alone linguistic units which cannot be deconstructed or broken down into smaller words. For example, in the word re-tell, the base word is *tell*.

Contractions are shortened forms of two words in which a letter or letters have been deleted. These deleted letters have been replaced by an apostrophe. Examples are *can't, didn't, I've* and *wouldn't*.

Comments

Definitions are included because the structural analysis components are explicitly taught in schools which advocate the phonics-centered approach and are also incorporated into the word work component of the schools which advocate the balanced literacy approach for instruction.

Definition questions, multiple choice questions which have only a single right answer, test whether you have memorized the appropriate terminology. They constitute for no less than 15% of the multiple choice question on the test. Therefore by taking the time to memorize these easy definitions, your scores are likely to improve.

Individual Students

ELL learners can construct these models for their native language root word families, as well for the English language words they are learning. ELL learners in the 5th and 6th grade may even appreciate analyzing the different root structures for contrasts and similarities between their native language and English.

Learners with special needs can focus in small groups or individually with a paraprofessional on building root word models.

Using Semantic and Syntactic Cues to Help Decode Words

Semantic Cues

Students will need use their base knowledge of word meanings—semantics—to help them decipher unknown words or text as well as to clarify reading when it does not seem to make sense. Some prompts the teacher can use which will alert the children to semantic cues include:
- Does that sentence make sense?
- Which word in that sentence does not seem to fit?
- Why doesn't it fit?
- What word might make sense in that sentence?

Syntactic Cues

The first strategy good readers use from their own knowledge base to help determine misreading is syntactic cues. Syntactic cues use the order of words and the student's knowledge of the oral English language to determine if what was read could be accurate. Some prompts the teacher can use to encourage and develop syntactic cues in reading include:
- You read (child's incorrect attempt). Does that sound right?
- You read (child's incorrect attempt). When we talk, do we talk that way?
- How would we say it?
- Recheck that sentence. Does it sound right the way you read it?

Knowledge of Greek and Latin Roots

Knowledge of Greek and Latin roots which comprise English words can measurably enhance children's reading skills and can also enrich their writing.

Word Webs

Sharon Taberski (2000) does not advocate teaching Greek and Latin derivatives in the abstract to young children. However, when she comes across (as is common and natural) specific Greek and Latin roots while reading to children, she uses that opportunity to introduce children to these rich resources.

For example, during readings on rodents (a favorite of first and second graders), Taberski draws her class's attention to the fact that beavers gnaw at things with their teeth. She then connects the "dent" root or derivative to the children's lives, other words they are familiar with or experiences. The children then volunteer *dentist, dental, denture.* Taberski begins to place these in a graphic organizer, or word web.

When she has tapped the extent of the children's prior knowledge of "dent" words, she shares with them the fact that *dens/dentis* is the Latin word for teeth. Then she introduces the word "indent," which she has already previewed with them as part of their conventions of print study. She helps them to see that the "indenting" of the first line of a paragraph can even be related to the "teeth" Latin root in that it looks like a "print" bite was taken out of the paragraph.

Taberski displays the word web in the Word Wall Chart section of her room. The class is encouraged throughout a week's time to look for other words to add to the web. Taberski stresses that for her, as an elementary teacher of reading and writing, the key element of the Greek and Latin word root web activity is the children's coming to understand that if they know what a Greek or Latin word root means, they can use that knowledge to figure out what other words mean.

She feels the key concept is to model and demonstrate for children how fun and fascinating Greek and Latin root study can be.

Greek and Latin Roots Word Webs
With an Assist from the World Wide Web

Older children in grades 3-6 can build on this initial print activity by searching online for additional words with a particular Greek or Latin root which has been introduced in class.

They can easily do this in a way that authentically ties in with their own interests and experiences by reading reviews for a book which has been a read-aloud online or by just reading the summaries of the day's news and printing out those words which appear in the stories online that share the root discussed.

The children can be encouraged to circle these instances of their Latin or Greek root and also to document the exact date and URL for the citation. These can be posted as part of their own online web in the word wall section study area. If the school or class has a website or webpage, the children can post this data there as a special Greek and Latin root word page.

Expanding the concept of the Greek and Latin word web from the printed page to the World Wide Web nicely inculcates the children in the habits of lifelong reading and researching online. This beginning expository research will serve them well in intermediate level content area work and beyond.

Syllabification as a Word Identification Strategy

Another way to help students identify words is to help them understand syllabification. Here is only one of many games that you can use.

Clap Hands, Count those Syllables as They Come!! (Taberski, 2000)

The objective of this activity is for children to understand that every syllable in a polysyllabic word can be studied for its spelling patterns in the same way that monosyllabic words are studied for their spelling patterns.

The easiest way for the K-3 teacher to introduce this activity to the children is to share a familiar poem from the poetry chart (or to write out a familiar poem on a large experiential chart).

First the teacher reads the poem with the children. As they are reading it aloud, the children clap the beats of the poem and the teacher uses a colored marker to place a tic (/) above each syllable.

Next, the teacher takes letter cards and selects one of the polysyllabic words from the poem which the children have already "clapped" out.

The children use letter cards to spell that word on the sentence strip holder or it can be placed on a felt board or up against a window on display. Together the children and teacher divide the letters into syllables and place blank letter cards between the syllables. The children identify spelling patterns they know.

Finally, and as part of continued small group syllabification study, the children identify other polysyllabic words they clapped out from the poem. They make up the letter combinations of these words. Then they separate them into syllables with blank letter cards between the syllables.

Children who require special support in syllabification can be encouraged to use many letter cards to create a large butcher paper syllabic (in letter cards with spaces) representation of the poem or at least a few lines of the poem. They can be told that this is for use as a teaching tool for others. In this way, they authenticate their study of syllabification with a real product that can actually be referenced by peers.

Techniques for Identifying Compound Words

The teaching of compound words should use structural analysis techniques such as the game described above. Here are some other strategies for helping students to identify and read compound words.

- Use songs and actions to help children understand the concept that compound words are two smaller words joined together to make one bigger word.
- Use games like Concentration, Memory and Go Fish for students to practice reading compound words.
- Use word sorts to have students distinguish between compound words and nonexamples of compound words.

Identification of Homographs

Homographs are words that are spelled the same but have different meanings. A subgroup within this area includes words that are spelled the same, have different meanings, and are pronounced differently. Some examples of homographs include "lie," "tear," "bow," "fair," "bass."

Teaching homographs can be interesting and fun for the students. Incorporate them into passages where the students can use the context clues to decipher the different meanings of the homographs. Games are also a good strategy for using to help students understand multiple meaning words. Jokes and riddles are usually based on homographs, and students love to make collections or books of these.

Semantic Feature Analysis

This technique for enhancing vocabulary skills by using semantic cues is based on the research of Johnson and Pearson (1984) and Anders and Bos (1986). It involves young children in setting up a feature analysis grid of various subject content words which is an outgrowth of their discussion about these words.

For instance, Cooper (2004) includes a sample of a Semantic Features Analysis Grid for vegetables.

Vegetables	Green	Have Peels	Eat Raw	Seeds
Carrots	-	+	+	-
Cabbage	+	-	+	-

Note: that the use of the + for yes, - for no, and possible use for + and - if a vegetable like squash could be both green and yellow.

Teachers of children in grade 1 and beyond can design their own semantic analysis grids to meet their students' needs and to align with the topics the kids are learning. First, select a category or class of words (could be planets, rodent family members, winter words, weather words).

Then, use the left side of the grid to list at least three or more items that fit this category. The number of actual items listed will depend on the age and grade level of the children with three or four items fine for K-1 and up to 10-15 for grades 5 and 6. Brainstorm with the children or, if better suited to the class, the teacher may list features that the items have in common. As can be noted from the example excerpted from *Cooper's Literacy: Helping Children Construct Meaning* (2004), these common features such as vegetables' green color, peels, and seeds are usually fairly easy to identify.

If they are not certain, show the children how to insert the notations +, -, and even ?. The teacher might also explore with the children the possibility that an item could get both a + and a -. For example, a vegetable like broccoli might be eaten cooked or raw depending on taste and squash can be green or yellow.

Whatever the length of the grid when first presented to the children (perhaps as a semantic cue lesson in and of itself tied in to a text being read in class), make certain that the grid as presented and filled out is not the end of the activity.

Children can use it as a model for developing their own semantic features grids and share them with the whole class. Child-developed grids can become part of a Word Work center in the classroom or even be published in a Word Study Games book by the class as a whole. Such a publication can be shared with parents during open school week and evening visits and with peer classes.

Contextual Redefinition

This strategy encourages children to use the context more effectively by presenting them with sufficient context *before* they begin reading. It models for the children the use of contextual clues to make informed guesses about word meanings.

To apply this strategy, you should first select unfamiliar words for teaching. No more than two or three words should be selected for direct teaching. You should then write a sentence in which sufficient clues are supplied for the child to figure out the meaning successfully. Among the types of context clues you can use are compare/contrast, synonyms, and direct definition.

Then present the words only on the experiential chart or as letter cards. Have the children pronounce the words. As they pronounce them, challenge them to come up with a definition for each word. After more than one definition is offered, encourage the children to decide as a whole group what the definition is. Write down their agreed upon definition with no comment as to its accurate meaning.

Then share with the children the contexts (sentences that you wrote with the words and explicit context clues). Ask that the children to read the sentences aloud. Then have them come up with a definition for each word. Do not comment as they present their definitions. Ask that they justify their definitions by making specific references to the context clues in the sentences. As the discussion continues, direct the children's attention to their previously agreed- upon definition of the word. Facilitate their discussing the differences between their guesses about the word when they saw only the word itself and their guesses about the word when they read it in context. Finally have the children check their use of context skills to correctly define the word by using a dictionary.

Development of Word Analysis Skills and Strategies, Including Structural Analysis

Structural analysis is a process of examining the words in the text for meaningful word units (affixes, base words, inflected endings). There are six types of word types which are formed and therefore can be analyzed using structural analysis strategies:

1. Common prefixes or suffixes added to a known word ending with a consonant
2. Adding the suffix –ed to words that end with consonants
3. Compound words
4. Adding endings to words that end with the letter e
5. Adding endings to words that end with the letter y
6. Adding affixes to multisyllabic words

When teaching and using structural analysis procedures in the primary grades, teachers should remember to make sound decisions on which to introduce and teach. Keeping in mind the number of primary words in which each affix appears and noting how similar they are will help you make the instructional process smoother and more valuable to the students.

Adding affixes to words can be started when students are able to read a list of one-syllable words by sight at a rate of approximately twenty words correct per minute. At the primary level, there is a recommended sequence for introducing affixes. The steps in this process are:

- Start by introducing the affix in the letter-sound correspondence format
- Practice the affix in isolation for a few days
- Provide words for practice which contain the affix (word lists, flash cards, etc.)
- Move from word lists to including passage reading, which include words with the affix (and some from the word lists/flash cards).

Word Study Group

This involves the teacher taking time to meet with children from grades 3-6 in a small group of no more than six children for a word study session. Taberski (2000) suggests that this meeting take place next to the Word Wall. The children selected for this group are those who need to focus more on the relationship between spelling patterns and consonant sounds.

Remember that this should not be a formalized traditional reading group that meets at a set time each week or biweekly. Rather the group should be spontaneously formed by the teacher based on the teacher's quick inventory of the selected children's needs at the start of the week. Taberski has templates in her book of *Guided Reading Planning Sheets.* These sheets are essentially targeted word and other skills sheets with her written dated observations of children who are in need of support to develop a given skill.

The teacher should try to meet with this group for at least two consecutive twenty-minute periods daily. Over those two meetings, the teacher can model a Making Words Activity. Once the teacher has modeled making words the first day, the children would then make their own words. On the second day, the children would "sort" their words.

Other topics for a word study group within the framework of the Balanced Literacy Approach that Taberski advocates are inflectional endings, prefixes and suffixes, and/or common spelling patterns.

This activity would be classified by theorists as a structural analysis activity because the structural components (i.e. prefixes, suffixes, and spelling patterns) of the words are being studied.

Discussion Circles

Cooper (2004) believes that children should not be "taught" vocabulary and structural analysis skills. Flesch and E.D. Hirsch , who are key theorists of the phonics approach and advocates of Cultural Literacy (a term coined and associated with E. D. Hirsch), believe that specific vocabulary words at various grade and age levels need to be mastered and must be explicitly taught in schools.

As far as J. David Cooper is concerned, all the necessary and meaningful (for the child and ultimately adult reader) vocabulary can't possibly be taught in schools (no apologies to Hirsch). To Cooper it is far more important that the children be made aware of and become interested in learning words by themselves. Cooper feels that through the child's reading and writing, the child develops a love for and a sense of "ownership" of words. All of Cooper's suggested structural analysis word strategies are therefore designed to foster the child's love of words and a desire to "own" more of them through reading and writing.

Discussion Circles is an activity which fits nicely into the balanced literacy lesson format. After the children conclude a particular text, Cooper suggests that respond to the book in discussion circles. Among the prompts, the teacher-coach might suggest that the children focus on words of interest they encountered in the text. These can also be words that they heard if the text was read aloud. Children can be asked to share something funny or upsetting or unusual about the words they have read. Through this focus on children's response to words as the center of the discussion circle, peers become more interested in word study.

Banking, Booking, and Filing It: Making Words My Own

Children can literally realize the goal of making words their own and exploring word structures through creating concrete objects or displays that demonstrate the words they own. Children can create and maintain their own files of words they have learned or are interested in learning.

The files can be categorized by the children according to their own interests. They should be encouraged to develop files using science, history, physical education, fine arts, dance, and technology content. Newspapers and web resources, which the teacher has approved, are excellent sources for such words. In addition, this provides the teacher with the opportunity to instruct the child in appropriate age and grade-level research skills. Even children in grades 2 and 3 can begin simplified bibliographies and webliographies for their "found" words. Children can learn how to annotate and note the page of a newspaper, book, or URL for a particular word.

They can also copy the word as it appears in the text (print or electronic). If appropriate, the child can place the particular words found for a given topic or content in an actual bank of the child's own making. The words can be printed on cards. This allows for differentiated word study and appeals to those children who are kinesthetic and spatial learners. Of course, children can also choose to create their own word books which include their specialized vocabulary and descriptions of how they identified or hunted down their words. Richard Scarry's "Watch" books can be anchor books to inspire this structural analysis activity.

ELL learners can share their accounts in their native language first and then translate (with the help of the teacher) these accounts into English with both the native language and the English language versions of the word exploration posted.

Write Out Your Words, Write with Your Words

Ownership of words can be demonstrated by having the children use them as part of their writings. The children can author a procedural narrative (a step-by-step description) of how they went about their word searches to compile the words they found for any of the activities. If the children are in grades K-1, or if the children are struggling readers and writers, their procedural narratives can be dictated. Then they can be posted by the teacher.

ELL students can share their accounts in their native language first and then translate (with the help of the teacher) these accounts into English with both the native language and the English language versions of the word exploration posted.

Children with special needs may model a word box on a specific holiday theme, genre or science/social studies topic with the teacher. Initially this can be done as a whole class. As the children become more confident, they can work with peers or with a paraprofessional to create their own individual or small team/pair word boxes.

Special needs children can create a storyboard with the support of a paraprofessional, their teacher, or a resource specialist. Using a tape recorder, they can also narrate their story of how they all found the words.

Word Study Museum within the Classroom

This strategy has been presented in detail so it can be used by the teachers within their own classrooms. In addition, the way the activity is described and the mention at the end of the description of how the activity can address family literacy, ELL, and special needs children's talents provides an example of other audiences a teacher should consider in curriculum design.

Almost every general education teacher and reading specialist will have to differentiate instruction to address the needs of special education and ELL learners. Family or shared literacy is a major component of all literacy instruction.

Children can create either a single or multiple exhibits, museum style, within their classrooms celebrating their word study. They can build actual representations of the type of study they have done including word trees (made out of cardboard or foam board), elaborate word boxes and games, word history timelines or murals, and word study maps. They can develop online animations, Kids Spiration graphic organizers, quick movies, digital photo essays, and PowerPoint presentations to share the word they have identified.

The classroom or the gym or cafeteria can be transformed into a gallery space. Children can author brochure descriptions for their individual, team or class exhibits. Some children can volunteer to be tour guides or docents for the experience. Other children can work to create a banner for the museum. The children can name the museum themselves and send out invitations to its opening. Invitations can be sent to parents, community, staff members, and peer or younger classes.

Depending on their age and grade level, children can also develop interactive games and quizzes focused on particular exhibits. An artist or a team of class artists can design a poster for the exhibit, while other children choose to build the exhibits. Another small group can work on signage and a catalogue or register of objects within the exhibit. Greeters who will welcome parents and peers to the exhibit can be trained and can develop their own scripts.

If the children are in grades 4-6, they can also develop their own visitor feedback forms and design word-themed souvenirs. The whole museum within the school or classroom can be captured digitally or with a regular camera. The record of this event can be hung near the word walls. Of course, the children can use many of their newly recognized and owned words to describe the event.

The Word Study Museum activity can be used with either a phonics-based or a balanced literacy approach. It promotes additional writing, researching, discussing, and reading about words.

It is also an excellent family literacy strategy in that families can develop their own Word Exhibits at home. This activity can also support and celebrate learners with disabilities. It can be presented in dual languages by children who are ELL learners and fluent in more than a single language.)

Development of Word Analysis Skills by Individual Students

This type of direct teaching of word definitions is useful when the children have dictionary skills and you know there are not sufficient clues about the words in the context to help the students define it. In addition, struggling readers and students from ELL backgrounds may benefit tremendously from being walked through this process that highly proficient and successful readers apply automatically

By using this strategy, you can also "kid watch" and note the students' prior knowledge as they guess the word in isolation. You can actually witness and hear how various students use context skills.

Through their involvement in this strategy, struggling readers gain a feeling of community as they experience the ways in which their struggles and guesses resonate with other peers' responses to the text.

Skill 5.5 Sight words

Strategies for Helping Students Decode Single Syllable Words that Follow Common Patterns and Multi-syllable Words

This activity is presented in detail so it can actually be implemented with children in an intermediate classroom. The detail will help you prepare for a potential constructed response question on a certification examination.

The CVC phonics card game developed by Jackie Montierth, a computer teacher in South San Diego for use with 5th and 6th grade students, is a good one to adapt to the needs of any group with appropriate modifications for age, grade level, and language needs.

The children use the vehicle of the card game to practice and enhance their use of consonants and vowels. Their fluency in this will increase their ability to decode words. Potential uses beyond whole classroom instruction include use as part of the small group word work component of the reading workshop and as part of cooperative team learning. This particular strategy also is particularly helpful for grade four and beyond English language learners who are in a regular English language classroom setting.

The card game works well because the practice of the content is implicit for transfer as the children continue to improve their reading skills. In addition, the card game format allows "instructional punctuation" using a student-centered high interest exploration.

Card Design: To create a deck, use the computer, 5"x 8" index cards, or actual card deck-sized oak tag cards. For repeated use and durability, be sure to laminate the cards.

The deck should consist of the following:
- 44 consonant cards (including the blends)
- 15 vowel cards (including 3 of each vowel)
- 5 wild cards (which can be used as any vowel)
- 6 final e cards

The design of this project can also focus on particular CVC words that are part of a particular book, topic, or genre format. In advance of playing the game, children can also be directed to review the words on the word wall or other words on a word map.

Procedure: Introduce the game first as part of a mini lesson. Read the rules and have a pair of children demonstrate. Have the children divide into pairs or small groups of no more than four per group. Each group needs one deck of CVC cards.

Have each group choose a dealer. The dealer shuffles the cards and deals five cards to each player. The remaining cards are placed face down for drawing during the play. One card is turned over to form the discard pile. Players may not show their cards to the other players. The first player to the left of the dealer looks at the cards and, if possible, puts down three cards which make a consonant-vowel-consonant word. For more points, four cards forming a consonant-vowel-consonant word can be placed down. The player must then say the word and draw the number of cards to replace the cards that were laid down. If the player is unable to form a word, the player draws a card from either the draw or discard pile. The player then discards one card. All players must have five cards at all times. Play moves to the left.

The game continues until one or more of the following happens:
1. There are no more cards in the draw pile.
2. All players run out of cards.
3. All players cannot form a word.

The winner is the player who has laid down the most cards during the game. Players may only lay down words at the beginning of their turn. Proper names may not be counted as words.

Variations: The game can be played with teams in a small group of four or fewer competing against one another (which is excellent for special needs or resource room students). It can also be done as a whole class activity where all the students are divided into cooperative teams or small groups who compete against one another. This second approach will work well with a heterogeneous classroom that includes special needs and/or ELL children.

Teachers of ELL learners can do this game in the native language first and then transition it into English, facilitating native language reading skills and second language acquisition. They can develop their own appropriate decks to meet the vocabulary needs of their children and to complement the curricula.

Skill 5.6   Terminology

Specific Terminology Associated With Phonics

Having a clear understanding of the terms associated with phonics is important. Let's review a few.

Phoneme: A phoneme is the smallest unit of sound in the English language. In print phonemes are represented by the letter and a slash. So, /b/ represents the sound the letter b would make.

Morpheme: A morpheme is the smallest unit of grammar in the English language. In other words, it is the smallest unit of meaning, not just sounds.

Consonant Digraph: A consonant digraph is two consonants of the English language placed together in a word to make a unique sound neither makes when alone. Examples: ch, th, sh, and wh.

Consonant Blend: A consonant blend occurs when two consonants are put together but each retains its individual sound. The two sounds go together in a seamless manner to produce a blended sound. Examples: st, br, cl.

Schwa sound: A schwa sound is a neutral vowel sound. It typically occurs in the unaccented syllable of a word. An example would be the sound of the /a/ at the end of the word sofa. It is represented in print by an upside down e /ə/.

COMPETENCY 6.0   SPELLING INSTRUCTION

Skill 6.1   Assessing spelling

Spelling is extremely important in the writing process. At first young children will use invented spelling; they write the words according to letter sounds. Several factors influence the development of spelling:

- Surrounding students with an environment rich in print
- Understanding the developmental stages of spelling
- Understanding that learning to spell is problem solving
- Teaching of the rules of spelling
- Promoting an awareness about spelling

Spelling should be taught within the context of meaningful language experiences. Giving children a list of words to learn to spell and then testing the children on the words every Friday will not aid in the development of spelling. Children must be able to use the words in context and they must have some meaning for the children. You should assess the ability of children to spell and determine their problems within a meaningful environment.

What are the main reasons for assessing spelling?
- To find out what the child knows about spelling patterns and strategies
- To determine what the teacher needs to teach
- To develop spelling growth over a period of time

For a spelling assessment to be accurate, it must have meaning for the children. Taking a list of misspelled words from a piece of writing is one example of a spelling list that the teacher can use. If the teacher keeps a list of words the children ask to spell, this can also be the basis for a word list.

Since spelling is something that is learned over time, you may notice that the children keep spelling the same words incorrectly again and again. Through explicit teaching of strategies and even learning tricks to help spell the words, eventually they will see success in spelling. Assessment is something that must take place over the course of a grade. Correct spelling is not something that children learn and retain automatically.

When assessing spelling, you'll want to look for these behaviors:
- Knowledge of sounds and symbols
- Development of visual memory
- Development of morphemic knowledge
- Mastery of high frequency words at specific grade levels
- Location and knowledge of how to use spelling resources
- Attempts at spelling unknown words
- Risk taking attempts in using invented spelling

Skill 6.2   Systematic spelling instruction

Spelling Pattern Word Wall

One of the understandings emergent readers come to about a word is that if they know how to read, write, and spell one word, they can read, write, and spell many other words as well.

Create in your classroom a spelling pattern word wall. The spelling word wall can be created by stapling a piece of 3" x 5" butcher block paper to the bulletin board. Then attach spelling pattern cards around the border with thumbtacks, so that the cards can be easily removed to use at the meeting area.

Once you decide on a spelling pattern for instruction, remove the corresponding card from the word wall. Then take a 1"x 3" piece of a contrasting color of butcher block paper and tape the card to the top end of a sheet the children will use for their investigation.

After the pattern is identified, the children can try to come up with other words that have the same spelling pattern. The teacher can write these on the spelling pattern sheet, using a different color marker to highlight the spelling pattern within the word. The children have to add to the list until the sheet is full, which might take two days or more.

After the sheet is full, the completed spelling pattern is attached to the wall. Once you decide on a spelling pattern for instruction, remove the corresponding card from the word wall. Then take a 1'x 3' piece of a contrasting color of paper and tape the card to the top end of a sheet the children will use for their investigation. Next read one of Wylie and Durrell's short rimes with the children and have them identify the pattern.

Some of the techniques teachers use to determine the words students need to spell include the following:
- Lists of misspelled words from student writing
- Lists of theme words
- Lists of words from the content areas
- Word bank

Skill 6.3   Spelling instruction in context

Beginning writers need to know that spelling is an important part of the writing process. However, insisting on correct spelling right from the beginning may actually hamper the efforts of beginning writers. In early spelling development, children should be allowed to experiment with words and use invented spelling. Spelling development is something that occurs over time as a developmental process. It does develop in clearly defined stages, which you should consider when planning lessons. Teachers should assess students' spelling knowledge and then plan mini-lessons to whole class and small groups as they are necessary.

Some of the ways teachers can provide spelling instruction in the context of meaningful reading and writing activities include:

- Shared reading
- Shared writing
- Reading chants
- Writing letters
- Writing daily news in the classroom

- Guided reading
- Shared reading
- Writing lists
- Writing invitations
- Poetry reading using rhyming words with the same spelling patterns

By planning spelling instruction, you will help children recognize word patterns, help then discern spelling rules, and help them develop their own tricks for remembering how to spell words. Direct instruction is necessary for students to develop the knowledge they need regarding the morphological structure of words and thus the relationships between words. Students also need to be taught graphophonic relationships to know the relationship between letters and sounds, the probability of letter sequences and the different letter patterns.

Developing visual methods of recognizing correct spelling is also an aid to helping students learn to spell when they can trace around the shape of a word. This helps them develop a visual memory as to whether or not the word looks as if it is spelled correctly. Memory aids (mnemonics) also aid in spelling development, such as in the word PAINT—Pat Added Ink Not Tar.

Along with direct teaching of spelling, you should model the process at all times. By talking about spelling and having students assist in class writing, you will help students develop the awareness that spelling is important. Some activities where teachers can use this approach include:

- Experience charts
- Writing notes to parents
- Writing class poems and stories
- Editing writing with students

Students also need to be encouraged to take risks with spelling. Rather than have students constantly asking how words are spelled, you can use "Have a Go Sheets." These sheets consist of three columns in which the students write the words as they think it is spelled. Then the **student asks the teacher** or another student if it is spelled correctly. If it is incorrect the student will tell the student which letters are in the correct place and the student will try again. After the third try, you can either tell the student how to spell the word and add this to the list of words the student has to learn or work on the necessary spelling strategy.

DOMAIN III.   **DEVELOPING READING COMPREHENSION AND PROMOTING INDEPENDENT READING**

COMPETENCY 7.0   READING COMPREHENSION

Skill 7.1   Assessing reading comprehension

Cooper defines comprehension as "a strategic process by which readers construct or assign meaning to a text by using the clues in the text and their own prior knowledge." We view comprehension as a process where the reader transacts with the text to construct or assign meaning. Reading and writing are both interconnected and mutually supportive. Comprehension is a strategic process in which readers adjust their reading to suit their reading purpose and the type or genre of text they are reading. Narrative and expository texts require different reading approaches because of their different text structures.

Strategic readers also call into play their metacognitive capacities as they analyze texts so that they are self aware of the skills needed to construct meaning from the text structure.

Knowledge of Reading as a Process to Construct Meaning

Two words synonymous with reading comprehension as related to the balanced literacy approach are "constructing meaning."

Cooper, Taberski, Strickland, and other key theorists and classroom teachers conceptualize the reader as interacting with the text and bringing prior knowledge and experience to it. Writing is interlaced with reading and is a mutually integrative and supportive parallel process—hence the division of literacy learning by the balanced literacy folks into reading workshop and writing workshop, with the same anchor "readings" or books being used for both.

Consider the sentence, "The test booklet was white with black print, but very scary looking."

According to the idea of constructing meaning as the reader read this sentence, the schemata (generic information stored in the mind) of tests the reader had experienced was activated by the author's notion that tests are scary. Therefore the ultimate meaning that the reader derives from the page is from the reader's own responses and experiences coupled with the ideas the author presents. The reader constructs a meaning that reflects the author's intent and also the reader's response to that intent.

It is also to be remembered that generally readings are fairly lengthy passages, composed of paragraphs which in turn are composed of more than one sentence. With each successive sentence, and every new paragraph, the reader refocuses. The schemata are reconsidered, and a new meaning is constructed.

Skill 7.2   Fluency and other factors affecting comprehension

Reading comprehension and reading fluently are necessary skills that students must acquire to become good readers. There are students who can read fluently, yet do not understand what they read, which means that teachers should ask questions about the text to ensure comprehension. When students do not read fluently, this can hamper comprehension because the student takes so long trying to figure out the words that the meaning is lost.

A lack of background knowledge is often one of the factors that affect comprehension. When students do not understand the topic at hand, they will have difficulty reading about the topic no matter how fluently they read. Other factors that affect the level of comprehension are:
- Lack of word recognition skills
- Inability to determine the meanings of words through context clues
- Insufficient level of vocabulary development

Through assessment teachers can determine the instruction students need before reading a text so that comprehension can take place.

Schemata, Prior Knowledge, Background, and Comprehension

Schemata are structures which represent generic concepts stored in our memory (Rumelhart, 1980). Young children develop their schemata through experiences. Prior knowledge and the lack of experiences in some cases influence comprehension. The more closely the reader's experiences and schemata approximate those of the writer, the more likely the reader is to comprehend the text. For many children from non-native English language speaking backgrounds and perhaps for those from struggling socio-economic family structures, schemata deficits indicate the need for intense teacher support as these children become emergent and early readers.

Often the teacher will have to model and scaffold for the child the steps to form a schemata from the information provided in a text.

Relationship Between Word Analysis Skills
and Reading Comprehension

The explicit teaching of word analysis requires that the teacher pre-select words from a given text for vocabulary learning. These words should be chosen based on the storyline and main ideas of the text. The educator may even want to create a story map for a narrative text or develop a graphic organizer for an expository text.

Once the story mapping and/or graphic organizing have been done, the educator can compile a list of words which relate to the storyline and/or main ideas.

The number of words that require explicit teaching should only be two or three. If the number is higher than that, the children need guided reading and the text needs to be broken down into smaller sections for teaching. When broken down into smaller sections, each text section should only have two to three words which need explicit teaching.

Some researchers, including Tierney and Cunningham, believe that a few words should be taught as a means of improving comprehension. However, the teacher can decide whether the vocabulary selected for teaching needs review before reading, during reading, or after reading.

Introduce vocabulary BEFORE READING if. . .

- Children are having difficulty constructing meaning on their own. Children themselves have previewed the text and indicated words they want to know.

- The teacher has seen that there are words within the text which are definitely keys necessary for reading comprehension

- The text, itself, in the judgment of the teacher, contains difficult concepts for the children to grasp.

Introduce vocabulary DURING READING if . . .

- Children are already doing guided reading.

- The text has words which are crucial to its comprehension and the children will have trouble comprehending it, if they are not helped with the text.

Introduce vocabulary AFTER READING if. . .

- The children themselves have shared words which they found difficult or interesting.

- The children need to expand their vocabulary.

- The text itself is one that is particularly suited for vocabulary building.

Strategies to support word analysis and enhance reading comprehension include the following

- Use of a graphic organizer such as a word map
- Semantic mapping
- Semantic feature analysis
- Hierarchical and linear arrays
- Preview in context
- Contextual redefinition
- Vocabulary self-collection

Skill 7.3   Facilitating comprehension

Use of Comprehension Skills Before, After, and During Reading

Cooper (2004) advocates that the children ask themselves what a text is about before they read it and, even during reading of the text, what the text is going to be about. The children should be continually questioning themselves whether the text has confirmed their predictions. Of course after completing the text, they can then review the predictions and verify whether they were correct.

Using another strategy, the children look over the expository text subheadings, illustrations, captions and indices to get an idea about the book. Then the children, before reading the text, decide whether they can find the answers to their questions.

Cooper (2004), Taberski (2000), Cox (2005) and other researchers recommend a broad array of comprehension strategies before, during, and after reading.

Cooper (2004) suggests a broad range of classroom posters on the walls plus explicit instruction to give children prompts to monitor their own reading. An example follows:

My Strategic Reading Guide

1. Do I infer/predict important information, use what I know, think about what may happen or what I want to learn?
2. Can I identify important information about the story elements?
3. Do I generate questions and search for the answers?
4. Does this make sense to me? Does this help me meet my purpose in reading?
5. If lost, do I remember fix-ups?
6. Re-read, read further ahead, look at the illustrations, ask for help, and think about the words, and evaluate what I have read.
7. Do I remember to think about how the parts of the stories that I was rereading came together?

Storyboard panels, which are used by comic strip artists and by those artists who do advertising campaigns as well as television and film directors, are perfect for engaging children K-6 in a variety of comprehension strategies before, during, and after reading. They can storyboard the beginning of a story, read aloud, and then storyboard its predicted middle or end. Of course, after they experience or read the actual middle or ending of the story, they can compare and contrast what they produced with its actual structure. They can play familiar literature identification games with a buddy or as part of a center by storyboarding one key scene or characters from a book and challenging a partner or peer to identify the book and characters correctly.

Use of Oral Language Activities to Promote Comprehension

Taberski advocates using the "Stopping to Think About" strategy with expository texts as well as fictional ones.

This strategy is centered on the readers using three "steps" as they go through the expository text. These steps may be expressed as questions.

1. What do I, the reader, think is going to happen?
2. What clues in the text or illustrations or graphics lead me to think that this is going to happen?
3. How can I prove that I am right by going back to the text to demonstrate that this does happen or is suggested by actual clues in the text?

Taberski (2000) deliberately uses expository texts that relate to her grade's social studies and science lessons to model for children how to "stop and think" about the way an expository text is organized. She sometimes deliberately reads a section of a text or a non-fiction book aloud until the end of its chapter, so that the children can consider what they have learned about the topic and how it is organized. Then together as a whole class or as a whole guided reading group, they make predictions about what is coming next.

Skill 7.4   Different levels of comprehension

**Knowledge of Levels of Reading Comprehension
(Literal, Inferential, and Evaluative) and Strategies for Promoting
Comprehension of Informational/expository Texts at All Three Levels**

There are five key strategies for child reading of informational/expository texts.

1. **Inferencing** is a process that involves the reader making a reasonable judgment based on the information given and engages children to literally construct meaning. You can develop and enhance this key skill in children with a mini lesson where you demonstrate this by reading an expository book aloud (i.e. one on skyscrapers for young children) and then demonstrate for them the following reading habits: looking for clues, reflecting on what the reader already knows about the topic, and using the clues to figure out what the author means/intends.

2. **Identifying main ideas** in an expository text can be improved when the children have an explicit strategy for identifying important information. They can make this strategy part of their everyday reading style, "walking" through the following exercises during guided reading sessions. Children should read the passage so that the topic is readily identifiable. It will be what most of the information is about.

   Next they should be asked to be on the lookout for a sentence within the expository passage that summarizes the key information in the paragraph. Then the children should read the rest of the passage or excerpt in light of this information and also note which information in the paragraph is less important. The important information the children have identified in the paragraph can be used to formulate the author's main idea. The readers may even want to use some of the author's own language in stating that idea.

3. **Monitoring** means self-clarifying: As they read, the children often realize that what they are reading is not making sense. They then need a plan for making sense out of the excerpt. Cooper and other balanced literacy advocates have a stop and think strategy which they use with children. A child reflects, "Does this make sense to me?" When the child concludes that it does not, the child then either re-reads, reads ahead in the text, looks up unknown words or asks for help from the teacher.

What is important about monitoring is that some readers ask these questions and try these approaches without ever being explicitly taught them in school by a teacher. However, these strategies need to be explicitly modeled and practiced under the guidance of the teacher by most, if not all, child readers.

4. **Summarizing** engages the reader in pulling together into a cohesive whole the essential bits of information within a longer passage or excerpt of text. Children can be taught to summarize informational or expository text by following these guidelines. First they should look at the topic sentence of the paragraph or the text and ignore the trivia. Then they should search for information which has been mentioned more than once and make sure it is included only once in their summary. Find related ideas or items and group them under a unifying heading. Search for and identify a main idea sentence. Finally, put the summary together using all these guidelines.

5. **Generating questions** can motivate and enhance children's comprehension of reading in that they are actively involved. The following guidelines will help children generate meaningful questions that will trigger constructive reading of expository texts. First children should preview the text by reading the titles and subheadings. Then they should also look at the illustrations and the pictures. Finally they should read the first paragraph. These first previews should yield an impressive batch of specific questions.

Next, children should get into a Dr. Seuss mode and ask themselves a "think" question. Make certain that the children write down the question. Then have them read to find important information to answer their "think" question. Ask that they write down the answer they found and copy the sentence or sentences where they found the answer. Also have them consider whether, in light of their further reading through the text, their original question was a good one or not.

Ask them to be prepared to explain why their original question was a good one or not. Once the children have answered their original "think" question, have them generate additional ones and then find their answers and judge whether these questions were "good" ones in light of the text.

Skill 7.5   Comprehension strategies

Use of Writing Activities to Promote Comprehension

K-W-L Strategy

This is a graphic organizer strategy which activates children's prior knowledge and also helps them target their reading of expository texts. This focus is achieved through having the children reflect on three key questions.

Before the child read the expository passage:
"What do I *K*now?" and
"What do I or we *W*ant to find out?"

After the child has read the expository passage:
"What have I or we *L*earned from the passage?"

What is excellent about this strategy, which is broadly used and easily implemented in almost any classroom, is that it is almost totally student- centered and powerfully focuses the children's attention on the actual reading of expository passages. The K-W-L strategy also helps the children prepare for a potential writing task.

When the teacher first introduces the K-W-L strategy, the children should be allowed sufficient time to brainstorm what all of them in the class or small group actually know about the topic. The children should have a three-columned K-W-L worksheet template for their journals and there should be a chart up front to record the responses from class or group discussion. The children can write under each column in their own journal and should also help the teacher with notations on the chart. This strategy enables the children to gain experience in note taking and keep a concrete record of new data and information they have gleaned from the passage about the topic.

Depending on the grade level of the participating children, the teacher may also want to channel them into considering categories of information they hope to find out from the expository passage. For instance, they may be reading a book on animals to find out more about the animal's habitats during the winter or about the animal's mating habits.

When children are working on the middle- section (*Want*) strategy sheet, the teacher may give them a chance to share what they would like to learn further about the topic and help them to express it in question format.

K-W-L is useful and can even be introduced as early as grade 2 with extensive teacher support. It not only serves to support the children's comprehension of a particular expository text but also models for children a format for note taking. Beyond note taking, when the teacher wants to introduce report writing, the K-W-L format provides excellent outlines and question introductions for at least three paragraphs of a report.

Cooper (2004) recommends this strategy for use with thematic units and with reading chapters in required science, social studies, or health text books.

In addition to its usefulness with thematic unit study, K-W-L is wonderful for providing the teacher with a concrete format to assess how well children have absorbed pertinent new knowledge within the passage (by looking at the third *Learn* section). Ultimately it is hoped that students will learn to use this strategy, not only under explicit teacher direction with templates of K-W-L sheets but also on their own by informally writing questions they want to find out about in their journals and then going back to their own questions and answering them after reading.

Both English Language Learners and struggling readers can benefit from the structure and format of the K-W-L approach. It allows them to share their prior experiences and knowledge of the topics covered in the expository text through natural conversation. It provides them with a natural device for the teacher or tutor to customize and to scaffold instruction to meet their linguistic and experiential backgrounds. Through the discussion and sharing of other children's comments, struggling readers and children from ELL backgrounds have an opportunity to learn how to use questions to "walk through" and take notes on expository writing.

Highly proficient readers can do a comparative expository news event study between print accounts, e-news reportage, and broadcast media coverage. They can prepare charts and their own news mock-up to show the similarities and contrasts between what aspects of the event get covered in what media format. They may also want to write to actual reporters and editors from the different media to share their insights and see if these professionals are willing to respond.

"If we want children to become strategic readers, then we create classrooms that reinforce the strategies we've demonstrated and allow children to practice on books that match their needs."—*Sharon Taberski*

Use of Text Features (e.g. Index, Glossary), Graphic Features (e.g. Charts, Maps), and Reference Materials

Traditionally, the aspects of expository text reading comprehension have been taught in a dry format using reference books from the school or public library, particularly the atlas, almanac, and dusty large geography volumes, to teach these necessary and meaningful skills.

Although these worthy library and perhaps classroom library books can still be used, it is much easier to take a simple newspaper to introduce and provide children with daily ongoing, authentic experiences in learning these necessary skills as they also keep up with real world events that affect their daily lives.

They can go on a chronological hunt through the daily newspaper and discover the many formats of schedules contained therein. For instance, some newspapers include a calendar of the week with literary, sports, social, movie, and other public events. Children can also go on scavenger hunts through various sections of the newspaper and on certain days find full blown timelines detailing famous individuals; careers, business histories, and milestones in the political history of a nation or even key movies made by a famous movie director up for an Oscar.

The nature of the newspaper reportage and the public's need to know the why and wherefore behind the story of natural disasters, company takeovers, political downfalls and uprisings leads newspapers to represent events graphically and to use cause /effect diagramming and comparison/contrast wording. If you want to make certain that the students come away with this material, you can pre-clip "teaching" stories from the news for the child and introduce them in a special news center.

After children have been walked through these comparison/contrast news writings and cause/effect diagramming as they have appeared in the newspaper, they can be challenged to find additional examples of these text structures in the news or challenged to reframe or rewrite familiar stories using these text structures. They can even use desktop publishing to re-author the stories using the same text structures.

If your class participates in a local Newspaper in Education program, where the children receive a free newspaper two to three times a week within the classroom, you can teach index skills using the index of the newspaper and having children compete or cooperate in small groups to find various features.

Map and chart skills take on much more relevance and excitement when the children work on these skills using sport charts detailing the batting averages and pass completions of their favorite players or perhaps the box scores of their older siblings' football and baseball games. Maps dealing with holiday weather become meaningful to children as they anticipate a holiday vacation.

Application of Comprehension Strategies for Electronic Texts

If the class gets newspapers in the classroom as part of an ongoing Newspapers in Education program, teachers can easily and naturally take the time to show children how their same news is covered online. All of the newspapers have e-news. Children can first do a K-W-L on what they know or think they know about e-news and then actually review their specific daily newspaper's site. With the support of the teacher or an older peer, they can examine the resource and perhaps note the following differences in electronic text:

- Use of moving pictures and video to document events
- Use of sound clips in addition to written text
- Use of music/sound effects not in printed text
- Links to other web resources and to other archived articles

Of course, this can lead to much rich discussion and to further detailed web versus print news resource analysis. For children in grades 5 and 6, this might even include a research investigation of a particular news story or event including broadcast media coverage.

Development of Reading Comprehension Skills and Strategies of Individual Students

While all readers can benefit from explicit expository reading strategies, the English Language Learner can truly get a gateway for understanding second language materials by working with a native English language speaking buddy on the question generating strategy. Both the buddy (a peer) and the teacher should alert and walk through with the English Language Learner student how much of a resource illustrations and pictures can be for constructing meaning.

If the teacher has time to work individually with the English Language Learner, the day's daily newspaper which is replete with graphics, photos and text is a wonderful tool for honing expository reading skills using these strategies.

The five strategies for enhancing expository reading skills are not beyond use with learners with special needs. However, rather than be offered in an array, these strategies would have to be presented one at a time—probably one on one with explicit teacher modeling and then done as shared reading and shared writing with the specific child.

Highly proficient readers might enjoy sharing their skills with other peers and could serve as the newspaper reading buddies for special needs students. They might not only support special needs grade level or younger peers in reading through a designated newspaper section every day but might also collaborate or oversee their peers or younger peers in designing a word search or crossword puzzle based on that particular section of the newspaper.

Use of editorial sports page cartoons is a good way to introduce special needs learners to opportunities for identifying point of view. They can also create their own takes on the topics of the editorial cartoons using an accessible, non-threatening storyboard format for their commentary.

COMPETENCY 8.0   LITERARY RESPONSE AND ANALYSIS

Skill 8.1   Assessing literary response and analysis

The Role of Literature in Developing Literacy

The balanced literacy approach advocates the use of "real literature"—recognized works of the best of children's fiction and non-fiction trade books and winners of such awards as the Newberry and Caldecott medals—for helping children develop literacy.

Balanced literacy advocates argue that:

- Real literature engages young readers and assures that they will become lifelong readers.
- Real literature also offers readers a language base that can help them expand their expressiveness as readers and as writers.
- Real literature is easier to read and understand than grade-leveled texts

There are districts in the United States where the phonics-only approach is heavily embedded. However, the majority of school districts would describe their approach to reading as the balanced literacy approach which includes phonics work as well as the use of real literature texts. To contrast the phonics and balanced literacy approaches as opposite is inaccurate, since a balanced approach includes both.

Visit online the key resources of the National Council of Teachers of English (NCTE) and the International Reading Association (IRA) to keep current with the latest research in the field.

Skill 8.2   Responding to literature

Sharon Taberski (2000) recommends that initially strategies for promoting comprehension of imaginative literary texts be done with the whole class.

Here are Taberski's four main strategies for promoting comprehension of imaginative literary texts. She feels that if repeated sufficiently during the K-3 years and even if introduced as late as grade 4 these strategies will even serve the adult lifelong reader in good stead.

Strategy One: "Stopping to Think" is reflecting on the text as a whole. As part of this strategy, the reader is challenged to come up with the answer to these three questions:

What do I think is going to happen? (Inferential)
Why do I think this is going to happen? (Evaluative and inferential)
How can I prove that I am right by going back to the story? (inferential)

Taberski recommends that teachers introduce these key strategies with books that can be read in one sitting and recommends the use of picture books for these instructive strategies.

Taberski also suggests that books which are read aloud and used for this strategy also contain a strong storyline, some degree of predictability, a text that invites discussion, and a narrative with obvious stopping points.

Strategy Two: story mapping, for promoting comprehension of imaginative and literary texts.

For stories to suit this strategy, they should have distinct episodes, few characters, and clear-cut problems to solve. In particular, Taberski tries to use a story where a single, central problem or issue is introduced at the beginning of the story and then resolved or at least followed through by the close of the story.

To make a story map of a particular story, Taberski divides the class into groups and asks one group of children to illustrate the "Characters" in the book. Another group of children are asked to draw the "Setting," while a third and fourth group of children tackle "Problem " and "Resolution." The story map may also help children hold together their ideas for writing in the writing workshop as they take their reading of an author's story to a new level.

Strategy Three: The character mapping strategy also used by Taberski focuses the children as readers on the ways in which the main character's personal traits can determine what will happen in the story. Character mapping works best when the character is a non-stereotypical individual, has been featured perhaps in other books by the same author, has a personality that is somewhat predictable, and is capable of changing behavior as a consequence of what happens.

Using writing to share, deepen, and expand understanding of literary texts is a cornerstone of the balanced literacy approach.

Strategy Four: Taberski advocates reading sections of stories aloud and then having the teacher pause to reflect on what's happened in the story and model writing down a response to it. The teacher can use a chart to record response to the events or characters of a particular story being read and the children can contribute their comments as well. Later on, the children can start reflective reader's notebooks or journals recording their reactions to their readings independently.

The best types of texts for this type of response are those that relate to age appropriate issues for young children (i.e. homework, testing, bullies, and friendship), a plot that can be interpreted in different ways, a text that is filled with questions, and a text full of suspense or wonder.

Development of Literary Response Skills

Literary response skills are dependent on prior knowledge, schemata, and background. Schemata (the plural of schema) are those structures which represent concepts stored in our memory.

Without schemata and experiences to call upon as they read, children have little ability to comprehend. Of course, the reader's schemata and prior knowledge have more influence on the comprehension of plot or character information that is implied rather than directly stated.

Prior Knowledge

Prior knowledge can be defined as all of an individual's prior experiences, learning, and development which precede his/her entering a specific learning situation or attempting to comprehend a specific text. Sometimes prior knowledge can be erroneous or incomplete. Obviously, if there are misconceptions in a child's prior knowledge, these must be corrected so that the child's overall comprehension skills can continue to progress. Prior knowledge of children includes their accumulated positive and negative experiences both in and out of school.

These might come from wonderful family travels, watching television, visiting museums and libraries, to visiting hospitals, prisons, and surviving poverty. Whatever the prior knowledge that the child brings to the school setting, the independent reading and writing the child does in school immeasurably expands his/her prior knowledge and hence broadens his/her reading comprehension capabilities.

As you prepare to begin any imaginative/literary text, you must consider the following about the students' level of prior knowledge:

1. What prior knowledge needs to be activated for the text, theme or for the writing to be done successfully?
2. How independent are the children in using strategies to activate their prior knowledge?

Holes and Roser (1987) have suggested five techniques for activating prior knowledge before starting an imaginative/literary text:

Free Recall: Tell us what you know about...

Unstructured Discussion: Let's talk about...

Structured Question: Who exactly was Jane Aviles in the life of the hero of the story?

Word Association: When you hear these words--hatch, elephant, who, think-- what author do you think of?

Recognition: Mulberry Street. What author comes to mind?

Previewing and predicting and story mapping are also excellent strategies for activating prior knowledge.

Skill 8.3   Literary analysis

Development of Literary Analysis Skills

You can sensitize and teach children about the features and formats of different literary genres in many exciting ways.

First, select fine children's literature as the basis for teaching literary analysis skills. Typically for younger children, you may turn to picture books. The best-illustrated picture book published in the U.S. each year wins the Caldecott award, named for Randolph Caldecott, was a 19th century English illustrator. There is one winning book selected yearly as well as one, two, or three Honor Books. You cannot go wrong in selecting "Caldecott books" to share with children. In recent years, more and more picture books are being written for older children as well.

Another award in children's literature which is critically important is the Newbery Medal, presented for the most distinguished children's book written by a U.S. author in any given year. The Newbery award-winning books tend to be suitable for intermediate and middle-level children. The award is named for John Newbery, an 18th century English bookseller. Like the Caldecott awards, there is one "big" winner as well as several honor books selected each year.

Next, you'll want to introduce various literary elements and devices to help the children understand the literature.

Analyzing Story Elements: Story elements include plot (including conflict and resolution), setting (including time and place), characters (flat and round/static and dynamic), and theme (the main idea of the story). Students can use graphic organizers such as story maps, compare/contrast displays, and sequence boxes to display their understanding of these critical features of fiction.

Analyzing Character Development: Characters in children's literature may be flat or round. A flat character is one-dimensional and is often defined by one characteristic. Rosie in *Rosie's Walk* is an example. A round character has multi-dimensions, like someone you know, such as Jess in *Bridge to Terabithia,*

Static characters do not change from the beginning to the end of the story, while dynamic ones do. Characters reveal themselves through their actions, through their interactions, and through their words.

Interpreting Figurative Language: Similes are direct comparisons between two things using "like" or "as." "Her eyes were like stars" is a simile. Metaphors are indirect comparisons, such as "The earth is a big blue marble." Personification is giving human characteristics to non-animal beings. Frances, Shrek, or the animals in *Mr. Gumpy's Outing* are all examples of personification.

Identifying Literary Allusions: Children can understand allusions best when they read a lot. A literary allusion when it appears in a story is also called *intertextuality.* That is when a reference, character, or symbol from one story appears or is alluded to in another. Recently, many popular children's books use literary allusions, from the Ahlbergs' *Each Peach Pear Plum* to Jon Scieszka's *The True Story of the Three Little Pigs.* Note that any character or plot element can become an allusion, not just a reference from fairy tales.

Analyzing the Author's Point of View: In fiction, point of view is the vantage point from which the narrator tells the story. We determine point of view by asking where is the narrator standing in relation to the characters? Is the narrator inside or outside of the story? If inside, is the narrator one of the characters? This is *first person point of view.* If outside, can the narrator "see" into anyone else's mind besides his/her own? If the narrator cannot see into the mind and heart of other characters, then the point of view is *third person limited.* Narrators who can see what other characters are thinking and feeling are using *third person omniscient point of view.*

Genre Switch-Reader and Writer Transformation: This strategy should be introduced as a read aloud with young children or with children who are struggling readers. In a similar fashion, it would be introduced as a read-aloud for ELL learners. Older children in grades 3-6 might just be "started off" by a teacher prompt and do the required reading on their own.

To begin, the teacher selects a particular genre book. If it is close to Halloween, a goblin or suspense story will do well. The teacher begins to read the story with the open invitation to the students to determine, as the story is being read, what type of story it is and what makes it that type of story.

Older children take notes in their reading journals, while younger children and those more in need of explicit teacher support contribute their ideas and responses as part of the discussion in class. Their responses are recorded on a chart.

As the reading continues, the story type components are listed on the chart (most of the responses are those which have been elicited from the children). At some point in what is either an oral read aloud, guided reading, or independent reading, the teacher directs the children's attention to the components which have emerged on the chart. They then use these components which are generally components of character—setting, plot, style, conflict, language—to identify the story genre.

The teacher provides the children with an opportunity to expound at length on why this story is an example of the genre which they have identified.
Once they have done so, the teacher challenges them to consider how this story with its set of given characters, plot, and setting would be changed if the genre were different. The teacher can challenge the class as a whole with the idea of changing the story to a radically different genre—i.e. from suspense to a fairy tale or a comedy or allow the children to come up another genre.

Then depending on the children's developed writing abilities, they might be given time to rewrite the story on their own or re-tell it in class prior to writing and illustrating it.

In the balanced literacy approach, this transformation of the story into another genre is done as part of the Writing Workshop component which uses the same reading material as the source for writing. The strategy results in the children experiencing an in-depth analysis of a particular genre as well as hands-on writing (or telling, if they can not yet write or can not yet write in English) experience of restyling that basic plot and characters into another genre. This authenticates the children's participation as readers and writers.

Use of Writing Activities
to Promote Literary Response and Analysis

In addition to the activities already mentioned, the following activities will promote literary response and analysis:

- Have children take a particular passage from a story and retell it from another character's perspective.

- Challenge children to suggest a sequel or a prequel to any given story they have read.

- Ask the children to recast a story so that the male characters become female characters (or vice versa). Have them explain how these changes alter the narrative, plot, or outcome.

- Encourage the children to transform a story or book into a Reader's Theater format and record it complete with sound effects for the audio-cassette center of the classroom.

- Have the children produce a newspaper as the characters of a given story would have reported the news in their community.

- Transform the story into a ballad poem or a picture book version for younger peers.

- Give ELL children an opportunity to translate stories into their native language or to author in English with a buddy a favorite story that was originally published in their native language.

COMPETENCY 9.0   CONTENT-AREA LITERACY

Skill 9.1   Assessing content-area literacy

Informational/Expository Texts

Expository texts are full of information which may or may not be factual and which may reflect the bias of the editor or author. Children need to learn that expository texts are organized around main ideas. Expository content is commonly found in newspapers, magazines, content textbooks, and informational reference books (i.e. atlas, almanac, yearbook of an encyclopedia).

Text Structures

The five types of expository texts (also called "text structures") to which the children should be introduced through modeled reading and a teacher facilitated walk through are:

Description Text usually gives the characteristics or qualities of a particular topic. It can be depended upon to be factual. Within this type of text, the readers have to use all of their basic reading strategies because these types of expository texts do not have explicit clue words.

Causation or Cause-Effect Text is one in which faulty reasoning may occur and the readers have to use inferential and self-questioning skills to assess whether the stated cause-effect relationship is a valid one. Clue words to look for are *therefore, the reasons for, as a result of, because, in consequence of, and since.* The readers must then decide whether the relationship is valid. For example, does the ventricle pump blood into the heart?

Comparison Text is an expository text which gives contrasts and similarities between two or more objects and ideas. Many social studies, art, and science text books in class and non-fiction books include this contrast. Key words to look out for are *like, unlike, resemble, different, different from, similar to, in contrast with, in comparison to,* and *in a different vein.* As children examine texts which are talking about illustrated or photographed entities, they should be able to review the graphic representations for clues to support or contradict the text.

Collection Text presents ideas in a group. The writer presents a set of related points or ideas. This text structure is also called a listing or a sequence. The author frequently uses clue words such as *first, second, third, finally,* and *next* to alert the reader to the sequence. Based on how well the writer structures the sequence of points or ideas, the reader should be able to make connections. The writer must make clear in the expository text how the items are related and why they follow in that given sequence.

Simple collection texts that can be literally modeled for young children include recipe making. A class of first graders, beginning readers and writers, were literally spellbound by a teacher's presentation of a widely known copyrighted collection text. The children were thrilled as the author followed the sequences of this collection text, and the children finally took turns stirring it until it was creamy and smooth. The children enjoyed eating their Cream Farina from a commercial cereal box which had cooking directions on it. The children had constructed meaning from this five-minute class demonstration and would now pay close attention to collection texts on other food and product instruction boxes because this text had become an authentic part of their lives.

Response Structure Expository Text presents a question or response followed by an answer or a solution. Of course, entire mathematics text books and some science and social studies text books are filled with these types of structures. Again, you as the teacher should walk the readers through the excerpt and sensitize them to the clue words which signal this type of structure. These words include, but are not limited to *the problem is, the question is, you need to solve for, one probable solution would be, an intervention could be, the concern is,* and *another way to solve this would be.*

Newspapers provide wonderful features which you can use as read-alouds to introduce children grades 3-6 to point of view distinctions, specifically editorials, editorial cartoons and key sports editorial cartoons. Children come to understand the distinction between fact and fiction when they examine a newspaper advertisement or a supermarket circular for a product they commonly use, eat, drink, or wear which includes exaggerated claims about what the product can actually do for the individual in question.

What is really intriguing about the use of newspapers as a model and an authentic platform for introducing children into recognizing and using expository text structures, features and references is that the children can demonstrate their mastery of these structures by putting out their own newspapers detailing their school universe using some of these text structures. They can also create their own timelines for projects or research papers they have done in class using newspaper models.

Fact vs. Opinion

Finally the fact versus opinion distinction can be nicely explored if you take the children online to look at some star web sites and walk them through some exaggerated claims made about their particular movie star favorites. If the children have access to the Internet, you should show them how to examine web sites, look at who developed a particular web site, and consider how credible the developers of the site are.

The Role of Oral Language Fluency in Facilitating Comprehension of Informational/expository Texts

Children on the middle and secondary levels of education, who are studying social studies content, have been exposed to what social studies educators call re-enactments. This is a Reader's Theater-version of history and cultural study based completely on fact and established historical texts and documents.

Even young children will enjoy and gain tremendous additional expository comprehension facility when they are asked to dramatize a well known historical document or song. They may act out the preamble to the Constitution or read aloud as a chorus the Declaration of Independence or dramatize the Battle Hymn of the Republic. This gives children an opportunity to examine in deep form the vocabulary, syntactic, and semantic clues of these texts. They then have to use their oral instruments (voices) to express the appropriate expression for the texts. If the children are in grades 4 and above, they can also be asked to "explain" in writing how they used the word, syntactic clues, and semantic clues to interpret their oral language recitation. Recitation and writing can be a powerful experience for children grades 4 and up as they build their expository reading and writing skills.

Skill 9.2   Different types of texts and purposes for reading

Use of Reading Strategies for Different Texts and Strategies

As children progress to the older grades (3-6), you should model for them that in research on a social studies or science exploration, you don't have to read every single word of a given expository information text. For instance, if the children are trying to find out about hieroglyphics, they might read only through those sections of a book on Egyptian or Sumerian civilization which deal with picture writing. With the assistance of a child, you can model how to go through the table of contents and the index of the book to identify only those pages which deal with picture writing. In addition other children should come to the front of the room or to the center of the area where the reading group is meeting. They should then, with the support of the teacher, skim through the book for illustrations or diagrams of picture writing which is the focus of their need.

Children can practice the skills of skimming texts and scanning for particular topics that connect with their grade social studies, science and mathematics content area interests.

Strategies for Promoting Comprehension Across the Curriculum by Expanding Knowledge of Content Area Vocabulary

Key Words

Cooper (2004) feels that the teacher should preview the content area text to identify the main ideas. Then the teacher should compile a list of terms related to the content thrust. These terms and words become part of the key concepts list.

Next, the teacher sees which of the key concept words and terms are already defined in the text. These will not require direct teaching. Words for which children have sufficient skills to determine their meaning through base, root, prefixes or suffixes also will not require direct teaching.

Instruction in the remaining key words, which should not be more than two or three in number, can be provided before, during, or after reading. If students have previewed the content area and identified those words they need support on, the instruction should be provided before reading. Instruction can also easily be provided as part of guided reading support. After reading support is indicated, the text offers the children an opportunity to enrich their own vocabularies.

Having children work as a whole class or in small groups on a content specific dictionary for a topic regularly covered in their grade level social studies, science, or mathematics, curriculum offers an excellent collaborative opportunity. They can design a dictionary/word resource that celebrates their own vocabulary learning. Such a resource can then be used with the next year's classes as well.

Skill 9.3   Study skills

One of the most important ways of helping students experience success in school, especially with reading and studying in the content areas, is to teach them how to study. This involves such skills as how to take notes, summarize, find information in reference materials, and use maps and graphics. A fundamental part of teaching study skills also involves teaching students to set goals, organize their material, and manage their time.

Teachers can make a fundamental connection between reading and writing and other areas of the curriculum when they incorporate these skills into content areas. Students must be able to organize their thoughts, to conduct research, and to write using various strategies. This not only helps in writing but in their study skills as well.

Some of the strategies that teachers can use to teach these skills within a literacy framework include:

- Modeling how to take notes and summarizing.
- Using exemplars so that the students have a clear idea of what is an example of excellence and what is not acceptable
- Teaching students how to set goals
- Teaching time management
- Holding class discussion about a topic
- Modeling writing using "Think alouds," such as "How will I begin?"
- Teaching how to create an outline. For young writers, this would consist of having two or three words for each point. Gradually outline writing will progress through using a topic, heading, three or four supporting ideas for each point, and ending with a conclusion or opinion.

Specific strategies that are of value in the classroom include:
- Using guided reading and writing
- Think Aloud
- Think, Pair, Share
- Read for information—pose a question and have students scan the text to find the answer
- Venn diagram
- K-W-L chart (see example)
- Mind Mapping
- T-chart
- OWL chart—Observe, Wonder and Learn
- Search chart—students organize research under headings, such as
    - Where to look
    - Questions to be answered
    - Information gathered
    - Conclusions

When reading, students need to use as many different strategies as possible to increase their comprehension. With good comprehension being the end goal of all reading, teachers can help their students by teaching them specific features of texts that they can use to clarify or enhance their understanding.

K-W-L Chart

Know	Want	Learn
In this box, the teacher or students list the information they already know about the topic to be discussed	In this box, the teacher or students list the questions they have about the topic, which may be answered through research or the activities already planned to be completed	In this box, the teacher or students list what information has been learned at the <u>end</u> of the teaching process. This becomes a nice reflective piece for both students and teachers and can even be used as a quick assessment for the teacher to ascertain all predetermined objectives were met.

Textual Features

Using specific textual features, students can begin to find information more easily, which allows them to create their own schema. Using this schema, they can analyze and organize the information in a manner that is tied directly to their own personal experience and prior knowledge. Once it is connected, it will then be easier for the students to recall and use the information when needed. Most texts provide brief introductions. These introductions can be used by the reader to determine if the information they are seeking is located within the passage to be read. By reading a short passage, the students can quickly ascertain the need for a complete reading or whether a quick skim will suffice.

As we teach students to write, we often spend a lot of time teaching them to write paragraphs with topic sentences and concluding sentences. However, we should also provide explicit directions for using these same features to better understand text. These parallels can help students better understand what they are reading and also help them develop their writing skills. Understanding that topic sentences tell the main idea of the paragraph and concluding sentences restate that idea can help students' comprehension as well.

When searching for information students can become much more efficient if they learn to use a glossary and index. Students can find the necessary facts in a more rapid manner and also clarify information that they may not understand on a first read.

Additionally, charts, graphs, maps, diagrams, captions, and photos in text can work in the same way as looking up unknown words in the glossary. They can provide more insight and clarify concepts and ideas the author is conveying.

Students may need to develop these skills to interpret the information accurately, which makes a natural cross-subject opportunity.

Content area subjects often have texts with a great deal of information: typically, much more information than is necessary for students to know at one time. In cases like this, students should develop specific study skills to help them take in the important information while weeding out the less important.

Highlighting is a difficult strategy for students to master. Even at the college level students have a hard time determining what is important and necessary. Key ideas or vocabulary are a good place to start with highlighting. Teaching students to highlight less information rather than more is also important. Highlighting a whole page of information is not an effective study skill.

Outlining is a skill many teachers use to help students understand the important facts. Sometimes you can provide the outline to the students to use as a guide when taking their own notes. In this way, the students know the important parts to key in to when reading. Developing outlines can be very difficult for some students. For those students mapping might be a more appropriate study aid.

Mapping involves using graphics, pictures, and words to represent the information in the text. The students can personalize and use colors and pictures that have meaning to them. This provides the natural bridge to prior knowledge and frames the information in a more personal way.

Note-taking skills also require direct instruction. Sometimes teachers assume students understand how to take notes based on a lecture format when in fact; the majority of students are trying to write down as much as they hear. Teachers can help in this process by taking the time to specifically teach and highlight the key factors.

Test-taking skills are another area where students sometimes lag in skill development. Start by teaching students to eliminate automatic wrong answers first and then narrow the choices. In open-ended questions, students need to be able to restate the question in their answer and understand they need to answer all parts of the question being asked.

Combining all of these approaches will allow the students the opportunity to read, take in new information, and use that information to respond appropriately.

COMPETENCY 10.0   STUDENT INDEPENDENT READING

Skill 10.1   Encouraging independent reading

Reading specialists need to have a large amount of material available to them to be able to meet the needs of the various students they may encounter. As children's needs span a wide range of skills, they may require many different materials, books (of varying levels and interests), and technological items. This information can be overwhelming to think about, let alone find, organize and manage in the classroom.

In regards to organizing materials, there are various accepted methods. In most cases, the texts should be leveled according to some standards. Many people use the Fountas and Pinnell leveling system or the Developing Readers Assessment system. Either one will provide you with lists of books and their corresponding levels; in fact, most major publishing companies provide this information for all of their materials. Knowing these levels will be helpful in meeting the instructional needs of the students in a more efficient manner.

The books can also be organized by author, genre, series, topics, or other ways that are helpful to both teacher and student. Crates can be purchased rather inexpensively or boxes can be used to hold the books. Labeling each container is helpful, though time consuming at the beginning.

Supportive materials, such as lesson plans, worksheets, and activity guides, can be stored in filing cabinets labeled by book title or kept in the same storage container as the books. Keeping all materials together can be difficult to manage, but it is the most efficient way to organize an overwhelming amount of information.

Selecting materials to meet the instructional needs of students is important. Assessment data, including running records, provide the basis for beginning instruction. Interest surveys are another method of gaining insight into the minds of your students to be able to meet their needs in that respect as well.

Technological advances allow not only for the purchase of activities and games that are software based but also for web-based reading support programs. These sites can be bookmarked for ease of use at later times with various groups of students. Technology is often quite inspirational to students and they enjoy completing activities involving computers, tape recorders, and other devices.

Fiction and Nonfiction Genres

As the reading specialist, you should familiarize yourself with various genres of literature, including those that specifically appeal to the students with whom you work. In addition, you should be able to locate appropriate resources that can support content area learning for students.

There are numerous fictional genres that may appeal to students in kindergarten through twelfth grade. They include:

Mystery	Fantasy	Drama
Historical Fiction	Fable	Mythology
Fairy tale	Poetry	Folklore
Legends	Realistic Fiction	Tall Tales
Science Fiction		

When reading any genre of fiction, students need to have well developed phonemic awareness, phonics, and fluency skills. Vocabulary and comprehension development will continue to occur throughout schooling and should be an integral part of the reading process. Texts for teaching reading specifically, should include many of the various genres, both nonfiction and fiction, and provide some authentic works of literature even if in a condensed format. It is imperative to expose students to various types of authentic literature. In the nonfiction realm, it is important for students to have access to materials that will support their learning in content areas as well as books that match their interests and learning desires. Some nonfiction genres include:

Essays	Narrative Nonfiction	Biography
Speech	Autobiographies	

Understanding and using these different types of nonfiction text will provide the students with the opportunity to explore various topics or support their learning in content specific classes. In addition to books, it may be necessary to use reference materials including:

Dictionaries	Thesauruses	Encyclopedias
Almanacs	Histories	Newspapers

**Strategies for Promoting Independent Reading
in the Classroom and at Home**

You can encourage children to adopt independent reading habits at home as well as in the classroom. For example, you can pre-select books for the children that are just right for them. Provide the children with a quiet, relaxing space within the classroom where they can go to read these books. Don't get upset if they seem to take a break or wander around the room after fifteen minutes. Adults take breaks as well. Encourage them to set up their own reading area at home, even it's just a corner.

Make certain that the children who are reading independently fill in their weekly logs. Beyond telling what books they were reading and how many pages they have read, have the children respond to the following prompts:

This week I was successful at...

Next week I plan to...

A response can also be an illustration or a sentence or two about the book.

Deliberately assign a child or a pair of children to read big books. These are a guaranteed success for the children because they have already been shared in class. Some children enjoy reading these independently using big rulers to point at words. This provides them with a sense of mastery over the words and ownership of their independent reading.

Some children enjoy working on their own strategy sheet such as a story map, character map, or storyboard panel to demonstrate how they can apply a strategy to their own independent learning.

Skill 10.2   Supporting at-home reading

You can encourage children to read for pleasure at home. One of the best ways is to read aloud from a novel each day, even with grades as young as Grade 2. For Kindergarten and Grade 1, choosing picture books by one author at a time will help students realize that different authors write on different topics and in different ways. Author-studies in all grades will encourage students to seek out books by that author and read them on their own.

Even within the content areas, a wealth of fiction relates to the theme at hand and provides the students with background information that will help them with their studies. For example, when studying Colonial America in Social Studies, you can use many picture books as introductions for the lessons. Having part of the class read aloud from a novel about that period in history will help students develop an interest in reading about the themes and help them understand how much enjoyment that reading can bring.

Monthly book clubs are also an excellent way of getting age-appropriate reading material into the students' hands. Since these book clubs offer the books at fairly inexpensive prices, parents realize that they can get more value for their money when they order each month. Book fairs at school provide students with the chance to win books for themselves and their classrooms.

Read-a-thons encourage reading because the students realize that by reading they are helping a cause. Some of these offers include prizes for the students. Perhaps the teacher or school could initiate this kind of motivation.

DOMAIN IV.   **SUPPORTING READING THROUGH ORAL AND WRITTEN LANGUAGE DEVELOPMENT**

COMPETENCY 11.0   RELATIONSHIPS AMONG READING, WRITING, AND ORAL LANGUAGE

Skill 11.1   Assessing oral and written language

As a teacher, you'll want to demonstrate the relationship between spoken and written language. Here are a few strategies that have proven effective. No doubt you'll discover even more.

- Writing down what the children say on a language chart.
- Highlighting the uses of print products found in the classroom such as labels, yellow sticky pad notes, labels on shelves and lockers, calendars, signs, and directions.
- Reading together big-print and oversized books to teach print conventions such as directionality.
- Practicing how to handle a book: how to turn pages, to find the top and bottom of pages, and to tell the difference between the front and back covers.
- Discussing and comparing with children the length, appearance, and boundaries of specific words. For example, children can see that the names Dan and Dora share certain letters and a similar shape.
- Having children match oral words to printed words by forming an echo chorus as the teacher reads poetry or rhymes aloud and they echo the reading.
- Having the children combine, manipulate, switch and move letters to change words.
- Working with letter cards to create messages and respond to the messages that they create.

The variation in literacy backgrounds that children bring to reading can make teaching more difficult. Often a teacher has to choose between focusing on the learning needs of a few students at the expense of the group and focusing on the group at the risk of leaving some students behind academically. This situation is particularly critical for children with gaps in their literacy knowledge who may be at risk in subsequent grades for becoming "diverse learners."

Areas of Emerging Evidence

- **Experiences with print (through reading and writing) help preschool children develop an understanding of the conventions, purpose, and functions of print.** Children learn about print from a variety of sources and in the process come to realize that print carries the story. They also learn how text is structured visually (i.e., text begins at the top of the page, moves from left to right, and carries over to the next page when it is turned). While knowledge about the conventions of print enables children to understand the physical structure of language, the conceptual knowledge that printed words convey a message also helps children bridge the gap between oral and written language.

- **Phonological awareness and letter recognition contribute to initial reading acquisition by helping children develop efficient word recognition strategies (e.g., detecting pronunciations and storing associations in memory).** Phonological awareness and knowledge of print-speech relations play an important role in facilitating reading acquisition. Therefore, phonological awareness instruction should be an integral component of early reading programs. Within the emergent literacy research, viewpoints diverged on whether acquisition of phonological awareness and letter recognition are preconditions of literacy acquisition or whether they develop interdependently with literacy activities such as story reading and writing.

- **Storybook reading affects children's knowledge about, strategies for, and attitudes towards reading.** Of all the strategies intended to promote growth in literacy acquisition, none is as commonly practiced, nor as strongly supported across the emergent literacy literature, as storybook reading. Children in different social and cultural groups have differing degrees of access to storybook reading. For example, it is not unusual for a teacher to have students who have experienced thousands of hours of story reading time along with other students who have had little or no such exposure.

Design Principles in Emergent Literacy

- **Conspicuous Strategies.** As an instructional priority, conspicuous strategies are a sequence of teaching events and teacher actions used to help students learn new literacy information and relate it to their existing knowledge. Conspicuous strategies can be incorporated in beginning reading instruction to ensure that all learners have basic literacy concepts. For example, during storybook reading teachers can show students how to recognize the fronts and backs of books, locate titles, or look at pictures and predict the story, rather than assume children will learn this through incidental exposure. Similarly, teachers can teach students a strategy for holding a pencil appropriately or checking the form of their letters against an alphabet sheet on their desks or the classroom wall.

- **Mediated Scaffolding.** Mediated scaffolding can be accomplished in a number of ways to meet the needs of students with diverse literacy experiences. To link oral and written language, for example, teachers may use texts that simulate speech by incorporating oral language patterns or children's writing. Or teachers can use daily storybook reading to discuss book-handling skills and directionality-concepts that are particularly important for children who are unfamiliar with printed texts. Teachers can also use repeated readings to give students multiple exposures to unfamiliar words or extended opportunities to look at books with predictable patterns, as well as provide support by modeling the behaviors associated with reading. Teachers can act as *scaffolds* during these storybook reading activities by adjusting their demands (e.g., asking increasingly complex questions or encouraging children to take on portions of the reading) or by reading more complex text as students gain knowledge of beginning literacy components.

- **Strategic Integration.** Many children with diverse literacy experiences have difficulty making connections between old and new information. Strategic integration can be applied to help link old and new learning. For example, in the classroom, strategic integration can be accomplished by providing access to literacy materials in classroom writing centers and libraries. Students should also have opportunities to integrate and extend their literacy knowledge by reading aloud, listening to other students read aloud, and listening to tape recordings and videotapes in reading corners.

- **Primed Background Knowledge.** All children bring some level of background knowledge (e.g., how to hold a book, awareness of directionality of print) to beginning reading. Teachers can use children's background knowledge to help children link their personal literacy experiences to beginning reading instruction, while also closing the gap between students with rich and students with impoverished literacy experiences. Activities that draw upon background knowledge include incorporating oral language activities (which discriminate between printed letters and words) into daily read-alouds, as well as frequent opportunities to retell stories, look at books with predictable patterns, write messages with invented spellings, and respond to literature through drawing.

Emergent literacy research examines early literacy knowledge and the contexts and conditions that foster that knowledge. Despite differing viewpoints on the relation between emerging literacy skills and reading acquisition, strong support was found in the literature for the important contribution that early childhood exposure to oral and written language makes to the facility with which children learn to read.

Skill 11.2   Oral language development

Oral language development occurs over time and at varying rates. Children start by developing their own rules and learn correct pronunciation and grammar by listening to and being corrected by adults. Over time they learn the correct syntax, but they do need time to develop their oral language skills. There are three basic components to oral language development:

- Phonological—combination of sounds
- Semantics—sounds and words go together to form other words
- Syntactics—combining words to form sentences

Students come to kindergarten in varying degrees of oral language development. Teachers should not try to focus on problems or the inability to pronounce certain words or letter sounds. If, however, after providing enormous support, the child cannot make the proper speech sounds, then he/she should be referred to a speech pathologist. This situation exists for only a small number of children. Many children will outgrow the oral language problems with the proper coaching and modeling provided by the teacher. Teachers should nurture oral language development by:

- Providing a wealth of oral language opportunities in the classroom
- Respecting the diversity of backgrounds and cultures that the students bring to the classroom.
- Engaging the students in conversation while instructing.
- Encouraging conversation between the students

Activities to Develop Oral Literacy Response

Retelling

Retelling needs to be very clearly defined so that the readers do not think that you want them to spill the whole story back in the retelling. Children should be able to talk comfortably and fluently about the story they have just read. They should be able to tell the main things that have happened in the story.

When children retell a story, you need ways to help them assess their understanding. Ironically, you can use some of the same strategies that you might suggest to the children. These strategies include back cover reading, scanning the table of contents, looking at the pictures, and reading the book jacket.

If the children can explain how the story turned out and provide examples to support these explanations, try not to interrupt with too many questions.

Children can use the text of the book to reinforce what they are saying and they can even read from it if they wish. Remember that some children need to re-read the text twice and their re-reading if for enjoyment.

When you plan to use the retelling as a way of assessment, then set the following ground rules and make them clear to the children. Explain the purpose of the retelling to determine how well the children are reading at the outset of the conference.

You can record in their assessment notebooks what the children say by writing key phrases they use. Record just enough to indicate their understanding of the story. You should also try to analyze what the children have not comprehended from the text. If the accuracy rate with the text is below 95 percent, then the problem is at the word level, but if the accuracy rate for the text is above 95 per cent, the difficulty lies at the text level.

Skill 11.3   Written language development

While some of the children coming to kindergarten can make their letters and even print their names, others have not yet reached this stage. There are stages to developing knowledge of the written language just as there are to the development of oral language. Average four- and five-year-olds are at the stage of making mock letters and words. The letters may be backwards or upside down and the words consist of letters that form the main sounds of the words. For example, the word "bat" may be written as "bt." Students do know that there are letters in their name showing that they understand letters form words. Even though they can copy words, reversing the letters is a frequent occurrence.

As children become more comfortable with using letters, they start using invented spelling and punctuation. The words they use are usually words from their environment, which is why the classroom needs to be rich in print.

As they progress through the language development to begin to write stories, rules for written language are gradually introduced to the class as teachers determine the needs based on assessment.

Spelling rules and the mechanics of writing are taught within the context of meaningful reading and writing activities. Strategies that teachers can use as they teach the rules of written language include:

- Use language experience to transfer the skills of oral language development to writing words on a page.
- Teach students to use the writing process.
- Model writing by saying the words aloud as you write them for the children
- Make shared writing a common class activity.
- Encourage students to respond to what they read in the form of writing activities.

Skill 11.4   Supporting English language learners

In addition to other information found in previous chapters about English language learners, here are a few more points to keep in mind.

Awareness of Strategies and Resources for Supporting Individual Students

Children who come from family backgrounds where English is not spoken lack a solid understanding of its syntactic structure. Therefore as they are being assessed using the oral running record, they may need additional support from their teacher in examining the structure and meaning of English. Children from a non-native English Language speaking background may often pronounce words that make no sense and just go on reading. They have to learn to stop to construct meaning. This child may have to be prompted to self-correct.

Children from non-native English Language speaking backgrounds can benefit from independent reading opportunities to listen to a familiar story on tape and read along. This also gives them practice in listening to Standard English oral reading. Often these children can begin to internalize the language structures by listening to the book on tape several times.

Highly proficient readers can sometimes support early readers through a partner relationship. Some children, particularly the emergent and beginning early readers, benefit from reading books with partners. The partners sit side by side and each one takes turns reading the entire text.

Use of talking book and author web resources provides special needs learners with visual or auditory handicapping conditions immediate contact with authors. This can lead to direct sharing in the joy of oral language story telling. In addition to the accessibility of the keyboard, children's responses to literature can be shared with a broad network of other readers, including close and distance peers. Technology literally invites special needs learners into the circle of connected readers and writers.

Development of the Reading Comprehension Skills and Strategies of Individual Students

ELL Learners bring to their classrooms different prior knowledge concerns than their native English language speaking peers. Some of the ELL students have extensive prior knowledge in their native language and can read well on or above their chronological age level in their native language. Other ELL learners come to the United States from cultures where reading was not emphasized or circumstances did not give families native language literacy opportunities.

ELL learners who have a positive attitude toward both their first and second language learning are called "crisscrossers," and of course they are a delight for their teachers.

Rigg and Allen (1999) offer the following four principles regarding the literacy development and prior knowledge of ELL-second language learners:

1. In learning a language you learn to do the things you want to do with people who are speaking that language.
2. A second language, like the first, does not develop linearly, but rather globally.
3. Language can develop in rich context.
4. Literacy develops parallel to language, so as speaking and listening for the second language develop, so do writing and reading.

As far as retelling, be aware that English language learners have the problem of not bringing rich oral English vocabulary to the stories they are decoding. Therefore, often they "sound the stories out" well but can not explain what they are about because they do not know what the words mean.

COMPETENCY 12.0   VOCABULARY DEVELOPMENT

Skill 12.1   Assessing vocabulary knowledge

The Role of Systematic, Noncontextual Vocabulary Strategies

Hierarchical and Linear Arrays

The very complexity of the vocabulary used in this strategy description may be unnerving for the teacher. Yet this strategy included in the Cooper (2004) literacy instruction is really very simple once it is outlined directly for children.

By using the term "hierarchical and linear" arrays, Cooper really is talking about how some words are grouped-based on associative meanings. The words may have a "hierarchical" relationship to one another. For instance, an undergraduate or a first grader is lower in the school hierarchy than the graduate student and second grader. Within an elementary school, the fifth grader is at the top of the hierarchy and the pre K or kindergartener is at the bottom of the hierarchy. By the way, the term for this strategy obviously need not be explained in this detail to K-3 children, but it might be shared with some grade and age-appropriate modifications with children in grades 3 and beyond. It will enrich their vocabulary development and ownership of arrays they create.

Words can have a linear relationship to one another in that they run a spectrum from bad to good. For example from K-3 experiences, consider "pleased-happy-overjoyed." These relationships can be displayed in horizontal boxes connected with dashes. Below is another way to display hierarchical relationships.

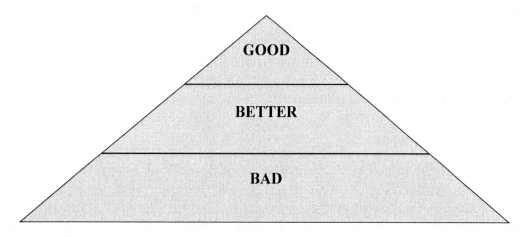

Once you get past the seemingly daunting vocabulary words, the arrays turn out to be another neat, graphic organizer tool which can help children "see" how words relate to one another.

To use this graphic organizer, you should pre-select a group of words from a read aloud or from the children's writing. Show the children how the array will look using arrows for the linear array and just straight lines for the hierarchy. In fact invite some children up to draw the straight hierarchy lines as it is presented, so they have a role in developing even the first hierarchical model.

Do one hierarchy array and one linear array with the pre-selected word with the children. Talk them through filling out (or helping you to fill out) the array. After the children have had their own successful experience with arrays, they can select the words from their independent texts or familiar, previously read favorites to study. They will also need to decide which type of array, hierarchical or linear, is appropriate. For 5th and 6th graders, this choice can and should be voiced using the now "owned" vocabulary words "hierarchical array" and "linear array."

This strategy is best used after reading since it will help the children expand their word banks.

Skill 12.2   Increasing vocabulary knowledge

Development of Vocabulary Knowledge and Skills

Hierarchical and linear array vocabulary development strategies lend themselves well to support the struggling learners or second language learners. The use of the arrays allows these learners to use a visual format to "see" and diagram word relationships. Furthermore the diagrams are easy to make, and they can be illustrated. With sufficient support and modeling, many special needs children can do simple linear and hierarchical arrays on their own. The arrays can also be attractively displayed in resource rooms and in regular education classrooms as a demonstration of these individual students' ownership of their words.

English Language Learners should first capably demonstrate their capacity to fill out hierarchical and linear arrays in their native language and then can work with this same format to hone their English Language vocabulary development. Their native language hierarchical relationships and arrays can be displayed in their general education classrooms.

Teachers may also want to encourage children grades 3 and beyond to make connections between some of the native, other than English, words, and words derived from them in English. This could be a rich "buddy" (ELL child and native English Language speaker) investigation or it could be one for ELL children alone. At any rate, use of the array with the ELL child's native language makes that child a second language vocabulary owner which immediately includes the child positively in ongoing vocabulary development.

Cooper (2004) suggests that teachers who have children from different language backgrounds use any unscheduled or "extra" time that emerges for read-alouds. Children should also learn to identify the purpose and organization to increase comprehension.

Author's purpose: Does the author want to inform, to entertain, or to persuade. One way to define the author's purpose is to have students examine the title, which can often set the tone of the passage. Reading newspaper headings is one way to practice determining the author's purpose.

Cause and effect: Cause and effect may occur in fiction, nonfiction, poetry, and plays. Sometimes one cause will have single or multiple effects. Other times, multiple causes lead to a single effect. Creating cause and effect diagrams helps you identify these components.

Chronological order: Recognizing the order of events in a selection. A text that is chronologically organized features a sequence of events that unfold over a period of time. For a student activity, you could read a passage to the students and then complete a timeline by matching the major events to their corresponding dates.

Probable passage: Probable passage is a strategy to improve comprehension, develop an awareness of story structure, and increase vocabulary development. For a student activity, you could prepare a story to be read to the students. Then put together a chart similar to the one below. Ask the students, "Can you predict the story you will be reading? Use the vocabulary words from your story frame to complete the probable passage by placing words into the blanks."

Vocabulary:
    Zeus
    recognized
    pardoned
    arena
    forest
    bound
    freed
    capture
    lion

Setting: _____

Characters: _____

Problem: _____

Solution: _____

Ending: _____

Graphic organizers: Graphic organizers help readers think critically about an idea, concept, or story by pulling out the main idea and supporting details. These pieces of information can then be depicted graphically through the use of connected geometric shapes. Readers who develop this skill can use it to increase their reading comprehension. See the graphic organizer in this section.

Selective underlining: Selective underlining is an effective tool for enhancing the recall of facts. It can be used both for initial reading and response and as a reference when studying for tests. Have students identify the main idea of various short stories and articles.

Story mapping: Story mapping is a technique used after a story has been read. It includes identifying the main elements and categorizing the main events in sequential order. A graphic representation is often used to illustrate the story structure and sequence of events.

When preparing to read a book, you should become acquainted with the elements of the story such as setting, characterization, style (language, both technically with regard to dialect but also structurally with regard to use of description, length of sentences, phrases, etc.), plot (particularly conflicts and pattern), tone (what is the *attitude* of the writer toward characters, theme, etc.) and particularly theme (the message or point the story conveys). Knowing the writer's biography is not essential but it is often helpful, especially in responding from the analyst's point of view.

Literature is written to evoke a personal response in readers. This is why so many books are sold. Once you have a grip on the story—a thorough understanding of the story—then an analysis of your own response to it is in order.

The following questions are useful:

1. Do you respond emotionally to one of the characters? Why? Is a character similar to someone you know or have known?
2. Is the setting evocative for you because of a place, situation, or milieu that you have experienced and that had meaning for you? Why?
3. Did the vocabulary, descriptions, or short or long sentences have impact on you? Why? For example, short, simple sentence after short, simple sentence may be used deliberately, but do you find it annoying?
4. Do you agree with the author's attitude toward the characters, setting, story, etc.? For example, has a character been written unsympathetically that you felt deserved more consideration? Does the author demonstrate distaste for the setting? Is this unjust? Or do you experience the same distaste?

Reading is personal. Responding to it personally adds important dimensions to an analysis for others.

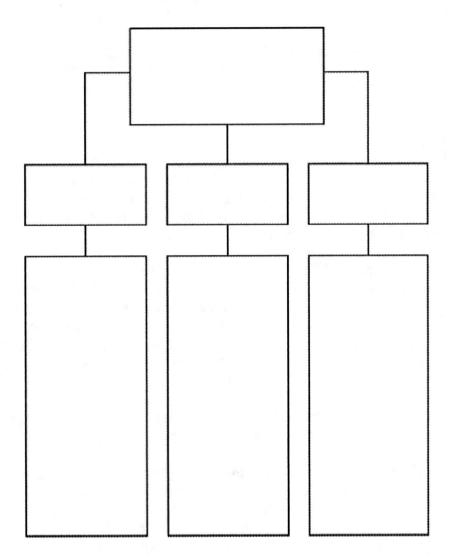

Skill 12.3   Strategies for gaining and extending meanings of words

Contextual Vocabulary Strategies

Vocabulary Self-Collection

This strategy is one in which children, even on the emergent level from grade 2 and up, take responsibility for their learning. It is also by definition a student-centered strategy, which demonstrates student ownership of their chosen vocabulary.

This strategy is one that you can introduce early in the year, perhaps even the first day or week. The format for self-collection can then be started by the children. It may take the form of a journal with photocopied template pages. It can be continued throughout the year.

To start, ask the children to read a required text or story. Invite them to select one word for the class to study from this text or story. The children can work individually, in teams, or in small groups. The teacher can also do the self-collecting so that this becomes the joint effort of the class community of literate readers. Tell the children that they should select words which particularly interest them or which are unique in some way.

After the children have had time to make their selections and to reflect on them, make certain that they have time to share them with their peers as a whole class. When the children have each shared their individual words, have them provide a definition for the word. Each word should be listed on a large experiential chart or even in a Big Book format, if that is age and grade appropriate. You should also share your word and provide a definition. Your definition and sharing should be somewhere in the middle of the children's recitations.

Use the dictionary to verify the definitions. When all the definitions have been checked, make a final list of child-selected (and single teacher-selected) words.

Once this final list has been compiled, the children can record it in their word journals or they may opt to record only those words they find interesting in their individual journals. You decide at the onset of the vocabulary self-collection activity whether the children have to record all the words on the final list or can eliminate some. Your decision made at the beginning must be adhered to throughout the year.

To further enhance this strategy, children, particularly those in grades 3 and beyond, can be encouraged to use their collected words as part of their writings or to record and clip the appearance of these words in newspaper stories or online.

This type of additional recording demonstrates that the children have truly incorporated the word into their reading and writing. It also habituates children to be lifelong readers, writers, and researchers.

One of the nice advantages about this simple but versatile strategy is that it works equally well with either expository or narrative texts. It also provides children with an opportunity to use the dictionary.

Assessment is built into the strategy. As the children select the word for the list, they share how they used contextual clues and through the children's responses to the definitions offered by their peers, you can assess their prior knowledge.

What is most useful about this strategy is that it documents that children can learn to read and write by reading and writing. The children take ownership of the words in the self-collection journals and that can also be the beginning of writer observation journals as they include their own writings. They also use the word lists as a start for writers' commonplace books. These books are filled with newspaper, magazine, and functional document clippings using the journal words.

This activity is a good one for demonstrating the balanced literacy belief that vocabulary study works best when the words studied are chosen by the child.

COMPETENCY 13.0   STRUCTURE OF THE ENGLISH LANGUAGE

Skill 13.1   Assessing English language structures

Language Development

The way language skills are developed depends on many factors, some internal (the age of the child), some external (immigration). Teachers can use a variety of approaches to accommodate individual differences.

Learning Approach

Early theories of language development were formulated from learning theory research. The assumption was that language development evolved from learning the rules of language structures and applying them through imitation and reinforcement. This approach also assumed that language, cognitive and social developments were independent of each other.

Thus, children were expected to learn language from patterning after adults who spoke and wrote Standard English. No allowance was made for communication through child jargon, idiomatic expressions, or grammatical and mechanical errors resulting from too strict adherence to the rules of inflection ("child's" instead of "children") or conjugation ("runned" instead of "ran"). No association was made between physical and operational development and language mastery.

Linguistic Approach

Studies spearheaded by Noam Chomsky in the 1950s formulated the theory that language ability is innate and develops through natural human maturation as environmental stimuli trigger acquisition of syntactical structures appropriate to each exposure level. The assumption of a hierarchy of syntax downplayed the significance of semantics. Because of the complexity of syntax and the relative speed with which children acquire language, linguists attributed language development to biological rather than cognitive or social influences.

Cognitive Approach

Researchers in the 1970s proposed that language knowledge derives from both syntactic and semantic structures. Drawing on the studies of Piaget and other cognitive learning theorists, supporters of the cognitive approach maintained that children acquire knowledge of linguistic structures after they have acquired the cognitive structures necessary to process language. For example, joining words for specific meaning necessitates sensory motor intelligence.

Children must be able to coordinate movement and recognize objects before they can identify words to name the objects or word groups to describe the actions performed with those objects.

Adolescents must have developed the mental abilities for organizing concepts as well as concrete operations, predicting outcomes, and theorizing before they can assimilate and verbalize complex sentence structures, choose vocabulary for particular nuances of meaning, and examine semantic structures for tone and manipulative effect.

Sociocognitive Approach

Other theorists in the 1970s proposed that language development results from sociolinguistic competence. Language, cognitive, and social knowledge are interactive elements of total human development. Emphasis on verbal communication as the medium for language expression resulted in the inclusion of speech activities in most language arts curricula.

Unlike previous approaches, the sociocognitive approach allowed that determining the appropriateness of language in given situations for specific listeners is as important as understanding semantic and syntactic structures.

By engaging in conversation, children at all stages of development have opportunities to test their language skills, receive feedback, and make modifications. As a social activity, conversation is as structured by social order as grammar is structured by the rules of syntax. Conversation satisfies the learner's need to be heard and understood and to influence others. Thus, the choices of vocabulary, tone, and content are dictated by the learner's ability to assess the language knowledge of listeners. The speaker is constantly applying his cognitive skills to using language in a social interaction. If the capacity to acquire language is inborn, without an environment in which to practice language, children would not pass beyond grunts and gestures, as did primitive man.

Of course, the varying degrees of environmental stimuli to which children are exposed at all age levels create a slower or faster development of language. Some children are prepared to articulate concepts and recognize symbolism by the time they enter fifth grade because they have been exposed to challenging reading and conversations with well-spoken adults at home or in their social groups. Others are still trying to master the sight recognition skills and are not yet ready to combine words in complex patterns.

Concerns for the Teacher

Because teachers must, by virtue of tradition and the dictates of the curriculum, teach grammar, usage, and writing as well as reading and later literature, the problem becomes when to teach what to whom.

The profusion of approaches to teaching grammar alone is mind-boggling. In the universities, we learn about transformational grammar, stratification grammar, sectoral grammar, and more. But in practice, most teachers, supported by presentations in textbooks and by the methods they learned themselves, keep coming back to the same traditional prescriptive approach - read and imitate - or structural approach - learn the parts of speech, the parts of sentence, punctuation rules, sentence patterns. After enough of the terminology and rules are stored in the brain, then we learn to write and speak. For some educators, the best solution is the worse—don't teach grammar at all.

The same problems occur in teaching usage. How much can we demand students communicate in only Standard English? Different schools of thought suggest that a study of dialect and idiom and recognition of various jargons is a vital part of language development. Social pressures, especially on students in middle and junior high schools, to be accepted within their peer groups and to speak the non-standard language spoken outside the school make adolescents resistant to the corrective, remedial approach. In many communities where the immigrant populations are high, new words are entering English from other languages even as words and expressions that were common when we were children have become rare or obsolete.

Regardless of differences of opinion concerning language development, language arts teachers will be most effective using the styles and approaches with which they are is most comfortable. And, if they subscribe to a student-centered approach, they may find that the students have a lot to teach them and each other.

Moffett and Wagner in the Fourth Edition of *Student-centered Language Arts K-12* stress the three I's: individualization, interaction, and integration. Essentially, they are supporting the socio-cognitive approach to language development. By providing an opportunity for students to select their own activities and resources, their instruction is individualized. By centering on and teaching each other, students are interactive. Finally, by allowing students to synthesize a variety of knowledge structures, they integrate them. The teacher's role becomes that of a facilitator.

Benefits of the Sociocognitive Approach

This approach has tended to guide the whole language movement, currently in fashion. Most basal readers use an integrated, cross-curricular approach to successful grammar, language, and usage. Reinforcement becomes an intradepartmental responsibility. Language incorporates diction and terminology across the curriculum. Standard usage is encouraged and supported by both the core classroom textbooks and current software for technology. Teachers need to acquaint themselves with the computer capabilities in their school district and at their individual school sites. Advances in new technologies require teachers to familiarize themselves with programs that would serve their students' needs. Students respond enthusiastically to technology.

Several highly effective programs are available in various formats to assist students with initial instruction or remediation. Grammar texts, such as the Warriner's series, employ various methods to reach individual learning styles. The school library media center should become a focal point for individual exploration.

Skill 13.2   Differences between written and oral English

The Relationship Between Oral and Written Vocabulary Development and Reading Comprehension

Biemiller's (2003) research documents that children entering 4th grade with significant vocabulary deficits demonstrate increasing reading comprehension problems. Evidence shows that these children do not catch up, but rather continue to fall behind.

Strategy One: Word Map Strategy

This strategy is useful for children grades 3-6 and beyond. The target group of children for this strategy includes those who need to improve their independent vocabulary acquisition abilities. The strategy is essentially teacher-directed learning where children are "walked through" the process. They are helped by the teacher to identify the type of information that makes a definition. They are also assisted in using context clues and background understanding to construct meaning.

The word map graphic organizer is the tool teachers use to complete this strategy with children. Word map templates are available online from the Houghton Mifflin web site and from READWRITETHINK, the web site of the NCTE (see Webliography section). The word map helps the children to represent visually the elements of a given concept.

The children's literal articulation of the concept can be prompted by three key questions: What is it? What is it like? What are some examples?

For instance, the word "oatmeal" might yield a word map with "What?" In a rectangular box you would write "a hot cereal you eat in the morning." "What is it like?" The answer is "hot, mushy, salty." To the question "What are some examples?" you would write "instant oatmeal you make in a minute, apple-flavor oatmeal, Irish Oatmeal."

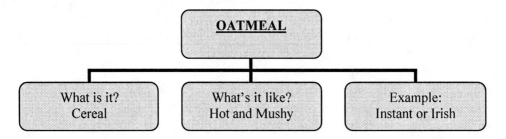

The procedure to be used in sharing this strategy with children is to select three concepts the children are familiar with. Then show them the template of a word map. Tell them that the three questions asked on the map and the boxes to fill in beneath them helps readers and writers to see what they need to know about a word. Next, help the children complete at least two word maps for two of the three concepts that were pre-selected. Then have the children select a concept of their own to map either independently or in a small group. As the final task for this first part of the strategy, have the children, in teams or individually, write a definition for at least one of the concepts using the key things about it listed on the map. Have the children share these definitions aloud and talk about how they used the word maps to help them with the definitions.

For the next part of this strategy, you should pick up an expository text or a textbook the children are already using to study mathematics, science or social studies. Either locate a short excerpt where a particular concept is defined or use the content to write model passages of definition on your own.

After the passages are selected or authored, duplicate and distribute them to the children along with blank word map templates. The children should be asked to read each passage and then to complete the word map for the concept in each passage. Finally, have the children share the word maps they have developed for each passage. Give them a chance to explain how they used the word in the passage to help them fill out their word map. End by telling them that the three components of the concept—class, description, example—are just three of the many components for any given concept.

This strategy has assessment potential because you can literally see how the students understand specific concepts by looking at their maps and hearing their explanations. The maps the students develop on their own demonstrate whether they have really understood the concepts in the passages. This strategy serves to ready students for inferring word meanings on their own. By using the word map strategy, children develop concepts of what they need to know to begin to figure out an unknown word on their own. It assists the children in grades 3 and beyond to connect prior knowledge with new knowledge.

This word map strategy can be adapted by the teacher to suit the specific needs and goals of instruction. Illustrations of the concept and the comparisons to other concepts can be included in the word mapping for children grades 5 and beyond. This particular strategy is also one that can be used with a research theme in other content areas.

Strategy Two: Preview in Context

This is a direct teaching strategy which enables you to guide the students as they examine words in context prior to reading a passage. Before beginning the strategy, select only two or three key concept words. Then read carefully to identify passages within the text that evidence strong context clues for the word.

Then present the word and the context to the children. As you read aloud, the children follow along. Once you have finished the read aloud, the children re-read the material silently. After the silent re-reading, coach the children to a definition of one of the key words selected for study. This is done through a child-centered discussion. As part of the discussion, asks questions which get the children to activate their prior knowledge and to use the contextual clues to figure out the correct meaning of the selected key words. Make certain that the definition of the key concept word is finally made by the children.

Next, help the children begin to expand the word's meaning. Have them consider the following for the given key concept word: synonyms, antonyms, other contexts or other kinds of stories/texts where the word might appear. This is the time for the children check their responses to the challenge of identifying word synonyms and antonyms. Have them go to the thesaurus or the dictionary to confirm their responses. In addition, have the children place the synonyms or antonyms they find in their word boxes or word journals. The recording of their findings will guarantee them ownership of the words and deepen their capacity to use contextual clues.

The main point to remember in using this strategy is that it should only be used when the context is strong. It will not work with struggling readers who have less prior knowledge. Through listening to the children's responses as you help them define the word and its potential synonyms and antonyms, you can assess their ability to use context clues successfully. The key to this simple strategy is that it allows the teacher to draw the child out and to grasp through the child's responses the individual child's thinking process. The more talk from the child the better.

The Relationship between Oral Vocabulary
and the Process of Identifying and Understanding Written Words

One way to explore the relationship between oral vocabulary and the comprehension of written words is through the use of Oral Records (which are discussed at length in the appendix).

In *On Solid Ground: Strategies for Teaching Reading K-3*, Sharon Taberski (2000) discusses how oral reading records can be used by the K-3 teacher to assess how well children are using cueing systems. She notes that the running record format can also show visual depictions for the teacher of how the child "thinks" as the child reads. The notation of miscues in particular shows how a child "walks through" the reading process. They indicate if and in what ways the child may require "guided" support in understanding the words he or she reads aloud.

Taberski notes that when children read they need to think about several things at once. First, they must consider whether what they are reading makes sense (semantic or meaning cues). Next, they must know whether their reading "sounds right" in terms of Standard English (syntactic and structural cues). Third, they have to weigh whether their oral language actually and accurately matches the letters the words represent (visual or graphophonic cues).

In taking the running record and having the opportunity first-hand to listen to the children talk about the text, you can analyze the relationship between the child's oral language and word comprehension. Information from the running record provides the teacher with a road map for differentiated cueing system instruction.

Skill 13.3   Applying knowledge of the English language to improve reading

Reading and the ELL Learner

Research has shown a positive and strong correlation between children's literacy in their native language and their learning of English. Put another way, the degree of native language proficiency and literacy is a strong predictor of English language development. Children who are literate and engaged readers in their native language can easily transfer their skills to a second language (i.e. English).

What this means is that teachers should not approach the needs of ELL learners in reading the same as they do native speakers. Those children whose families are not from a focused oral literacy and reading culture in the native language will need additional oral language rhymes, read-alouds, and singing as supports for reading skills development in both their native and the English language.

In reading research and theory, new distinctions and definitions appear often. The body of reading knowledge changes over time. The information and definitions in this guide are those accepted in the year of its publication and the time of its authoring and updating. As changes occur in accepted theories, they will be made in the guides and in the certification exams.

"If you believe that you learn to read by reading, you must learn to want to read. Reading to children, therefore models both the "how" and "why" of reading."— Helen Depree and Sandra Iversen, *Early Literacy in the Classroom*

"The long talk that parents have put off about the ways of the world might need to be an introduction to the facts about the English alphabet."—Terrence Moore, Ashbrook Center Fellow, Principal of Ridgeview Classical Schools in Fort Collins, Colorado

GLOSSARY

These definitions are critical for success on all multiple choice questions on the examinations. Proper use of these terms is crucial for success in tackling a constructed response involving balanced literacy.

Ability Grouping—grouping of children with similar needs for instructional purposes. Ability groups do not remain constant throughout the year, but change as the children's needs within them change.

Alliteration—occurs when words begin with the same consonant sound, as in *Peter Piper picked a pair of pickled peppers*.

Alphabetic Principle—the idea that written spellings represent spoken words.

Anchor Book—a balanced literacy term for a book that is purposely read repeatedly and used as part of both the reading and writing workshop. It is a good idea to use certain books that become the children's familiar and cherished favorites for both reading and writing.

Assonance—occurs when words repeat the same vowel sound, as in *how now brown cow*.

Authentic Assessment—assessment activities which reflect the actual workplace, family community and school curriculum.

Balanced Literacy Lesson Format—The Balanced Literacy Approach has its own specific format for the delivery of the literacy lesson, whether it is a reading or writing workshop lesson. The format begins with a 10-15 minute mini-lesson which the teacher delivers to the whole class. This mini-lesson is then followed by a thirty-minute small group (when the children break into small groups to work) lesson. It concludes with a 10-minute share during which the whole class reconvenes to share what they have done in the small groups. One can refer to this format as the whole-small-whole group approach.

Benchmarks—school, state, or nationally mandated statements of the expectations for student learning and achievement in various content areas.

BICS (Basic Interpersonal Communication Skills)—ELL term, bilingual education; learning second language skills and becoming proficient in a second language through face-to-face interaction, translation through speaking, listening, and viewing.

Blending—the process of hearing separate phonemes and being able to merge them together to read the word.

Book Features—Children need to be familiar with the following book features: front and back cover, title and half-title page, dedication page, table of contents, prologue and epilogue, and foreword and after notes. For factual books, children need to be familiar with labels, captions, glossary, index, headings and subheadings of chapters, charts and diagrams, and sidebars.

Checklist—an assessment form which lists targeted learning and social behaviors as indicators of achievement, knowledge or skill. They can be professionally or teacher prepared.

Cinquain—a five line poem that can be read and then used as a model for writing. Generally line 1 of this format is a single word, line 2 has 2 words, which describe the title of line 1, line 3 is comprised of 3 words which are movement words, line 4 has 4 words which express feeling and line 5 has a single word which is a synonym for line 1's single word.

Comprehension—occurs when the reader correctly interprets the print on the page and constructs meaning from it. Comprehension depends on activating prior knowledge, cultural and social background of the reader, and the reader's ability to use comprehension monitoring strategies.

Concepts About Print—include how to handle a book, how to look at print, directionality, sequencing, locating skills, punctuation, and concepts of letters and words.

Consonant Diagraphs—two consecutive consonants that represent one new speech sound. In the word "digraph" the *ph* which sounds like /f/ is a digraph.

Contexts—sentences deliberately prepared by the teacher which include sufficient contextual clues for the children to decipher meaning.

Contextual Redefinition—using context to determine word meaning.

Cooperative Reading—Children read with a partner or buddy. It can be silent or oral reading.

Crisscrossers—an ELL term for second language learners who have a positive attitude toward both first language and second language learning. These second language learners, children from ELL backgrounds, are comfortable navigating back and forth between the two languages as they learn.

Cues—As they self monitor their reading comprehensions, readers have to integrate various sources of information or cues to help them construct meaning from text and graphic illustrations.

Decoding—"sounding out" a printed sequence of letters based on knowledge of letter sound correspondences.

Diphthongs—two vowels in one syllable where the two sounds are heard. For instance in the word *house,* both the "o" and the "u" are heard.

Differentiated Instruction—the need for the teacher, based on observation of individual student's work, progress, test results, fluency, and other reading/literacy behaviors, to provide modified instruction and alternative strategies or activities. These activities are specifically developed by the teacher to address the individual student's different needs.

Directionality—occurs when children use their fingers to indicate left to right direction and return sweep to the next line.

Early Readers—recognize most high frequency words and many simple words. They use pictures to confirm meaning. Using meaning, syntax, and phonics, they can figure out most simple words. They use spelling patterns to figure out new words. They are gaining control of reading strategies. They use their own experiences and background knowledge to predict meanings.
They occasionally use story language in their writing. This stage follows emergent reading.

Emergent Readers—the stage of reading in which the reader understands that print contains a consistent message. The reader can recognize some high frequency words, names, and simple words in context. Pictures can be used to predict meaning. The emergent reader begins to attend to left to right directionality and features of print and may identify some initial sounds and ending sounds in words.

Encode—to change a message into symbols. For example, readers encode oral language into writing.

English as a Second Language (ESL)—a way of teaching English to speakers of other languages using English as the language of instruction.

Expository Text—is non-fiction that provides information and facts. This text type is what newspapers, science, mathematics and history texts use. Currently there is much focus, even in elementary schools, on teaching children how to comprehend and author expository texts. They must produce brochures, guides, recipes, and procedural accounts on most elementary grade levels. The teaching of reading of expository texts requires working with a particular vocabulary and concept structure that is very different from that of the narrative text. Therefore time must be taken to teach the reading of expository texts and contrast it with the reading of narrative texts.

First Language—an ELL term for the language any child acquires in the first few years of life. It is through this acquired language that the child acquires phonological and phonemic awareness.

Fluent Readers—identify most words automatically. They can read chapter books with good comprehension. They consistently monitor, cross-check, and self-correct reading. They can offer their own interpretations of text based on personal experiences and prior reading experiences. Fluent readers are capable of reading a variety of genres independently. Furthermore, they can respond to texts or stories by sharing pertinent examples from their lives. They can also readily make connections to other books which they have read. Finally, they are capable of beginning to create spoken and written writings which are in the style of a particular author.

Formal Assessment—a test or an observation of a performance task which is done under controlled and regulated conditions.

Functional Reading—the reading of instructions, recipes, coupons, classified ads, notices, signs, and other documents which we have to read and correctly interpret in school and in society.

Grade Equivalent/Grade Score—a score transformed from a raw score on a standardized test into the equivalent score earned by an average student in the norming group.

Graphic Organizers—graphic organizers express relationships among various ideas in visual form including sequence, timelines, character traits, fact and opinion, main idea and details, differences and likenesses. Graphic organizers are particularly helpful for visual learners.

Guided Reading—one of the key modes of instruction in the balanced literacy theory approach. During guided reading, the teacher "guides" the child through silent reading of a text by giving them prompts, asking target questions, and even helping the child start an answer to a specific prompt or question. At the end of each guided reading section or excerpt of the text, the child stops to talk with the teacher about the text. By definition, guided reading is an interactive discussion between the child and the teacher. This mode of reading instruction is generally used when children need extra support in constructing meaning because the text is complex or because their current independent reading capacities are still limited.

High Frequency—frequently used words. These words appear many more times than do other words in ordinary reading material. Examples of such words include *as, in, of,* and *the*. These words are also sometimes called service words. These words are also part of sight vocabulary words. A classic best-known high frequency word list was generated by Dolch (1936).

Independent Reading—a set period of time within the daily literacy block when children read books with 95%-100% accuracy on their own. This reading of books by themselves which they can understand without teacher support promotes lifelong literacy and love of learning. This, in turn enhances reading mileage, builds fluency, and helps children orchestrate integrated cue strategies.

Informal Assessment—observations of children made under informal conditions; these can include kid watching, checklists, and individual child/teacher conversations.

Informal Reading Inventory (IRI)—a series of reading excerpts that can be used to determine a child's reading strengths and needs in comprehension and decoding. Many published reading series have an IRI to go with their series.

Justified Print—the positioning of print on the page so that every line of text reaches the right margin evenly; can be harder to read than ragged right paragraph alignment (as used in this guide).

Kid Watching—term used within the balanced literacy approach for the teacher's deliberate, detailed, and recorded observations of individual student and class literacy behaviors, often done during small group work. The teacher then reconfigures lessons on experiences to meet the students' individual and group needs.

Kinesthetic—Learning is tactile, as contrasted with an activity where the learner sits still or attempts to sit still in one place. Cutting and moving syllable or word strips or using sandpaper letters are kinesthetic activities.

Language Experience—occurs when children give dictation to the teacher who writes their words on a chart or their drawings. This shows children that words can be written down.

Learning Logs—daily records of what students have learned.

Listening Post—sets of headphones attached to a single tape player. Children can go to centers where they listen to audiotapes of books while reading the print book. These posts are in many libraries as well.

Literature Circles—a group discussion involving four to six children who have read the same work of literature (narrative or expository text). They talk about key parts of the work, relate it to their own experience, listen to the responses of others, and discuss how parts of the text relate to the whole.

Manipulation—moving around or switching sounds within a word or words within a phrase or sentence.

Meaning Vocabulary—words whose meanings children understand and can use.

Miscue—an oral reading error made by a child which differs from the actual printed text.

Miscue Analysis—when the teacher keeps a detailed recording of the errors or inaccurate attempts of a child reader during a reading assessment. These are recorded within a running record. This helps the teacher see whether the cues—syntactic, semantic, or graphophonemic—the child is using are accurate.

Monitoring Reading—various strategies that children use to monitor their readings. A sample are maintaining fluency by bringing prior knowledge to the story to make predictions, using these predictions to do further checking, searching, self-correcting as the story progresses, and using problem-solving word study skills to make links from known words to unknown words.

Morphemes—the smallest units of meaning in words. There are two types of morphemes: free morphemes, which can stand alone such as *love;* and bound morphemes, which must be attached to another morpheme to carry meaning such as *ed* in *loved.*

Narrative Text—one of the two basic text structures. The narrative text tells or communicates a story. Narrative texts are novels, short stories and plays. Some poems are narratives as well. The narrative text needs to be taught differently than the expository text because of its structure.

One–to–One Matching—matching one spoken word with one written word.

Onset Rime Blending (Onset)—Everything before the vowel and rime (the vowel and everything after it). For example, the word "sleep" can be broken into /sl/ and /eep/. Word families are built using rimes. The /eep/ word family would include *jeep, keep* and *weep.*

Orthography—a method of representing spoken language through letters and diacritics.

Percentile—If a child scores at the 56th percentile for his/grade level, his/her score is equal to or above that of 56 percent of the children taking that standardized test and below that of 46 percent of the children on whose scores the test was normed.

Performance Assessment—having children do a task that demonstrates their knowledge, skills, and competency. Having children author their own alphabet book on a particular topic would be a performance assessment for knowledge of the alphabet.

Phoneme—The speech sound units that make a difference in meaning. The word "rope" has three phonemes /r/, /o/, and /p/. Change one phoneme, say /r/ to /n/, and you have a different word *nope.*

Phonemic Awareness—the understanding that words are composed of sounds. Phonemic awareness is a specific type of phonological awareness dealing only with phonemes in a spoken word.

Phonics—the study of relationships between phonemes (speech sounds) and graphemes (letters) that represent the phonemes. It is also decoding or the sounding out of unknown words that are written.

Phonological Awareness—the ability to recognize the sounds of spoken language and how they can be blended together, segmented, and switched or manipulated to form new combinations and words.

Phonological Cues—readers use their knowledge of letter/sound and sound/letter relationships to predict and confirm reading.

Phonology—the study of speech structure in language that includes both the patterns of basic speech units (phonemes) and the tacit rules of pronunciation.

Portfolios—collections of a child's work over time. They include a cover letter, reflections from the child and teacher, and other supportive documents including standards, performance task examples, prompts and sometimes peer comments.

Primary Language—an ELL term; the language an individual is the most fluent in and at ease with. This is usually, but not always, the individual's first language.

Prompts—when the teacher intervenes in the child's independent reading to help the child pronounce or comprehend a specific word or prompt. On a reading record, the teacher notes the prompt. When the teacher wants to match a child with a particular book or determine the child's stage of reading/level, the teacher does not use prompts.

Question Generating Strategy For An Expository Text—First the child previews the text by reading titles, subheads, looking at pictures or illustrations, and reading the first paragraph. Next the child asks a "think" question and then records the question. Then the child reads to find information that might answer the "think" question. The child may write down the information found or think about another question that is answered by what the child is reading. The child continues to read using this strategy.

Reading for Information—Reading with the purpose of extracting facts and expert opinion from the text. Children should be introduced to the following information reading resources: web resources that are age and grade appropriate for children, the concept of the table of contents, chapter headings, glossaries, pictures, maps, charts, diagrams and text structures in an information text. They should be taught to use notes, graphs, organizers, and mind maps to share information extracted from a text.

Recode—To change information from one code into another, as recoding writing into oral speech.

Recognition Vocabulary—the group of words which children are able to correctly pronounce, read orally, and understand on sight.

Record of Reading Behavior—a running record; an objective observation during which the teacher records, using a standard set of symbols, everything the child reader says as the child reads a book selected by the teacher.

Reflection—to analyze, discuss, and react to one's learning on any grade or age level.

Retelling—can be written or oral. Children are expected and encouraged to tell as much of a story as they can remember. Re-telling is far more extensive than just summarizing. Children should include the beginning, middle, and end plot lines and should be able to tell about the book's characters.

Rubric—a set of guidelines or acceptable responses for the completion of any task. Usually a rubric ranges from 0 to 4 with 4 being the most detailed response and 0 indicating a response to the task which lacked detail or was in other ways insufficient.

Scaffolding—refers to the teacher support necessary for the child to accomplish a task or to achieve a goal which the child could not accomplish on his/her own. Vygotsky termed this window of opportunity the "zone of proximal development." Ultimately as the child becomes more proficient or capable, the scaffold is withdrawn. The goal of scaffolding is to help the child to perform the reading task independently and internalize the behavior. During shared reading, the task is scaffolded by the teacher's reading to the children aloud. As the teacher reads, the teacher scaffolds the initial decoding and helps with the meaning making/construction.

Searching—children pause to search in the picture, print, or their memory for known information. This can happen as the child tackles an unknown word or after an error.

Second Language—ELL term; a language acquired or learned simultaneously with or after a child's acquisition of a first language.

Segmenting—the process of hearing a spoken word and identifying its separate phonemes or syllables.

Self-Correction—children begin to correct some of their own reading errors. Generally this behavior is accompanied by the re-reading of the previous phrase or sentence.

Semantic Cues—children use their prior knowledge, sense of the story, and pictures to support their predicting and confirming the meaning of the text.

Semantic Web—a visual graphic organizer the teacher uses to introduce a reading on a specific topic. It visually represents many other words associated with a target word. The web can help activate the children's prior knowledge and extend or clarify it. It can also serve to check new learning after guided or independent reading.

Spatial Learning—using images, color, or layout to help readers whose learning style is spatial.

Standard Score—how far a child's grade on a standardized test is from the average score (mean) on the test in terms of the standard deviation. If a child scores 70 on a standardized test and the standard deviation is 5 and the average (mean) score is 65, the child is one standard deviation above the average.

Standardized Test—a test given under specified conditions allowing comparisons to be made. A set of norms or average scores on this test will be used for comparisons.

Stop and Think Strategy—a balanced literacy strategy for constructing meaning. As the text is being read, the child asks, "Does this make sense to me? If it does not make sense to me, I should then try to re-read it or read ahead. I can also look up words that I don't know or ask for help." Generally the teacher models this strategy with the whole class as a mini lesson and then posts it posted in the classroom for continued reference by the children.

Strategic Readers—A lengthy glossary explanation of this term has been provided because it can appear in a variety of multiple choice questions on the examination as well as part of a constructed response question.

As defined by researchers Marie Clay and Sharon Taberski, strategic readers are self improving and do the following as they read:

- Monitor their reading to see if it makes sense semantically, syntactically, and visually.
- Look for and use semantic, syntactic, and visual clues.
- Uncover and identify new things about the text.
- Cross check and use one cueing system against another.
- Self-correct their reading when what they first read does not match the semantic, syntactic and visual clues
- Solve for and identify new words using multiple cueing systems

Beyond these behaviors, strategic or self-improving readers use many strategies to construct meaning. When their reading experience is going well, they know the words and understand the text or story; they are working continuously (even if they are not conscious of it) at maintaining meaning. If and when the strategic or self-improving reader runs into an unfamiliar word, then the reader has many strategies to identify that word. Becoming a successful strategic reader is a goal that can and should be shared with children as early as the middle of the first grade, although the term "self-improving reader" might be used at that point.

Text Features—children need to be alerted to the following text features which may initially appear strange to them. The features of text include the following:

- A period which marks the end of a "telling sentence"
- A question mark that is at the end of a sentence that asks a question
- An exclamation mark used to express surprise or excitement at the end of a sentence
- Capital letters which begin a sentence and the names of persons, places, and things
- Bold, italicized, or underlined text to highlight key ideas
- Quotation marks which show dialogue
- A hyphen used to break a long word up into its syllables
- A dash used to show a break in an idea, or to indicate a parenthetical element or an omission
- An ellipse, which shows an omission or break in the text
- A paragraph in nonfiction which shows a new point being made

Transitional Readers—recognize an increasing number of "hard" words that are content related. They can provide summaries of the stories that they read. They are more at ease with handling longer, more complex, connected text with short chapters. Transitional readers can read independent level texts with correct phrasing, expression, and fluency. When they encounter unfamiliar words, they have a variety of strategies to figure out the unfamiliar words. Their reading demonstrates that they are able to integrate meaning, syntax, and phonics in a consistent manner so that they can understand the texts they are reading.

Venn Diagram—a diagram consisting of two or three intersecting circles to visually represent similarities and differences for texts, characters, and topics. No author study is complete without Venn diagrams comparing different authors' works. This is the most commonly used graphic organizer in elementary schools today. It can be used effectively as part of an answer to a constructed response question.

Visual Cues—occurs when readers use their knowledge of graphemes to predict and confirm text. The graphemes may be words, syllables or letters.

Word Analysis—the analysis of words employing letters, phonic structures, contextual clues, or dictionary skills.

Word Identification—how the reader determines the pronunciation and the meaning of an unknown word.

Word Recognition—the process of determining the pronunciation and some degree of the meaning of an unknown word.

Word Work—the term that the balanced literacy approach uses for the study of vocabulary.

DIRECTORY OF THEORISTS AND RESEARCHERS

Introduction

Many questions on the teacher certification examinations can be correctly answered only if you know the theorist or the research that is referenced. The teaching of reading owes much to the work, principles, and guidelines of teacher educators and university field researchers who have changed the style, methods, and practice of teaching reading. While those listed in this directory are by no means all the major researchers (page constraints would make a complete listing impossible), the individuals listed below are those whose contributions are frequently referenced on the certification tests and whose work is evident in today's elementary classroom teaching and learning of reading.

Phonics-Centered Approach

In 1955 Rudolph Flesch gained national prominence when he published *Why Johnny Can't Read.* This book went on to become a best seller and has now become a classic which is very readable and still speaks to current concerns. Flesch became the spokesperson for a war that periodically resurfaces in the reading world.

Flesch, Chall (1967) Stahl (1992), Adams (1990), and Johnson and Bauman (1984) believe that a phonics-based approach is crucial for reading success. Flesch and others feel that the balanced literacy advocates are seriously undermining the crucial role that phonics plays in the children's development as successful decoding readers. However, it must be noted that while balanced literacy does emphasize the use of literature based reading programs, it in no way dismisses phonics from its reading program; indeed phonics is included in the crucial "word work" component of the reading and writing workshop.

The phonics advocates point to the fact that most research shows that early and systematic instruction in phonics skills results in superior reading achievement in elementary school and beyond.

Adams (1990) detailed what type of phonics instruction is needed.

To learn to read skillfully, children need practice in seeing and understanding decodable words in real reading situations and with connected text ... [P]honics instruction [needs to be] part of a reading program that provides ample practice in reading and writing. Encouraging children with connected text can also show them the importance of what they are learning and make the lessons in phonics relevant and sensible. Phonics centered advocates believe that children should begin to learn letter associations in kindergarten with most useful phonics skills being taught by first grade. These basic skills should then be reviewed in second grade and beyond.

Consonant sounds should be taught first, since they are more reliable in their letter-sound associations.

Short vowel sounds appear more frequently in beginning reading materials, so they should be introduced before long vowels. Phonics advocates believe that most beginning readers need to be taught letter sound associations explicitly. Phonics advocates also believe that beginning readers need to read stories that have words to which phonics skills apply. This allows them to practice their phonics skills as they write and spell words. They should also play lots of letter-sound association games.

Phonics advocates claim that when phonics is abandoned reading, scores drop and balanced literacy advocates counter with the fact that they have never advocated abandoning the teaching of phonics.

As Jeanne Chall, a professor at Harvard's Graduate School of Education notes: "a beginning reading program that does not give children knowledge and skill in recognizing and decoding words will have poor results."

Theorists and Researchers

Adams, Marilyn Jager—Noted for her research on early reading, Adams lists five basic types of phonemic awareness tasks which should be covered by the end of first grade. These include ability to hear rhymes and alliterations, ability to do oddity tasks, ability to orally blend words, ability to orally segment words, ability to do phonemic manipulation tasks.

Clay, Marie M.—A New Zealand-born researcher in the field of special needs emergent literacy and in the development of assessment tools for these children. Her research in this field is felt throughout the Reading Recovery movement and involves the use of her *Reading Recovery: A Guidebook for Teachers in Training* in the majority of graduate emergent literacy courses and in many classrooms in the U.S. including those that do not have a Reading Recovery teacher.

Her doctoral thesis focused on what was to become her life's work, emergent reading behavior. At the crux of her research for the dissertation, Clay reviewed and detailed the progress week by week of one hundred children during their first year of school (1966). An important outcome of the dissertation was her development of reliable observation tools for the assessment and analysis of changes over time in children's literacy learning. These assessments are the crux of *An Observation Survey of Early Literacy Achievement* (1993) which is an essential work for the primary school educator. The assessments have been validated and reconstructed for learners from the Spanish, Maori, and French languages. A special appendix in this guide includes the *Record of Reading Behavior* tool she created with Kenneth Goodman.

Reading Recovery is a key Clay contribution to the field of foundations of reading teaching. The movement, which is discussed in detail in this section, was born out of the concerns of classroom educators who were upset that even with excellent programs and expert teaching, they were not able to positively influence the literacy progress of some of their young children. Clay posed the question of investigating what would happen if the design and delivery of traditional reading education were changed for these struggling young learners.

The whole thrust of the Reading Recovery movement has been to improve the early identification and instructional delivery for these struggling young readers. Her goal was to develop a system which would bring those children scoring the lowest in assessment measures to the level of the average readers within their classes.

With the support of Barbara Watson and others, the program was developed in three years. The first field tests of the program took place in the late 1970s in Auckland schools. To date, circa 2005, the program is operating in most English-speaking countries and has been reconstructed for use in Spanish and French.

Janet S. Gaffey and Billie Askew have said of Marie Clay (1991) that her contribution "has been to change what is possible for individual learners when teaching permits different routes to be taken for desired outcomes."

Reading Recovery has been identified by the International Reading Association as a program that not only teaches children how to read but also reduces the number of children who are labeled as "learning disabled." It further lowers the number of children who are placed in remedial reading programs and classes.

Clay Reading Recovery lessons are designed to promote accelerated learning so that children can catch up to their peers and continue to learn independently.

The hallmark of the Reading Recovery program is that the Reading Recovery teacher works with one student at a time over a 12 to 20 week period. Each daily 30 minute lesson is tailored to address the needs of the individual student. Therefore Reading Recovery teachers generally teach no more than four or five students per day in individual lessons.

The Clay Observation of Early Childhood Achievement (1993) is used to assess children's strengths and weaknesses. Reading Recovery teachers devote the first ten minutes of their sessions with individual children to assessment as the children engage in reading and writing. A running record of the child's progress is taken every day and is used to plan future lessons.

The lessons themselves include the use of familiar stories. Children engage in assembling and in sequencing cut up stories. They work with letters or write a story. Teaching style involves the teacher demonstrating strategies and the child then developing effective strategies to continue reading independently. Key components of each lesson include phonemic awareness, phonics, spelling, and comprehension study. Much time is devoted to problem solving so that the children's decoding is purposeful. Children are given time to practice and demonstrate fluency skills.

Ultimately what sets Reading Recovery aside is the fact that it is one-to-one tutoring. This is also what makes it effective for children, and of course, what raises issues about it are costs for the school systems which may want to adopt it. Obviously the districts and education systems have to decide whether they want to pay the costs of this and other individualized tutoring systems now in the primary school years or pay later as these children become adults whose literacy skills are not sufficient for proactive citizenship.

Fountas, Irene C and Gay Su Pinnell—These two researchers have developed a leveling system for reading texts, which arranges them by level of difficulty. Beyond a specific analysis of set titles, the theorists have explained in several published works how to use their leveling system to meet and assess the progress of various readers. They also provide detailed explanations and support for reading teachers of young children K-3 in using reading records and benchmark texts.

They are the key articulators of the balanced literacy model that includes reading and writing workshop. Among their other contributions to the field are guidelines for creating sets of leveled books, assessment rubrics, strategies for fostering "word solver" skills in child readers, and methods for teaching phonics and spelling in the literacy classroom.

Routman, Regie—Routman's contributions to Reading Foundations are the result of over three decades of experience as an elementary school teacher, a reading specialist, a learning disabilities tutor, a Reading Recovery teacher, a language arts and mentor teacher and a staff developer. Because of these various experiences, her insights into reading resonate with a broad spectrum of school community members.

Routman's works are conversational, teacher-to-teacher sharings of her daily experiences in classrooms. In her published books on the teaching of reading (i.e. *Reading Essentials*-Heinemann, 2002), Routman shows teachers how to teach consistently with the findings in reading research, yet also with highly practical "scripted lessons" and teaching tips which make the classroom come alive. She advocates literature based-teaching and meaning-centered approaches for learning.

In addition, she is a strong advocate of using poetry from grades one and beyond as an integral thread for a reading program. She is the author of *Kids' Poems: Teaching Children to Love Writing Poetry* (Scholastic, 2000) which includes separate volumes of poetry for grades K-4.

Routman believes in teaching reading to meet specific children's needs regardless of the particular reading program in place. She is a strong advocate for the use of small guided reading groups and reading for understanding. Phonics and other word analysis strategies are part of her reading framework, but not at its core. Her focus for the reading classroom is on the development and the use of the classroom library as the center for an independent reading program, shared reading and reading aloud.

Routman has designed informal reading evaluations on books/texts her students are reading (her published works are known for their appendices replete with templates for evaluations, projects, reports, book lists, suggested texts by topics and more). Her classroom model includes matching children with specific library books as well as linking assessment with instruction. Finally she is a researcher who sees reading as intimately linked to writing.

Routman is also involved with the politics of literacy. This vision of literacy involves the image of the teacher as an informed professional, who regularly reads the latest professional books, collaborates with colleagues in school and beyond, and deals with the most recent research developments. Interestingly, Routman is one researcher who also feels that an informed professional can and should know when to question research. Other aspects of the politics of literacy as Routman conceptualizes them are communicating effectively with parents and dealing with testing and standards mandates.

Two of her published works, *Conversations: Strategies for Teaching, Learning, and Evaluating* (Heinemann, 2000) and *Invitations: Changing as Teachers and Learners k-12* (Heinemann, 1991 and 1994) are essential for the elementary reading teacher's bookshelf and can take the teacher through several years of work.

Taberski, Sharon—Taberski is an experienced elementary teacher educator who is also a member of the Primary Literacy Standards Committee run by the National Center on Education and the Economy and the University of Pittsburgh. Her works in the field are served up as wonderfully accessible and necessary advice from "the veteran teacher across the hall" who loves her students and is delighted to help a new colleague.

Unlike many theorists in the field of reading, Taberski's work is not focused around a prescribed set of skills but rather around a series of interconnected interactions with the learner.

Among these interactions which are detailed and clearly communicated in her book *On Solid Ground* (2000-Heinemann) are the following:

- Assessment—Procedures for assessing children's reading to inform teaching, scheduling and managing reading conferences, taking oral reading records, and using retellings as discussion tools.
- Demonstration—Taberski developed and field tested strategies for using shared reading and read aloud as platforms for figuring out words and comprehending texts. She is a strong advocate of small group work-guided reading, word-study groups and teaching children one on one.
- Practice—In the Taberski framework, independent reading is used as a time for practice. Students play key roles in this practice and she has a set of detailed and easily adaptable guidelines for matching children with books for independent reading. Her work includes booklists and ready to use information that is available for reproduction.
- Response—Students should know that they are doing well and that they must focus their efforts to improve skills. Taberski explains how her students use writing and dialogue as tools for independent reading.

Vail, Priscilla—Noted for her research in the study of dyslexia and its myths, Vail has articulated ways in which children can develop their reading skills as they cope with this disorder and techniques parents and educators can use to support reading development. She has also worked on specific test taking skills for children coping with dyslexia and other special needs. Her strategies can be infused in the regular education program to enhance all students' reading achievement schools. She is a proponent of phonics instruction and skills within the context of an integrated whole language approach (once called integrated language arts).

Another focus of Vail's research is the link between language and thinking. She is concerned with how a child's receptive language, expressive language and metacognition can be fostered. She has developed assessment methods for each of these capacities and activities to help strengthen them in children grades k-4.

BIBLIOGRAPHY OF PRINT RESOURCES

Professional Books

Adams, M. (1990). *Beginning to read: Thinking and learning about print.* Cambridge, MA: MIT Press.

Anders, P., & Boss, C. (1986). Semantic feature analysis: An interactive strategy for vocabulary development and reading comprehension, *Journal of Reading*, 29, 610-616.

Blevins, W. (1997). *Phonemic awareness activities for early reading success.* New York: Scholastic.

Block, Cathy Collins. (2002). *Comprehension instruction: Research based practices.* New York: The Guilford Press.

Boyd-Bastogne, P. (2004). Focused Anecdotal Record Assessment (ARA): A Tool for Standards Based Authentic Assessment. *Reading Teacher, 58* (3), pp. 230-239.

Calkins, Lucy McCormick. (2001). *The art of teaching reading.* New York: Longman.

This author beautifully explains the reading workshop and its relationship to the writing workshop as she shares wonderful snapshots of mini lessons, conferring, conferencing, independent reading, guided reading, book talks, prompts, coaching, and classroom library use. Exceedingly readable and direct.

Camborne, Brianne. (2002). "Conditions for literacy learning." *The Reading Teacher*, 55, (8): 758-62.

Cambourne, Briane. (1993). *The whole story: Natural learning and the acquisition of literacy in the classroom.* Auckland, NZ: Ashton, Scholastic.

Campbell, Robin. (2004). *Reading and writing for real purposes.* Portsmouth, NH: Heinemann.

This work focuses on how children who deftly absorb and interconnect symbols and sounds of their universes can be supported in K-1 classes to extend this ability into phonics learning. Campbell demonstrates how immersion in a highly literate classroom filled with print and language stimuli allows kids to build accurate letter-sound relationships. The book provides a framework for teaching phonics using proven field-tested Campbell strategies.

Among these strategies are early mark making, read-alouds, playing with language in rhyme and song, writing and reading in a variety of genres, exploring environmental and classroom print, and using students' own names. Samples of student work are included.

Chancey, C. (1994). Language development, metalinguistic awareness, and emergent literacy skills of 3 year old children in relation to social class. *Applied Psycholinguistics*, 15, 371-394.

Clay, Marie M. (1993). *An observation survey of early literacy achievement.* Portsmouth, NH: Heinemann.

Clay, Marie M. (1993). *Reading recovery: A guidebook for teachers in training.* Portsmouth, NH: Heinemann.

Cooper, J. David. (2004). *Literacy-helping children construct meaning.* Boston, MA: Houghton Mifflin. (5th Edition).

With numerous charts, tables, templates, and excerpts form actual texts, this book explains what the balanced literacy approach to the teaching of reading and writing is. It offers the new teacher exact schedules, strategies, guidelines, assessment tools, bibliographies, research, and even scripts for conferring with children.

Cooper is a clear and crisp writer who does not overwhelm the reader, but rather engages the reader. Even veteran teachers would return again and again to this text for support and refreshing insights.

Cox, Carole. (2005). *Teaching language arts.* Boston, MA: Pearson.

A compendium of state-of-the-art lesson plans, web resources, online case studies, teaching ideas and extensive templates. All of these materials are aligned to the balanced literacy reading and writing workshop model.

The book also includes teaching ideas for the ELL reader, children with learning disabilities, and speakers of non-standard dialects. The book also features snapshots of second language learners as well as bi-literacy web resources.

Cullinan, Bernice E. (1998). *Three voices: An invitation to poetry across the curriculum.* New York: Stenhouse. K-6 and beyond.

Two classroom educators and a noted researcher in children's literature demonstrate how poetry can be used in the classroom to teach various aspects of reading and to nurture lifelong literacy. Thirty-three grade and age appropriate strategies are included which have been field tested in classrooms across the country.

Cunningham, Patricia M. (2000). *Phonics they use: Words for reading and writing.* 3rd Edition. New York: Addison Wesley Longman.

Evidence based reading instruction. (2002) Articles from International Reading Association. Newark, Delaware: *International Reading Association.*

Ezell, H. K., & Justice, L. M. (2000). Increasing the print focus of adult -child shared book reading through observational learning. *American journal of Speech Pathology*, 9, 36-37.

Flesch, Rudolf. (1985). *Why Johnny can't read.* New York: Harper and Row.

Fountas, Irene C., & Gay Su Pinnell. (2001). *Guiding readers and writers 3-6.* Portsmouth, NH: Heinemann.

This work includes 1000 leveled books with guidelines for using them as part of a reading and writing workshop. The book explains how to use various genres in the classroom and how to use visual graphic organizers for the teaching of reading and writing.

Fountas, Irene. C. & Gay Su Pinnell. (1999). *Matching books to readers using leveled books in guided reading K-3.* Portsmouth, NH: Heinemann.

This major contribution to the field has a list of 7,500 grade and age appropriate books. In addition the authors include word counts to be used for keeping running records, text characteristics, guidelines for leveling of additional books and suggestions for developing classroom library collections.

Other works by these researchers also published by Heinemann include: *Voices on word matters: Learning about phonics and spelling in the literacy classroom* (1999) and *Word matters: Teaching phonics and spelling in the reading/writing classroom* (1998).

Fry, Edward Bernard, Kress, Jacqueline, Fountakidis, Dona Lee. (2000). *The reading teacher's book of lists.* San Francisco, CA: Wiley Press.

This book is an invaluable resource for the working classroom educator. It includes ready to use lists that cover a multiplicity of teacher needs. Among them are spelling demons, readability graphs, phonics, useful words, reading math, vowel lists, anagrams, portmanteaus (Do you know what they are and how well they can work in word study?), web sites, classic children's literature, and more. Even a veteran teacher educator will find useful and new resources. This is also wonderful for developing independent word study investigations and literature explorations.

Ganske, Kathy. (2000). *Word Journeys: Assessment-guided phonics, spelling, and vocabulary instruction.* New York, NY: Guilford Press.

This book offers a practical approach for assessing children's spelling. The author has created a DSA (Development Spelling Analysis) tool which teachers can use to evaluate individual children's spelling progress and to differentiate instruction. The book includes snapshots of children at different levels of spelling development.

Hall, Susan. (1994). *Using picture books to teach literary devices.* Westport, CT: Oryx Press.

How to help every child become a reader. Just Publishing. K-6 and beyond.

This accessible text draws on materials developed by the U.S. Department of Education to share research, resources, referrals, and suggestions for supporting all children to become lifelong and engaged readers. It offers specific suggestions and resources for assisting struggling readers including those with special needs and those from ELL backgrounds.

Hoyt, Linda. (2002). *Make it real: Strategies for success with informational texts.* Portsmouth, NH: Heinemann.

Kimball-Lopez, Kimberley. (1999). *Connecting with traditional literature.* Boston: Allyn and Bacon.

Labov, L. (2003). When ordinary children fail to read. *Reading Research Quarterly*, 38, 128-31.

Macmillan, B. M. (2002). Rhyme and reading. A critical review of the research methodology. *Journal of Research in Reading, 25*(1), 4-42.

Makor, Barbara. *Primary phonics readers.*

Short storybooks that K-2 can own and read independently. They feature phonetically controlled texts, sounds and spellings that are grade and age appropriate and high interest child-centered themes. As children progress through the series of twenty titles, they review and enhance their mastery of phonetic elements, sight words, and sequences at a more rapid pace. This material is compatible with the majority of phonics programs.

Moffett, James and Betty Jane Wagner. *Student-Centered Language Arts K-12.* 4th ed. Boston: Houghton Mifflin, 1992.

Munro, J. (1998). Phonological and phonemic awareness: Their Impact on learning to read prose and spell. *Australian Journal of Learning Disabilities*, 3, 2, 15-21.

Owacki, G, and Y. Goodman. (2002*). Kidwatching: Documenting children's literacy development.* Portsmouth, NH: Heinemann.

Owocki, Gretchen. (2003). *Strategic instructions for k-3 students.* Portsmouth, NH: Heinemann.

Paperback nursery rhyme sampler, Whispering Coyote Press.

Essential for a Pre K-1 classroom and useful even in grades 1 and 2; these classic nursery rhymes promote phonemic and phonological awareness and children's ownership of their reading through song and movement.

Quindlen, Anna. (1998). *How reading changed my life.* New York: Ballantine Books, 1998.

Routman, Regie. (2000). *Conversations: Strategies for teaching, learning, and evaluating.* Portsmouth, NH: Heinemann.

Routman, Regie. (1994). *Invitations: Changing as teachers and learners K-12.* Portsmouth, NH. Heinemann.

Routman, Regie. (1996). *Literacy at the crossroads: Crucial talk about reading, writing, and other teaching dilemmas,* Portsmouth, NH: Heinemann.

Routman, Regie. (2002). *Reading essentials.* Portsmouth, NH: Heinemann.

Schultz, C. (2000). *How partner reading fosters literacy development in first grade students.* Action Research project, Saginaw Valley State University, University Center, Michigan.

Schumm, Heanne Shay. *The reading tutor's handbook*. Free Spirit. K-6 and beyond.

This guide offers step-by-step instructions, templates and handouts for providing children with differentiated reading support. It is not only helpful for teachers, but also can be shared with paraprofessionals, teachers, interns, and parents as a support framework for the classroom reading program.

Short, K., J. Harste and C. Burke. (1996). *Creating classrooms for authors and inquirers*. Portsmouth, NH: Heinemann.

Statman, Ann. *Handprints: Leveled storybooks for early readers* Educators Publishing Service Grades K-2.

These fifty titles which come with five teacher's guides were leveled using the Fountas and Pinnell Guided Reading Leveling System. The stories reflect real world situations and people young readers know. They include sentence structure, pictures and cues that focus strategic reading. Print size, sentence positioning, and word spacing are appropriate for the level of the particular storybook. The titles build a strong sight vocabulary through the use of high frequency words. Language used within the series progresses from natural to formal book language.

Taberski, Sharon. (2000). *On solid ground: Creating a literacy environment in your K-3 classroom*. Portsmouth, NH: Heinemann.

Terban, Marvin. *Time to rhyme: A rhyming dictionary*. Boyd Mills Press. Grades 1-3.

This book is easily enough formatted so that it can be used to introduce children in the early elementary grades to the use of a rhyming dictionary as a reference tool. Its simple word groupings encourage writing which can also reinforce and reciprocally enhance reading skills through the reading and writing workshop.

Trelease, Jim. (2001). *The Read-Aloud Handbook*. 4th Ed. New York: Penguin.

Vail, Patricia. *Reading comprehension: Students needs and teacher's tools*. Educators Publishers Service K-6 and beyond.

This is a compendium of explanations of specific instructional practices, terms, student projects, learning games, and resources which are critical for successfully teaching reading.

Wilde, Sandra. (2000). *Miscue analysis made easy: Building on student strengths.* Portsmouth, NH: Heinemann.

Wilde, Sandra. (2000). *Reading made easy.* Portsmouth, NH: Heinemann.

Alphabet Books

A major genre of fiction and non-fiction for the teacher of reading is the alphabet book. The appeal, concepts, and efficiency of these books as models for reading and writing merit them a special section in this bibliography. Even those whose text is simple enough for Pre K-2 can serve as anchor books and models for writing workshop in grades 3-6.

Aigner-Clark, Julie. (2002). *Baby Einstein: The ABCs of art*. Illustrations by Nadeen Zaidi. New York: Hyperion Books.

Beaton, Clare. *Zoe and her zebra*. Barefoot Books. Pre K-1.

This board book features a character young children can identify with named Zoe. Her adventures are told in a simple, repetitive text with a soft literally "touchy" felt art.

Bunting, Eve. *Girls A to Z*. Boyd Mills Press. Pre K-1.

This book uses the alphabetic format to promote the opportunity for girls to select various professions and careers ranging from astronaut to zookeeper. Bunting's text is breezy and rhymes.

Cheney, Lynne. (2002). *America: A patriotic primer*. New York: Simon and Schuster Books. Illustrated by Robin Priess Glasser.

Cheney, Lynne. *A is for Abigail: An almanac of amazing American women*. New York: Simon and Schuster Books. Ages 4-8.

Glaser, Milton. (2003). *The Alphazeds*. Miramax. Ages 4-8.

Grimes, Nikki. *C is for City*. Illustrated by: Pat Cummings. Boyd Mill Press. K-3.

This alphabet rhyme book doubles as a guide to city activities. With its built in invitations to readers to search for alphabetical items, it is perfect for use as an informal assessment tool or an interactive/paired reading anchor text.

Inkpen, Mick. (2000). *Kipper's A to Z*. San Diego: Harcourt. Ages 3-7.

Isadora, Rachel. (1999). *ABC pops! (Picture Books)*. Disney Press. Ages 4-8.

Johnson, Stephen. (1995). *Alphabet city*. Penguin Books. All ages.

Kelley, Marty. *Summer sinks*. Zino Press. Prek-1.

This work describes the summer season in terms of things which "stink" about it, including ants, bugs, and sweat. Fun to read and add to as the alphabet letters are learned and vocabulary is built up.

Martin, Mary Jane. *From Anne to Zach*. Boyd Mills Press.

In this captivating book which can serve as a touchstone text for model collaborative authoring, children learn the letters of the alphabet through other children's names.

Melmed, Laura Krauss and Frane Lesser. (2003) *Capital! Washington DC from A to Z.* New York: Harper Collins.

Musgrove, Margaret. (1976). Illustrated by Leo and Diane Dillon. *Ashanti to Zulu. African Traditions.* New York: Dial Books for Young Readers.

This is a Caldecott-winning book which uses the alphabetic format for a richly detailed and researched study of 26 African Peoples. It includes a map and pronunciation guide and illustrations that were researched in the Schomberg Center and the American Museum of Natural History. Even the frame design for each illustration reflects the African Kano knot which signifies endless searching.

Paratore, Colleen. *26 big things hands do*. Minneapolis, MN: Free Spirit.

What is delightful about this alphabet book is that it presents the alphabet letters as positive actions children can perform with their own small hands to help others. These actions include applauding, giving gifts, planting, and volunteering. Of course, alphabet study can continue with adding other "helping actions" to the word wall or substituting them in the text.

Pelham, David, (1991). *A is for animals*. New York: Simon and Schuster

Seeley, Lorna. *The book of shadow boxes*. Peachtree.

Within the shadow of each letter's shadow box lies a hidden treasure for the young reader to find. The book is intricately and exquisitely designed and conceptualized by Ms. Seeley. Its visual fascination extends well beyond the elementary grades as it of course fosters not only the alphabetic principle but also reading comprehension and literacy response.

Sneed, Brad. (2002). *Picture a letter*. New York: Penguin Books.

Seuss. *ABC*. Random House. Ages 2-up.

Thornhill, Jim. *The wildlife ABC and 123: A nature alphabet and counting book.* Maple Tree Press. K-1 with additional nature notes on the species for the teacher/parent.

In addition to fostering the alphabetic principle, the book nicely mixes geographic, multicultural, and scientific knowledge into a beautifully designed text. It uses children's fascination with nature to foster reading and math literacy.

Zschock, Martha and Heather. (2002). *Journey around New York from A to Z. Beverly*. Mass: Commonwealth Editions

Zschock, Martha. (2001). *Journey Around Boston from A to Z.* Beverly Mass: Commonwealth Editions.

Trade Books

These books foster particular aspects of reading skills, fluencies, and competencies.

Blackstone, Stella. *Where's the cat?* Barefoot Books. Pre-k.

> This book which focuses its primary school readers on searching for a lost cat provides excellent use of repetitive language and encourages interactive reading.

Campbell, Bebe Moore. (2003). *Sometimes my mommy gets angry.* New York, New York: G. P. Putnam's Sons.

> This is a moving story about a young girl whose mother suffers from mental illness. It is told in a way that is easy to read, along with beautiful illustrations. The main character is Annie. Sometimes her mother is very happy and other times very angry and sad. Annie has learned what to do when her mom is having a bad episode. She has books to read, a special stuffed animal, and some secret snacks. Annie also has a strong support system in place with friends, neighbors, her teacher and grandmother.

> This book is a good introduction to the issue of mental illness. It is especially important in that students see how this young girl is able to cope with this difficult part of her life. "Sometimes my mommy has a dark cloud inside of her. I can't stop the rain from falling, but I can find sunshine in my mind."

> Teachers can introduce students to this issue with this poignant book. Students can brainstorm different scenarios and discuss how they can be resolved. They can discuss who their support network includes and what it takes for a person to be strong enough to weather such a storm.

> The book is a much needed resource for children in times where Annie's situation is far more common than is generally known. Annie's capacity to make effective, affirming social decisions makes the work an inspirational touchstone for other peers who need to confront their parents' emotional crises. Children might be inspired to author poetry or create deliberately fictionalized narrative accounts about how they have confronted various crises.

> In offering an upper elementary grade and age appropriate narrative of a peer dealing with an emotionally ill parent, this book provides readers confronting similar family and caregiver issues with an opening for discussion and for hopeful outreach. Just reading this account may well be the first step necessary to assist a youngster in acknowledging a "hidden problem" and getting crucial adult assistance in dealing with the crisis.

Garza, Carmen Lomas. (1990). *Family pictures: Cuadros de familia*. Children's Book Press.

This book tells the story of the author's childhood growing up in a Hispanic community in Texas. The book is written in both Spanish and English, accompanied by the author's incredible paintings. The paintings are unique, somewhat folksy, colorful, and totally entrancing. They bring you into Carmen's world. Once inside it, you don't want to leave.

There is so much to explore in this book; it works well with the study of "myself and family," community, communities around the world, Mexico, family traditions, and customs. It emphasizes social and emotional learning and how a young girl can find her way in the world. The traditions followed by her community and family were not necessarily accepted or understood by white America. Yet these values gave her the strength to be her own person and to rely on both her relationships and rich inner life to express herself.

There are so many activities that this book inspires. Children can study the origins of the piñata, and make one. They can make a cookbook of recipes from Mexico or from their own homes. Children can also be encouraged to design their own book of family pictures. They can emphasize special occasions that they celebrate or focus on family traditions which reflect their cultural backgrounds. The richness and lushness of the paintings invites the readers to construct meaning and to create their own narratives, procedural accounts, poetry, and dialogues inspired by one or more of the paintings.

Picture walk through the illustrations. Given the Spanish/English text, this strategy can be an engaging spatial entry point for descriptive and narrative spoken and written presentations. The lushly detailed illustrations of family rites and celebrations can be springboards for children's literary and artistic renditions of equivalent family pictures and events which are prompted by Carmen's selections.

Use of dual language text for the book validates children's and family member's responses in languages other than English. Obviously, this book and its format are inspirational for ELL/Bilingual learners and for special needs learners who can be captivated by the paintings.

The power of this book lies in its accessing and modeling the magic of family rites and rituals for a broad spectrum of linguistics, intrapersonal, spatial, and kinesthetic learners from monolingual, bilingual and special needs backgrounds. Common to all of its audience members are the social and emotionally celebratory components of Family Pictures.

Glaser, Shirley, & Glaser, Milton. (2003). *The alphazeds words*. Hyperion Books.

This book is incredible in so many ways! It is an alphabet book that can be read by or to little ones and not so little ones. It starts with an empty room. One by one, each letter of the alphabet enters the room, each with its own distinct look, fantastic illustrations and typography by the designer Milton Glaser. Each of these letters also has its own distinct personality. A is angry, B is bashful, J is jealous, and so on. The room gets quite crowded. How do all of these different personalities manage to get along and coexist? Not too well apparently, as there is shouting, pushing, hitting and kicking. In the midst of all the chaos, the light in the room goes out and there is silence.

> "When the light came back on, something
> extraordinary had happened. Four letters
> had gotten together to comfort one another.
> Together they had managed to create something
> larger and more important than themselves.
> *"They had made the first word."*

This is a great lesson on how each of us can be an individual, yet when we work together, something wonderful can happen. This book illustrates an incredible lesson in social and emotional maturity and helps the child realize that it isn't just about "me."

There are many different activities that a teacher can use with this book. The children can work in groups to make their own alphabet book of emotions. They can then present the book as a group, discussing the roles each of them played, and how they each used their unique talents to make the book.

Older children, grades 3 and up, can research and present as a group some important discoveries that were made more special because they involved people working together. They can also work on a project about cooperative learning, perhaps surveying class and schoolmates on how they feel they learn the best.

Hest, Amy. (1985). *The purple coat*. New York: Macmillan Publishing Co.

In the autumn of every year, Gabrielle travels with her mother to New York City to visit her Grandpa who owns a tailor shop. Once there, he always makes her a new coat, but this year Gabrielle decides the usual navy blue coat won't do. The Purple Coat follows Gabrielle in her attempt to establish her own identity.

Lionni, Leo. (1980). *Inch by Inch*. Astor-Honor Publishing Co. Inc.

In *Inch by Inch*, an inchworm (which is a caterpillar, or larval stage, of the fall cankerworm, which becomes a moth) keeps itself from being eaten by various birds by proving its worth as a measuring device.

Lupton, Hugh. *The story tree: Tales to read aloud*. Barefoot Books. K-3

These seven multicultural stories are accessible enough to children to encourage their eventually taking over the read aloud sharing on their own. This book is also a good one for family literacy sessions and for parent volunteers to read aloud in the classroom.

Martin Jr., Bill, & John Archambault. (1966). *Knots on a counting rope*. New York, New York: Henry Holt and Company.

This beautifully illustrated book reaches out in so many different directions, and we can all learn so much from it. *Knots on a Counting Rope* is the story of a Native-American boy who is blind and is learning from his grandfather how to survive in this world. Boy-Strength-of-Blue-Horses insists on hearing the story of his birth over and over again.

Every time his grandfather retells the story of the boy's birth, he adds a knot to his counting rope. Each time he hears the story, Boy-Strength-of-Blue-Horses gains more confidence in himself. The story emphasizes the Native-American tradition of storytelling, and there are numerous art, math and social studies lessons that offshoot from this book.

Of course, the telling and retelling of the story celebrate the young blind hero's strengths and weaknesses and ability to set goals with optimism. Stories of one's birth related by others are powerful demonstrations of social skills of the highest order.

This book also deals extensively with social and emotional learning. Children learn that those with disabilities need to be treated with sensitivity while learning to find their place in the world. One way in which children's social and emotional learning is strengthened is by understanding themselves and those around them. To facilitate this, each child will interview at least one family member about when he/she was born. The accounts collected with appropriate photos or memorabilia can then be shared in class and perhaps even authored into a *Knots on a Counting Rope* style book format.

Children can also retell the story of the boy using the counting system of cultures other than Native American. This literary response will incorporate cultural study, respect and empathy into ongoing reading and writing workshop efforts.

McCully, Emily Arnold. (1992). *Mirette on the high wire.* G.P. Putnam's & Sons.

Mirette helps her mother run a boardinghouse for acrobats, jugglers, actors, and mimes. Her life changes when she discovers a boarder crossing the courtyard on air. She begs him to teach her how he does it. He refuses to teach her, but she begins practicing on her own. As she improves, he begins to help her. In the end she helps him overcome his fear of the high wire.

Rabe, Bernice. (1981). *The balancing girl.* E.P. Dutton.

Margaret, a girl in a wheel chair is excellent at balancing all kinds of objects. Margaret shows her friend Tommy how good she is at balancing at the school carnival.

Ringgold, Faith. (1991). *Tar Beach.* New York, New York: Crown Publishers.

A favorite, this book is moving in its words, art, and the beautiful story it tells. This is an effective book to use for younger grades to connect with myself, my family and my community. It can also be used in connection with a mapmaking unit. The children can be encouraged to make a map of their neighborhood from an aerial view.

A starting point for a discussion would be why the author portrayed New York from such a vantage point. In this beautiful book, the narrator, Cassie Louise Lightfoot, lets her dreams and ambitions take her to places in New York City that she ordinarily would not be able to be part of because of her circumstances. As a result of her self-motivation and self- awareness, Cassie is able to go as far as her dreams will let her. In this book Cassie also shows strengths in the areas of emotional sensitivity as well as inter- and intra-personal relationships.

Children can author their own Tar Beach equivalent night fantasies and then share them with one another through an exhibit or big books.
Although Cassie's family is obviously poor since they have to picnic on their roof, Cassie's dreamlike lushly illustrated flight over Harlem validates the beauty of their family life and of the city landscape which is accessible to all. This is an invaluable lesson in the importance of the wealth inherent in the appreciation of family connections and the beauty of nature and public architectural designs! A song of family and of the city!

Schories, Pat. *Breakfast for Jack/Jack and the missing piece*. Front Street.

These wordless stories help pre-literate children, ELL learners new to this country and special needs children explore the basic elements of story-character, setting, and plot. The lack of words allows the children to "construct their own meaning," and create their own different stories which "fit" the illustrations.

Steinberg, Laya. *Thesaurus Rex*. Barefoot Books.

This book introduces a dinosaur with an interest in words whose story is told through a wonderful rhyming text which can be used for fostering phonemic awareness and for choral readings.

Uhlberg, Myron. *The printer*. Peachtree.

This story celebrates the conventions of print in that the boy narrator's father is a deaf man who speaks with his hands and as a job chooses to turn lead type letters into words and sentences. An excellent book to support family literacy and an appreciation for the conventions of print.

Van Allsburg, Chris. (1988). *Two bad ants*. Houghton Mifflin Co.

In Two Bad Ants, news comes to the ant world of a great discovery in a far away place. A delicious crystal has been found. A group of ants set out to bring back this crystal to their queen. Two ants are overwhelmed by the treasure and stay behind in this dangerous alien world. It is a tale of choices, consequences and the discovery of life's real treasures.

Walter, Mildred Pitts. (2004). Illustrated by Larry Johnson. *Alec's primer*. Lebanon, NH: University Press of New England.

This is the true account of a Virginian slave who was taught to read by his owner's daughter. He later fought in the Civil War on the Union side and became a landowner himself in Vermont. The beautifully written narrative is complemented by the vibrant paintings of Larry Johnson which include authentic period details.

Webliography

Balanced Literacy
http://www.thekcrew.net/balancedliteracy.html
Established in 1996, this site is organized according to the components of the balanced literacy approach. It also has an excellent listing of professional books that can assist with various aspects of teaching reading.

Carol Hurst
http://www.carolhurst.com/index.html
This is a terrific resource for exploring the children's literature works which are at the crux of author and genre study. It can be used for material to supplement period studies and discussions of authors' lives. Older children will be able to explore it on their own.

Inspiration Software
http://www.inspiration.com
http://www.inspiration.com/freetrial/index.cfm
This is the home site for the Inspiration and Kidspiration mind mapping software. These online templates and capacities assist the reading teacher with customizing the various graphic organizers discussed throughout the book, and with gaining the ability to design customized graphic organizers for a particular theme, study or student group. A free trial version of this resource which is child friendly can be downloaded.

Read, Write, Think
http://www.readwritethink.org/lessons/
This resource maintained by the NCTE, National Council of Teachers of English, has a growing database of age and grade specific literacy lesson plans. It also includes all the graphic organizers cited in this book and many more, ready to download.

Reading Online
http://www.readingonline.org
This online web resource which is sponsored by the International Reading Association is full of specific reading teaching ideas, lessons and new research. It includes summaries of conference presentations and even tips on how to use technology to teach reading.

Visual Thesaurus
http://www.visualthesaurus.com/online/
This is really both an online dictionary and a thesaurus.

Resources for Read Aloud, Shared Reading, and Independent Reading available on the Internet include the following:

Mighty Books
http:// www.mightybook.com/library_4to6.htm.
This is a library of books read aloud by the computer. Children can listen to these books or practice reading with a buddy as the computer broadcasts the text. Of course, this type of read aloud would only be used in addition to the vibrant read-aloud of the teacher.

Mother Goose Rebus Rhymes-Enchanted Learning Software
http://www.enchantedlearning.com/Rhymes.html
These are online nursery rhymes ready for reading to the children and posting throughout for room or for literacy center display.

SEDL-RCI Framework of Reading
http://www.sedl.org/reading/framework/assessment.html
This is an excellent resource for readings in the theories and methods of foundations. There are topic aligned links to specific theorists which can be included at the close of your lesson planning and may be reviewed before certification tests.

Tools for Teaching and Testing:
To Help You Teach the Foundations of Reading
and Succeed in Constructed Response
Certification Examinations

The Record of Reading Behavior: A close up look at a key assessment tool.

Often in the constructed response question on a foundations of education certification test or on a general elementary certification test, the educator is asked to analyze a record of reading behavior or to construct an appropriate one from data given in an anecdote. Furthermore with the current climate of accountability, it is a good idea for new teachers and for career changers to examine closely the basic elements of recording reading behavior.

While various formats are acceptable for emergent literacy assessment used throughout the country, the one selected for use here is based on the work of Marie Clay and Kenneth Goodman. These two are key researchers in the close observation and documentations of children's early reading miscues (reading mistakes).

Remember that the teacher should not just "take the Record of Reading Behavior" and begin filling it out as the child reads from a random book prior to beginning of the observation. There are specific steps for taking the record and analyzing its results.

1. Select a text

If you want to see if the child is reading on instructional level, choose a book that the child has already read. If the purpose of the test is to see whether the child is ready to advance to the next level, choose a book from that level which the child has not yet seen.

2. Introduce the text

If the book is one that has been read, you do not need to introduce the text, other than by saying the title. But if the book is new to the child, you should briefly share the title and tell the child a bit about the plot and style of the book.

3. Take the record

Generally with emergent readers' grades 1-2, there are only 100-150 words in a passage used to take a record. Make certain that the child is seated beside you so that you can see the text as the child reads it.

If desired, you may want to photocopy the text in advance for yourself, so you can make direct notations on your text while the child reads from the book. After you introduce the text, make certain that the child has the chance to read the text independently. Be certain that you do not "teach" or help the child with the text, other than to supply an unknown word that the child requests you supply. The purpose of the record is to see what the child does on his or her own. As the child reads the text, you must be certain to record the reading behaviors the child exhibits.

In taking the record, keep in mind the following: Allow enough time for the child to work independently on a problem before telling or supplying the word. If you wait too long, you could run the risk of having the child lose the meaning and interest in the story as he or she tries to identify the unknown word.

It is recommended that when a child is way off track, you say, "Try that again" (TTA). If a whole phrase is troubling, put it into square brackets and score it as only one error.

The notation for filling out the Record of Reading behavior involves noting the child's response on the top with the actual text below it.

Comprehension Check

This can and should be done by inviting the child to retell the story. This retelling can then be used to ask further questions about characters, plot, setting, and purpose which allow you to observe and to record the child's level of comprehension.

Calculating the Reading Level and the Self-correction Rate

Calculating the reading level lets you know if the book is at the level on which the child can read it independently or comfortably with guidance or if the book is at a level where reading it frustrates the child.

Generally, an accuracy score of 95-100% suggests that the child can read the text and other books or texts on the same level.

An accuracy score of 90-94% indicates that the text and texts likely will present challenges to the child but, with guidance from you, a tutor, or parent, the child will be able to master these texts and enjoy them. This is instructional level.

However, an accuracy score of 89% or less tells you that the material you have selected for the child is too hard for the child to control alone. Such material needs to be shared with the child in a shared reading situation or read to the child.

Keeping Score on the Record

Insertions, omissions, substitutions, and teacher-told responses all count as errors. Repetitions are not scored as errors. Corrected responses are scored as self corrections.

No penalty is given for a child's attempts at self correction that results in a finally incorrect response but the attempts should be noted. Multiple unsuccessful attempts at a word score as one error only.

The lowest score for any page is zero. If a child omits a line or lines, each word omitted is counted as an error. If the child omits a page, deduct the number of words omitted from the total number of words which you have used for the record.

Calculating the Reading Level

Note the number of errors made on each line on the Record of Reading Behavior in the column marked E (for Error).

Total the number of errors in the text and divide this number into the number of words that the child has read. This will give you the error rate.

If a child read a passage of 100 words and made 10 errors, the error rate would be 1 in 10. Convert this to an accuracy percentage, or 90%.

Calculating the Self Correction Rate

Total all the self-corrections.

Next, add the number of errors to the number of self-corrections and divide by the number of self-corrections.

A self correction rate of 1 in 3 to 1 in 5 is considered good. This rate indicates that the child is able to help himself or herself as problems are encountered in reading.

Analyzing the Record

This record should assist the educator in developing a detailed date specific picture of the child's progress in reading behavior. It should be used to help the educator individualize instruction for the specific child.

As you review the errors, consider whether the child made the error because of semantics (cues from meaning), syntactic (language structure), or visual information difficulties.

As you analyze self corrections, consider what led the child to make that self-correction. Check out and consider what cues the child does use effectively and which the child does not use well.

Consider the ways in which the child tackles a word which is unknown. Characterize that behavior and consider how the teacher can assist the child with this issue.

If a child can retell at least three quarters of a story, this is considered adequate for retelling.

Analysis of reading behavior records can and should support the educator in designing appropriate mini lessons and strategies to help the child with his or her recorded errors and miscues.

Sample Questions – Multiple Choice

Explanation of Rigor
Easy: The majority of test takers would get this question correct. It is a simple understanding of the facts and/or the subject matter is part of the basics of an education for teaching Reading.
Average Rigor: This question represents a test item that most people would pass. It requires a level of analysis or reasoning and/or the subject matter exceeds the basics of an education for teaching Reading.
Rigor: The majority of test takers would have difficulty answering this question. It involves critical thinking skills such as a very high level of abstract thought, analysis or reasoning, and it would require a very deep and broad education for teaching Reading.

1. **A key theorist whose work has helped teacher's document children's oral reading progress throughout the school year is (Average Rigor) (Skill 1.1)**

    A)   Jerome Bruner.

    B)   Daniel J. Chard.

    C)   J. David Cooper.

    D)   Marie Clay.

2. **The reliability of a test is measured by (Average Rigor) (Skill 1.1)**

    A)   the number of children who can pass it.

    B)   the number of children who fail it.

    C)   the degree to which it measures what it is supposed to measure over time.

    D)   None of the above

3. Paul is a new teacher. He has just started his logs and assessments for his children's phonemic awareness. He asks a reading teacher to look over his log, but the log is returned to him. (Average Rigor) (Skill 1.1)

A) Paul gave the log to the wrong colleague.

B) The colleague would not help him out by reviewing it.

C) The log did not have the dates the child's behavior was observed and had no stated performance standards.

D) The log didn't have a cover letter from Paul.

4. The teacher is very concerned about identifying a book that is "just right" for Jay to read independently. This means that Jay should be able to read this book with: (Average Rigor) (Skill 1.1)

A) below 92% accuracy.

B) 100% accuracy.

C) 95-100% accuracy.

D) 92-97% accuracy.

5. Jay really wants to read a book that he can only read with 94% accuracy. He could get to read this book as: (Average Rigor) (Skill 1.1)

A) an independent reading.

B) a guided reading.

C) a shared reading.

D) All of the above.

6. Norm-referenced tests (Average rigor) (Skill 1.1)

A) give information only about the local samples results.

B) provide information about the local test takers did compared to a representative sampling of national test takers.

C) make no comparisons to national test takers.

D) None of the above.

7. **Validity in assessment means (Average Rigor) (Skill 1.1)**

   A) the test went off without any previewing of the questions or leaks on its contents.

   B) the majority of test takers passed.

   C) the correct time was allowed for the children to complete the test.

   D) the test assessed what it was supposed to assess and measure.

8. **"Bias" in testing occurs when (Rigorous) (Skill 1.1)**

   A) the assessment instrument is not an objective, fair and impartial one for a given cultural, ethnic, or special needs participant.

   B) the testing administrator is biased.

   C) the same test is given with no time considerations or provisions for those in need of more time or those who have handicapping conditions.

   D) All of the above

9. **A standardized test will be (Rigorous) (Skill 1.1)**

   A) given out with the same predetermined questions and format to all.

   B) helps with placement for special services.

   C) may be taken over a lengthier test period (i.e. 4 hours instead of three or two if given out in exactly the same format with the same content).

   D) All of the above.

10. **Reading portfolios can include which of the following: (Rigorous) (Skill 1.1)**

    A) checklists and surveys

    B) rubrics

    C) miscue analysis

    D) All of the above

11. "Self correct" in reading means (Easy) (Skill 1.2)

   A) the teacher corrects on the record the errors the child makes.

   B) the child goes back and corrects errors made in a running record.

   C) the reading specialist teaches this to the child.

   D) a and b.

12. Sometimes children can be asked to demonstrate their understanding of a text in a non-written format. This might include all of the following *except*: (Easy) (Skill 1.2)

   A) a story map.

   B) a Venn diagram.

   C) storyboarding a part of the story with dialogue bubbles.

   D) Retelling or paraphrasing.

13. Mrs. Young is a first grade teacher trying to select a books that are "just right" for her students to read independently. She needs to consider which of the following: (Rigorous) (Skill 1.2)

   A) Illustrations should support the meaning of the text.

   B) Content that relates to student interest and experiences

   C) Predictable text structures and language patterns

   D) All of the above

14. Julia has been hired to work in a school that serves a local public housing project. She is working with kindergarten children and has been asked to focus on shared reading. She selects (Rigorous) (Skill 1.2)

   A) chapter books.

   B) riddle books.

   C) alphabet books.

   D) wordless picture books.

15. **Mr. Mandrake is subbing for Ms. Matley. He sees by the schedule that he is supposed to start the day after the morning meeting with a Read-Aloud. He notes a large picture on the easel and grabs the book just two minutes before the Read-Aloud is to start. He shouldn't heave a sigh of relief because (Rigorous) (Skill 1.2)**

A) he needs to be familiar with the book so that he can plan the read-aloud.

B) he does not know if the class has already heard this book.

C) he has not planned vocabulary, themes, or activities to go with the book.

D) All of the above.

16. **When taking a child's running record, the kinds of self corrections the child makes (Average Rigor) (Skill 1.3)**

A) are not important, but the percentage of accuracy is important.

B) may show something about which cueing systems the child relies on.

C) can be meaningful if analyzed over several records.

D) Both B and C

17. **Ms. Rivers is preparing for a parent teacher conference. She does all of the following *except* (Average Rigor) (Skill 1.3)**

A) Collects individual child running records.

B) Puts away all the book bags and leveled pots so the classroom will be more spacious.

C) Puts out by each child's seat the child's weekly log and spelling folder.

D) Sets up work samples by each child's place.

18. **Ms. James is seated with a child by her side. The child is reading aloud from an open book. Ms. James is teaching in a school that has embraced the Balanced Literacy Approach. Therefore it is most likely that Ms. James is writing and recording (Rigorous) (Skill 1.3)**

   A) the child's use of expression in reading aloud.

   B) the child's errors and miscues.

   C) her observations of the child's attitude toward reading.

   D) the child's feelings about the particular passage being read.

19. **Once a teacher has carefully recorded and documented a running record (Rigorous) (Skill 1.3)**

   A) there is nothing further to do as long as the teacher keeps the running record for conferences and documentation of grades.

   B) The teacher should review the running record and other subsequent ones taken for growth over time.

   C) The teacher should differentiate instruction for that particular student as indicated by growth over time and evidence of other needs.

   D) Both b and c

20. A delegation from the United Kingdom has come to the United States and since they are considering adapting the balanced literacy approach, they are very interested in seeing the small group demonstrated. Mr. Adams knows that he should bring them into Greg's room when Greg is doing which activity? (Average Rigor) (Skill 2.1)

A) A mini lesson.

B) A conference with individual students.

C) A time when children are divided into small and independent study groups.

D) A read-aloud.

21. Mr. Adams was pleased with Ms. Ramirez's reading lesson, but he realized that she would have visually represented the comparisons she was trying to get the children to make better, if she had used (Rigorous) (Skill 2.1)

A) a big book.

B) more expressive language.

C) a better literary example.

D) a graphic organizer.

22. A "decodable text" is (Rigorous) (Skill 2.1)

A) a text that a child can read aloud with correct pronunciations.

B) a text that a child can answer questions about with a high percentage of accuracy.

C) text written to match the sequence of letter-sound relationships that have been taught.

D) None of the above.

23. In terms of a balanced literacy classroom, a "leveled bin" indicates (Easy) (Skill 2.2)

A) a plant set at child's eye level for descriptive writing purposes.

B) a bin with books the child has selected.

C) a bin with books leveled by the teacher.

D) a bin with all kinds of reading materials including magazines and packaging on a child's level.

24. In a balanced literacy classroom, new vocabulary would most likely appear on (Easy) (Skill 2.2)

    A)   an experiential chart.

    B)   a class newspaper.

    C)   the word wall.

    D)   outside the room on a bulletin board.

25. Among the literary strategies that teachers can use to activate prior knowledge are (Easy) (Skill 2.2)

    A)   predicting and previewing a story.

    B)   story mapping.

    C)   Venn diagramming.

    D)   linear arrays.

26. In Ms. Francine's class, dictionary use is a punishment. Her principal observes her class and is (Average Rigor) (Skill 2.2)

    A)   pleased with the way that Ms. Francine approaches dictionary use.

    B)   unconcerned with this approach to the use of the dictionary

    C)   convinced that the teacher should model her own fascination and pleasure in using the dictionary for the children.

    D)   delighted by the fact that children are being forced to use the dictionary.

27. As part of a study for a unit on the history of Massachusetts, Mr. Gentry is using the early childhood book *26 Letters and 99 Cents* by Tina Hoban. He wants his readers to study it and create a more detailed guide to their state using its concept. This is a technique frequently used in (Rigorous) (Skill 2.2)

    A)   reading and writing workshop.

    B)   writing process instruction.

    C)   readers workshop.

    D)   technical writing.

28. **Ability grouping means (Rigorous) (Skill 2.2)**

   A) grouping of children according to the results of an IQ test.

   B) grouping of children with similar test results for instructional purposes.

   C) grouping of children according to their oral reading accuracy rate.

   D) grouping of children with similar needs for instructional purposes.

29. **The major difference between phonemic and phonological awareness is (Average Rigor) (Skill 3.1)**

   A) one deals with a series of discrete sounds and the other with sound-spelling relationships.

   B) one is involved with teaching and learning alliteration and rhymes.

   C) phonemic awareness is a specific type of phonological awareness that deals with separate phonemes within a given word.

   D) phonological awareness is associated with printed words.

30. **Phonological awareness includes all of the following skills *except* (Average Rigor) (Skill 3.1)**

   A) rhyming and syllabification

   B) blending sounds into words

   C) understanding the meaning of the root word

   D. removing initial sounds and substituting others

31. **All of the following are true about phonological awareness *except* (Average Rigor) (Skill 3.1)**

   A) it may involve print.

   B) it is a prerequisite for spelling and phonics.

   C) activities can be done by the children with their eyes closed.

   D) it starts before letter recognition is taught.

32. The theorist in early reading (emergent reading) who has identified five tasks for phonemic awareness is (Average Rigor) (Skill 3.1)

    A) John Munro

    B) Brian Cambourne

    C) Marilyn Jager Adams

    D) Lucy Calkins

33. A teacher is asking children to look at the beginning letters of words. She then asks the child to connect the beginning letter to the text and story and to think about what word would make sense there. This is an example of (Average Rigor) (Skill 3.1)

    A) a balanced literacy approach.

    B) a phonemic approach.

    C) a phonic approach.

    D) an ELL-differentiated approach.

34. An oddity task is one in which children (Rigorous) (Skill 3.1)

    A) identify the odd number in a mathematical series and talk about how they did it.

    B) perform a creative exercise designed for differentiated learning styles.

    C) recognize which sound is odd in a series of like sounds.

    D) design a different activity for themselves.

35. By definition, which children in a classroom will have trouble with syntactic cues? (Average Rigor) (Skill 3.2)

    A) Those from families who do not have household libraries.

    B) Those not in a top reading group.

    C) Those from ELL backgrounds.

    D) All of the above.

36. Ronald's parents are hearing impaired. He probably will need (Average Rigor) (Skill 3.2)

A) extensive work with the use of picture cues

B) work with songs, rhymes and read alouds to promote phonemic awareness.

C) no extra work or support.

D) None of the above.

37. Gracie seems to be struggling with her reading, even in first grade, although her mother works at a publishing firm and her dad is an editor. Her speech is also full of mispronunciations, although her parents were born in the school neighborhood. Gracie should be checked by (Average Rigor) (Skill 3.2)

A) a reading specialist.

B) a speech therapist or an audiologist

C) a pediatrician.

D) a psychologist.

38. Most of the children in first-year teacher Ms. James's class are really doing well in their phonemic awareness assessments. However, Ms. James is very concerned about three children who do not seem to be able to distinguish between spoken words that "sound alike" but are different. Since she is a first-year teacher, she feels her inexperience may be to blame. In truth, the reason these three children have not yet demonstrated phonemic awareness is most likely that (Rigorous) (Skill 3.2)

A) they are not capable of becoming good readers.

B) they are bored in class.

C) they may be from an ELL background.

D) Ms. James does not pronounce the different phonemes clearly enough.

39. Four of Ms. Wolmark's students have lived in other countries. She is particularly pleased to be studying Sumerian proverbs with them as part of the sixth grade unit in analyzing the sayings of other cultures because (Rigorous) (Skill 3.2)

A) this gives her a break from teaching and the children can share sayings from other cultures they and their families have experienced.

B) this validates the experiences and expertise of ELL learners in her classroom.

C) This provides her children from the US with a lens on other cultural values.

D) All of the above.

40. "Beautiful Beth is the Best Girl in the Bradley Bay area." This sentence could be used to help children learn about (Easy) (Skill 3.3)

A) assonance.

B) alliteration.

C) rhyming pairs.

D) None of the above

41. Andrew is just starting school, but it looks like he will be successful in reading because (Average Rigor) (Skill 3.3)

A) he comes from a family which cares about his progress.

B) he is phonemically aware and knows his alphabet.

C) he has been in pre-school.

D) he is well behaved.

42. As a parent walked through the first grade floor of her school, she kept hearing repeated clapping. Most likely the children were (Average Rigor) (Skill 3.3)

A) clapping to show respect for one another.

B) rehearsing for how they would clap at a play.

C) clapping out syllables of multi-syllabic words.

D) All of the above.

43. The term graphophenemic awareness refers to (Easy) (Skill 4.1)

A) handwriting skills.

B) letter to sound recognition.

C) alphabetic principle.

D) Phonemic awareness

44. The best way for a teacher to track a student's progress in demonstrating the alphabetic principal/ graphophonemic awareness is to (Rigorous) (Skill 4.1)

A) provide group assessments

B) maintain individual records

C) assess with standardized tests

D) have the student assessed by a team of teachers

45. Environmental print is available at all of the following except (Easy) (Skill 4.2)

A) within a newspaper.

B) on the page of a library book.

C) on a supermarket circular.

D) in a commercial flyer.

46. Book handling skills include ALL of the following except (Easy) (Skill 4.2)

A) putting a cellophane or plastic cover on a book.

B) identifying the back cover of the book.

C) reading the book jacket.

D) reading dedication page and the title page of the book.

47. The best way for a primary grade teacher to model directionality and one to one word matching would be (Easy) (Skill 4.2)

A) using a regular library or classroom text book.

B) using her own person reading book.

C) using a big book.

D) using a book dummy.

48. **An effective way to build vocabulary and to make connections with mandated science and mathematics material is to teach Greek and Latin roots using (Average Rigor) (Skill 4.2)**

   A) semantic maps.

   B) hierarchical arrays.

   C) linear arrays.

   D) word webs.

49. **A district observer notes that fifth graders are showing younger peers in the third grade how to hold a book and walk around with it, they assume (Average Rigor) (Skill 4.2)**

   A) that the fifth graders are particularly theatrical.

   B) that the fifth graders are proud of how they read stories aloud.

   C) that the fifth graders are training the younger children in book holding.

   D) that this has nothing to do with instruction.

50. **Dictionary study (Average Rigor) (Skill 4.3)**

   A) can begin in grades 1 or 2.

   B) can begin in pre-K using the lush picture dictionaries.

   C) should start on grade three level.

   D) A and B.

51. **Greg Ball went to an author signing where Faith Ringgold gave a talk about one of her many books. He was so inspired by her presence and by his reading of her book *Tar Beach* that he used the book for his reading and writing workshop activities. His supervisor wrote in his plan book, that he was pleased that Greg had used the book as an/a _____ book. (Average Rigor) (Skill 4.3)**

   A) basic book.

   B) feature book.

   C) anchor book.

   D) focus book.

52. **The work of Chard and Osborn (1999) in establishing guidelines for children with reading disabilities has shown that it is essential for them to (Rigorous) (Skill 4.3)**

    A) Read wordless picture books.

    B) Learn at least 10 sight words.

    C) Work intensely on the alphabetic principle.

    D) Focus on using syntactic clues.

53. **To decode is to (Easy) (Skill 5.1)**

    A) construct meaning.

    B) sound out a printed sequence of letters.

    C) use a special code to decipher a message.

    D) None of the above.

54. **A theorist who believes that there is a finite body of approved literature children should be taught on various grade levels and has produced books about what everyone needs to know to be literate on various grade levels is (Rigorous) (Skill 5.1)**

    A) Rudolf Flesch

    B) J. David Cooper

    C) John Dewey

    D) E. D. Hirsch

55. The science fair is coming up and Ms. Gardner is trying to find time in her busy schedule to work on her class's earth worm diary project. With all of the mandated tests and assemblies, she has not found time to start her students on their earth worm research. Within the context of reading instruction, she can (Rigorous) (Skill 5.1)

A) begin a thematic study unit.

B) start with a read aloud of the *Diary of an Earth Worm* by Doreen Cronin.

C) scaffold the research process by going online with her children using an approved search engine to find matches for earthworm sites.

D) All of the above.

56. The first grade class is on a neighborhood walk. As the children approach the neighborhood Kentucky Fried Chicken chain, Danny reads from the store window "Kentucky Fried Chicken Hot and Crunchy." Danny has never read or been taught to read this before. The most likely explanation for Danny's being able to read this is that he is (Easy) (Skill 5.2)

A) an advanced reader who is self improving.

B) his parents have taught him to read the signs and materials at the Kentucky Fried Chicken store.

C) he is in the logographic phrase of phonics learning.

D) this was just a lucky guess on his part.

57. An observer enters Julia's first grade classroom. Children are working with oak tag strips and placing the word letters on these strips on a sentence strip holder. Then they seem to be involved in some kind of counting. The observer is confused. This activity is taking place during the reading block. Julia explains that (Average Rigor) (Skill 5.2)

A) the children are counting letters.

B) this is word sorting and the children are grouping words by length, common letters and sound.

C) the children are combining mathematics counting and word study.

D) the children are doing a strategy sheet based on a particular word family

58. Randy is proud of how many new vocabulary words he has learned. He enjoys playing with a device his teacher has, since it helps him to show all the words he can create from various letters. The device is a (Average Rigor) (Skill 5.2)

A) word strip.

B) letter holder for making words.

C) word mask.

D) None of the above.

59. A natural role for a highly proficient reader would be (Average Rigor) (Skill 5.2)

A) to assist the teacher with cleaning the classroom and organizing the student folders.

B) to develop charts for the teacher by copying needed poems for full class study.

C) tutor and support struggling readers.

D) work on personal own interests while the teacher works with the rest of the class.

60. Margaret is the winning PS 123 orator. She loves reciting poetry by Shel Silverstein. Who would guess that she is also a poet in her first language? Margaret's first language is definitely (Average Rigor) (Skill 5.2)

A) English.

B) French.

C) Spanish.

D) not English.

61. The sequence of learning phonics skills includes (Rigorous) (Skill 5.2)

A) letter naming.

B) letter sounds.

C) variant vowels and diphthongs.

D) All of the above.

62. Asking a child if what he or she has read makes sense to him or her, is prompting the child to use (Easy) (Skill 5.4)

A) phonics cues.

B) syntactic cues.

C) semantic cues.

D) prior knowledge.

63. "Ballgame" is a _____word. Its meaning is derived from the combination of "Ball" and "Game." (Easy) (Skill 5.4)

A) contraction

B) compound

C) portmanteau

D) palindrome

64. Cues in reading are (Easy) (Skill 5.4)

A) vowel sounds.

B) digraphs.

C) sources of information used by readers to help them construct meaning.

D) None of the above.

65. The word "bat" is a _____word for "batter-up." (Easy) (Skill 5.4)

A) suffix

B) prefix

C) root word

D) inflectional ending

66. **A bound morpheme is (Average Rigor) Skill 5.4**

    A) a prefix.

    B) a contraction.

    C) an inflectional ending that can be added to a base word to change its case, gender, number, tense or form.

    D) a root word.

67. **A key theorist who supports a phonics centered approach is (Average Rigor) (Skill 5.4)**

    A) Marie Clay.

    B) Sharon Taberski.

    C) Shelley Harwayne.

    D) Rudolf Flesch.

68. **Children "own" words when all of the following happen *except* (Average Rigor) (Skill 5.4)**

    A) they find these words on their own.

    B) the teacher provides a mandated word list.

    C) they use the words in their own writings.

    D) the words appear in literature that interests them.

69. **In order to get children to compile specialized vocabulary, they can use (Average Rigor) (Skill 5.4)**

    A) newspapers.

    B) Internet resources and approved web-sites that focus on the special interest.

    C) experts they can interview.

    D) All of the above.

70. **When you ask a child if what he or she has just read "sounds right" to him or her, you are trying to get that child to use (Average Rigor) (Skill 5.4)**

    A) phonics cues.

    B) syntactic cues.

    C) semantic cues.

    D) prior knowledge.

71. If children are engaged in creating a museum within classroom project to exhibit their work, they are (Average Rigor) (Skill 5.4)

A) not doing any reading or writing.

B) doing many authentic reading, writing, and researching tasks.

C) not likely to visit a real museum.

D) All of the above.

72. A discussion circle can convene (Average Rigor) (Skill 5.4)

A) after the children have finished reading a text as a group.

B) before the children read a text as a group.

C) While the reading of the text is going on.

D) All of the above.

73. While the supervisor is pleased overall with Barbara's first year of teaching, he feels that given the fact that two of her students are transfers from Mexico and one student has a hearing impairment, she has to plan for (Rigorous) (Skill 5.4)

A) extra homework for all of them.

B) extra time for the hearing impaired child.

C) a buddy to work with the two students from Mexico.

D) differentiated instruction to meet these students varied special needs.

74. **Based on individual conferences with many children, the teacher realizes that although they are all self-improving readers, they need help in better use of the context to define words. The teacher decided to try the use of (Rigorous) (Skill 5.4)**

A) a dictionary to look up words.

B) a thesaurus to use with the dictionary.

C) contextual redefinition training.

D) instruction in how to effectively use a dictionary.

75. **As Ms. Wolmark looks at the mandated vocabulary curriculum for the 6th grade, she notes that she can opt to teach foreign words and abbreviations which have become part of the English language. She decides (Rigorous) (Skill 5.4)**

A) to forego that since she is not a teacher of foreign language.

B) to teach only foreign words from the native language of her four ELL students.

C) to use the ELL students' native languages as a start for an extensive study of foreign language words.

D) to teach 2-3 foreign language words that are now in English and let it go at that.

76. **Structural analysis is (Rigorous) (Skill 5.4)**

   A) the "sounding out" a printed sequence of letters based on knowledge of letter sound correspondences

   B) when the teacher keeps a detailed recording of the errors or inaccurate attempts of a child reader during a reading assessment

   C) the process of hearing a spoken word and identifying its separate phonemes or syllables.

   D) the process of examining the words in the text for meaningful word units (affixes, base words, inflected endings).

77. **Tim is not in the same ability group as his best friend Alex. He starts to cry even though he is a second grader. The teacher comforts him by telling him the truth that (Rigorous) (Skill 5.5)**

   A) he is just as smart as Alex.

   B) he can play with Alex during recess.

   C) ability groups change as the children's needs in them change during the year.

   D) Tim is smarter than his best friend Alex.

78. **Two consonants placed together in a word to make a unique sound is a (Easy) (Skill 5.6)**

   A) consonant digraph

   B) consonant blend

   C) morpheme

   D) phoneme

79. Young children often spell words they write according to the way the letters sound. This is called (Easy) (Skill 6.1)

A) spelling lists

B) incorrect spelling

C) developmental spelling

D) invented spelling

80. The thirty-seven dependable spelling patterns called "rimes" were identified by (Rigorous) (Skill 6.2)

A) Calkins

B) Wylie and Durrell

C) Clay and Flesch

D) Flesch

81. The best ways to select words students need to learn to spell include all of the following *except* (Rigorous) (Skill 6.2)

A) misspelled words from student writing

B) lists of theme words

C) lists from a spelling textbook

D) lists of words from content areas

82. Direct teaching of a concept or strategy means (Average Rigor) (Skill 6.3)

A) the teacher teaches the concept or strategy as part of a genre lesson.

B) the teacher teaches the concept as part of the writing workshop.

C) the teacher explicitly announces to the class that this strategy will be taught.

D) the teacher teaches the strategy to a small group of children or to an individual child.

83. There are two basic types of text structure: (Easy) (Skill 7.1)

A) Fiction and non-fiction.

B) Primary and pre-K.

C) Expository and narrative.

D) Wordless and text rich.

84. Vocabulary should be introduced after reading if (Average Rigor) (Skill 7.2)

   A) The children have identified words from their reading which were difficult and which they need explained.

   B) The text is appropriate for vocabulary building.

   C) The teacher would like to teach vocabulary after the reading.

   D) A and B

85. A teacher discovers after considering his class's prior knowledge of the story material that he would need to teach 12 words at least before he starts teaching the story to the whole group. This indicates (Rigorous) (Skill 7.2)

   A) the children will need a read-aloud.

   B) the children will need independent reading.

   C) the children will need guided reading.

   D) the children will need shared reading.

86. Factors that affect the level of comprehension a student demonstrates when reading a story include all of the following *except* (Rigorous) (Skill 7.2)

   A) lack of background knowledge

   B) inability to spell words correctly

   C) lack of word recognition skills

   D) inability to determine the meanings of words through context clues.

87. Teachers should select at least _____words for pre-reading vocabulary discussion. (Rigorous) (Skill 7.2)

   A) 12.

   B) 15.

   C) 2-3.

   D) 8-10.

88. Two steps a teacher might take before selecting words for study are (Rigorous) (Skill 7.2)

A) reading the story and story mapping.

B) asking advice from a veteran teacher and the grade leader.

C) looking in a teacher's guide and copying out the words listed there.

D) All of the above are correct.

89. A second grader is writing his first book review. He has conferred with his teacher several times while he was writing the book review. Now he is rehearsing it with the teacher before he reads it aloud to the class. The child's learning of how to compose and deliver a book review has been   (Rigorous) (Skill 7.2)

A) done independently.

B) assisted by family support.

C) done in a cooperative group setting.

D) scaffolded by the teacher.

90. The concerned parent whose child had a visual impairment wanted as much help for him as the teacher and the school district could give her. She begged: "Please, he didn't attend pre-school; he has no prior knowledge." Strictly speaking this is (Rigorous) (Skill 7.2)

A) correct, since he didn't get pre-school experiences.

B) incorrect, since prior knowledge covers everyone's experiences.

C) Incorrect, since he did have prior knowledge experiences but these didn't match those of many of his peers, so he would need to enhance his prior knowledge.

D) both B and C

91. A strategy is   (Average Rigor) (Skill 7.4)

A) a practice or routine the teacher can continually refer to.

B) a practice or routine a child can continually refer to or use.

C) a sheet or template for a practice the child can continually fill out.

D) All of the above.

92. **Making inferences from the text means that the reader (Average Rigor) (Skill 7.4)**

    A) is making informed judgments based on available evidence.

    B) is making a guess based on prior experiences.

    C) is making a guess based on what the reader would like to be true of the text.

    D) All of the above.

93. **The Stop and Think Strategy means that the child reader will (Average Rigor) (Skill 7.4)**

    A) read through until the end of the story or text.

    B) ask himself or herself if what he or she has read makes sense to him or her.

    C) stop after reading some text and write down his/her concerns.

    D) All of the above

94. **To help children with "main idea" questions, the teacher should (Rigorous) (Skill 7.4)**

    A) Give out a strategy sheet on the main idea for children to place in their reader's notebooks.

    B) Model responding to such a question as part of guided reading.

    C) Have children create "main idea questions" to go with their writings.

    D) All of the above.

95. **The five key strategies for a child reading of informational/ expository texts include (Rigorous) (Skill 7.4)**

    A) identifying key information from the pictures or illustrations

    B) having a plan for making sensible meaning from the passage

    C) Looking for points of trivia within the text.

    D) None of the above

96. The strategy in which a graphic organizer is used to help identify what students know, what they want to know, and what they learned is referred to as (Easy) (Skill 7.5)

    A) a bubble map

    B) a reading log

    C) a K-W-L- chart

    D) a Venn diagram

97. When they are in 6th grade, children should be able to independently go through an unfamiliar collection and (Average Rigor) (Skill 7.5)

    A) use only the table of contents.

    B) use the first line indices, and find a poem by author and subject.

    C) use only the glossary.

    D) None of the above.

98. One of the many ways in which a child can demonstrate comprehension of a story is by (Average Rigor) (Skill 7.5)

    A) filling in a strategy sheet.

    B) retelling the story orally.

    C) retelling the story in writing.

    D) All of the above.

99. A fifth grade teacher has subscribed to an online version of a local newspaper. She can help the students examine this resource and how it compares to the print version by noting the following differences. (Rigorous) (Skill 7.5)

    A) Use of video to document events

    B) Use of sound clips in addition to written text

    C) Links to other web resources

    D) All of the above

100. Mark is a brand new teacher who is not from the neighborhood where his school is located. He is a bit nervous as this is his first teaching assignment. He does not yet know how to relax enough to get his students to activate prior experience. He should (Rigorous) (Skill 8.2)

A) try a free recall question: "Tell us what you know about..."

B) try an unstructured question: "Let's talk about..."

C) use word association: "What do you associate X with?"

D) All of the above.

101. Ms. Angel has to be certain that her fourth graders know the characteristics of the historical fiction genre. She can best support them in becoming comfortable with this genre by (Easy) (Skill 8.3)

A) providing sequel and prequel writing opportunities using that genre.

B) reading them many different works from that genre.

C) Both A and B.

D) having them look up the definition of that genre in a literary encyclopedia.

102. An excellent research project that can combine dictionary study with science research would be (Average Rigor) (Skill 9.2)

A) a student-authored dictionary terms and phrases about earthworms.

B) a teacher-developed specialized dictionary of words and phrases about earthworms.

C) a collection of articles on earthworms put together by the school librarian.

D) Both B and C.

103. **Factual book features children should learn include (Average Rigor) (Skill 9.3)**

    A) captions.

    B) glossaries.

    C) diagrams.

    D) All of the above.

104. **Teaching students how to set goals, modeling how to take notes, and how to create an outline are all examples of (Rigorous) (Skill 9.3)**

    A) study skills.

    B) comprehension strategies.

    C) read aloud strategies.

    D) discussion skills.

105. **Historical fiction, mythology, folklore, realistic fiction, mystery, and legends are known as (Easy) (Skill 10.1)**

    A) reading styles.

    B) young adult topics.

    C) genres.

    D) booklists.

106. **Nonfiction genres include all of the following *except* (Easy) (Skill 10.1)**

    A) essays

    B) poetry

    C) speech

    D) biography

107. **The Developing Readers Assessment System for leveling books was developed by (Rigorous) (Skill 10.1)**

    A) Calkins and Clay

    B) Fountas and Pinnell

    C) Wylie and Durrell

    D) Flesch and Clay

108. **Monthly book clubs, book fairs, read-a-thons, and the class library are all examples of (Rigorous) (Skill 10.2)**

    A) ways to foster reading outside class.

    B) ways to raise money for the school library.

    C) ways to raise money for the classroom library.

    D) None of the above.

109. As Ms. Maxwell enters a first grade class, the teacher is busily writing down what the children are saying. The teacher is probably doing this to **(Easy) (Skill 11.1)**

    A) demonstrate how to copy down speech.

    B) make a connection and promote awareness of the relationship between spoken and written language.

    C) authenticate the children's comments.

    D) raise the children's self esteem.

110. To encode means that you **(Average Rigor) (Skill 11.1)**

    A) decode a second time.

    B) construct meaning from a code.

    C) tell someone a message.

    D) None of the above.

111. Author's viewpoint questions stump Gary. His teacher can help him by asking him during their reading conferences **(Average Rigor) (Skill 11.1)**

    A) if Gary feels the book he is reading is right for him.

    B) what the author would say about what the character is doing in the story.

    C) how the story can be changed to another genre.

    D) if Gary wants to read more books by this author.

112. **Ms. Clark is seen by outside observers from her district, seated in front of her class of sixth graders with a notebook in her lap and an easel. She reads aloud from a book and then writes down a series of questions. As she reads along, she sometimes writes down the answers to her own questions. This is most likely (Average Rigor) (Skill 11.2)**

    A)   a sign that Ms. Clark is uncertain of her own comprehension capacity.

    B)   she is modeling self questioning for the children.

    C)   she is aware that she is being watched and wants to make a good impression.

    D)   All of the above.

113. **The stage at which average four and five year old children write letters backwards, upside down or create their own letters is called (Rigorous) (Skill 11.3)**

    A)   making invented spellings

    B)   making mock letters and words

    C)   creating developmental spelling

    D)   language development

114. **At a faculty meeting Ms. Riley found out that she might have crisscrossers in her class and that Mr. Brown had them and he was happy about it. (Rigorous) (Skill 11.4)**

    A)   Crisscrossers are students who have skipped a grade.

    B)   Crisscrossers are students with excellent skills in reading and in Math.

    C)   Crisscrossers are second language learners who have a positive attitude toward first and second language learning.

    D)   Crisscrossers are second language learners who are only positive about English Language Learning.

115. The teacher is working on a life science unit in grade five and using many print and electronic sources for information. Some of these words have a linear and some of them a hierarchical relationship to one another. The teacher has spent much time explaining how the words connect with one another. At this point, it would be a good idea to (Rigorous) (Skill 12.2)

A) use a root family diagram or tree.

B) work with the base words.

C) use hierarchical and linear arrays.

D) start semantic mapping for a particular concept.

116. A technique used after a story has been read. It includes identifying the main elements and categorizing the main events in sequential order. A graphic representation is often used to illustrate the story structure and sequence of events is called   (Rigorous) (Skill 12.2)

A) story mapping

B) hierarchy organizer

C) K-W-L chart

D) Venn diagram

117. Taking responsibility for a child's own learning will usually involve the child in (Average Rigor) (Skill 12.3)

A) reading and writing on his/her own.

B) developing a personal literacy project which will later be shared with the teacher and peers and family.

C) putting away books and materials when directed.

D) Both A and B.

118. If a student has a poor vocabulary, the teacher should recommend first that (Skill 13.1, Average Rigor)

A. the student read newspapers, magazines and books on a regular basis.

B. the student enroll in a Latin class.

C. the student write the words repetitively after looking them up in the dictionary.

D. the student use a thesaurus to locate synonyms and incorporate them into his/her vocabulary

119. The synonyms *gyro, hero,* and *submarine* reflect which influence on language usage? (Skill 13.1 Average Rigor)

    A. Social

    B. Geographical

    C. Historical

    D. Personal

120. Which aspect of language is innate? (Skill 13.1 Rigorous)

    A. Biological capability to articulate sounds understood by other humans

    B. Cognitive ability to create syntactical structures

    C. Capacity for using semantics to convey meaning in a social environment

    D. Ability to vary inflections and accents

121. The arrangement and relationship of words in sentences or sentence structures best describes (Skill 13.1, Rigorous)

    A. style.

    B. discourse.

    C. thesis.

    D. syntax.

122. The teacher should choose words for pre-story discussion and exploration based on (Average Rigor) (Skill 13.2)

    A) the teacher's interest.

    B) whether the teacher feels the children have prior knowledge of or experience with the words.

    C) a pre-existing grade level required vocabulary list.

    D) words that will impress his or her supervisor.

123. "Sounds right" can sound wrong to (Rigorous) (Skill 13.2)

A) any reader who is not a fluent or early reader.

B) an ELL reader.

C) a struggling reader.

D) None of the above.

124. Maria was an outstanding student in her elementary school in Brazil. Now she is nervous about starting fourth grade in the US, although she learned English as a second language in Brazil. She and her parents should be relieved to know that (Rigorous) (Skill 13.3)

A) she will get extra help in the United States with her English.

B) there is a positive and strong correlation between a child's native language and his/her learning of English.

C) her classmates will help her.

D) she will have a few months to study for the reading test.

125. A very bright child in a grade one class came from a family which did not a have a strong oral story telling or story reading tradition in its native language. This child would need support in developing (Rigorous) (Skill 13.3)

A) letter-sound correspondence skills.

B) schemata for generic concepts most children have in their memories and experiences based on family oral traditions and read a loud.

C) oral expressiveness.

D) Both B and C.

Answer Key

1	D	26	C	51	C	76	D	101	C
2	C	27	C	52	C	77	C	102	A
3	C	28	D	53	B	78	A	103	D
4	D	29	C	54	B	79	D	104	A
5	A	30	C	55	D	80	B	105	C
6	B	31	A	56	C	81	C	106	B
7	D	32	C	57	B	82	D	107	B
8	D	33	C	58	B	83	C	108	A
9	D	34	C	59	C	84	D	109	B
10	D	35	C	60	D	85	C	110	B
11	B	36	B	61	D	86	B	111	B
12	D	37	B	62	C	87	C	112	B
13	D	38	C	63	B	88	D	113	B
14	D	39	D	64	C	89	D	114	C
15	D	40	B	65	C	90	D	115	C
16	D	41	B	66	C	91	D	116	A
17	B	42	C	67	D	92	A	117	D
18	B	43	C	68	B	93	B	118	A
19	C	44	B	69	D	94	D	119	B
20	C	45	B	70	B	95	B	120	A
21	A	46	A	71	B	96	C	121	D
22	A	47	C	72	A	97	B	122	B
23	C	48	D	73	D	98	D	123	B
24	C	49	C	74	C	99	D	124	B
25	A	50	D	75	C	100	B	125	B

Rigor Analysis Table

	Easy %20	Average Rigor %40	Rigorous %40
Question #	11, 12, 23, 24, 25, 40, 43, 45, 46, 47, 53, 56, 62, 63, 64, 65, 78, 79, 83, 96, 101, 105, 106, 109	1, 2, 3, 4, 5, 6, 7, 16, 17, 20, 26, 29, 30, 31, 32, 33, 35, 36, 37, 38, 39, 41, 42, 48, 49, 50, 51, 57, 58, 59, 60, 66, 67, 68, 69, 70, 71, 72, 82, 84, 91, 92, 93, 97, 98, 102, 103, 110, 111, 112, 117, 118, 119, 122	8, 9, 10, 13, 14, 15, 18, 19, 21, 22, 27, 28, 34, 44, 52, 54, 55, 61, 73, 74, 75, 76, 77, 80, 81, 85, 86, 87, 88, 89, 90, 94, 95, 99, 100, 104, 107, 108, 113, 114, 115, 116, 120, 121, 123, 124, 125

Explanation of Rigor

Easy: The majority of test takers would get this question correct. It is a simple understanding of the facts and/or the subject matter is part of the basics of an education for teaching Reading.

Average Rigor: This question represents a test item that most people would pass. It requires a level of analysis or reasoning and/or the subject matter exceeds the basics of an education for teaching Reading.

Rigorous: The majority of test takers would have difficulty answering this question. It involves critical thinking skills such as a very high level of abstract thought, analysis or reasoning, and it would require a very deep and broad education for teaching Reading.

Answers with Rationales

1. **A key theorist whose work has helped teacher's document children's oral reading progress throughout the school year is (Average Rigor) (Skill 1.1)**

   A) Jerome Bruner.

   B) Daniel J. Chard.

   C) J. David Cooper.

   D) Marie Clay.

   The answer is D. Understanding the value and importance of the concepts of print for beginning readers developed out of the work of Marie Clay in New Zealand. Assessment of these skills typically occurs in kindergarten and into first grade as necessary.

2. **The reliability of a test is measured by (Average Rigor) (Skill 1.1)**

   A) the number of children who can pass it.

   B) the number of children who fail it.

   C) the degree to which it measures what it is supposed to measure over time.

   D) None of the above

   The answer is C. The degree to which it measures what it is supposed to measure over time. Reliability is the consistency of the test. This is measured by whether the test will indicate the same score for the child who takes it more than once.

3. **Paul is a new teacher. He has just started his logs and assessments for his children's phonemic awareness. He asks a reading teacher to look over his log, but the log is returned to him. (Average Rigor) (Skill 1.1)**

   A) Paul gave the log to the wrong colleague.

   B) The colleague would not help him out by reviewing it.

   C) The log did not have the dates the child's behavior was observed and had no stated performance standards.

   D) The log didn't have a cover letter from Paul.

   The answer is C. The log did not have the dates the child's behavior was observed and had no stated performance standards. Records of Independent Reading and Writing can include the children's journals, notebooks or logs of books read with the names of the authors, titles of the books, date completed, and pieces related to books completed or in progress.

4. **The teacher is very concerned about identifying a book that is "just right" for Jay to read independently. This means that Jay should be able to read this book with: (Average Rigor) (Skill 1.1)**

   A) below 92% accuracy.

   B) 100% accuracy.

   C) 95-100% accuracy.

   D) 92-97% accuracy.

   The answer is D. For a book to be considered on a child's independent level the student must be able to read it with 92-97% accuracy. A higher percentage would be too easy and a lower percentage would mean the text was too difficult.

5. **Jay really wants to read a book that he can only read with 94% accuracy. He could get to read this book as: (Average Rigor) (Skill 1.1)**

A) an independent reading.

B) a guided reading.

C) a shared reading.

D) All of the above.

The answer is A. For a book to be considered on a child's independent level the student must be able to read it with 92-97% accuracy. A higher percentage would be too easy and a lower percentage would mean the text was too difficult.

6. **Norm-referenced tests (Average Rigor) (Skill 1.1)**

A) give information only about the local samples results.

B) provide information about the local test takers did compared to a representative sampling of national test takers.

C) make no comparisons to national test takers.

D) None of the above.

The answer is B. Norm-referenced tests are measure children against one another. Scores on this test are reported in percentiles. Each percentile indicates the percent of the testing population whose scores were lower than or the same as a particular child's score. Percentile is defined as a score on a scale of 100 showing the percentage of a distribution that is equal to it or below it.

7. **Validity in assessment means (Average Rigor) (Skill 1.1)**

A)   the test went off without any previewing of the questions or leaks on its contents.

B)   the majority of test takers passed.

C)   the correct time was allowed for the children to complete the test.

D)   the test assessed what it was supposed to assess and measure.

The answer is D. Validity is how well a test measures what it is supposed to measure. Teacher made tests are therefore not generally extremely valid, although they may be an appropriate measure for the validity of the concept the teacher wants to assess for his/her own children's achievement.

8. **"Bias" in testing occurs when (Rigorous) (Skill 1.1)**

A)   the assessment instrument is not an objective, fair and impartial one for a given cultural, ethnic, or special needs participant.

B)   the testing administrator is biased.

C)   the same test is given with no time considerations or provisions for those in need of more time or those who have handicapping conditions.

D)   All of the above

The answer is D. Bias in testing occurs when the information within the test or the information required to respond to a multiple choice question or constructed response (essay question on the test) is information that is not available to some test takers who come from a different cultural, ethnic, linguistic or socio-economic background than do the majority of the test takers.

9. **A standardized test will be (Rigorous) (Skill 1.1)**

   A) given out with the same predetermined questions and format to all.

   B) helps with placement for special services.

   C) may be taken over a lengthier test period (i.e. 4 hours instead of three or two if given out in exactly the same format with the same content).

   D) All of the above.

   The answer is D. Standardized tests are generally:
   - Uniformly administered
   - time efficient
   - best for younger children
   - helps with placement
   - permits comparisons across groups
   - used for policy decisions by administrators for special services

10. **Reading portfolios can include which of the following: (Rigorous) (Skill 1.1)**

    A) checklists and surveys

    B) rubrics

    C) miscue analysis

    D) All of the above

    The answer is D. Portfolios often contain six categories of materials: work samples, records of independent reading and writing, checklists and surveys, self evaluation forms, rubrics, miscue analysis, and informal reading inventories.

11. **"Self correct" in reading means (Easy) (Skill 1.2)**

    A)   the teacher corrects on the record the errors the child makes.

    B)   the child goes back and corrects errors made in a running record.

    C)   the reading specialist teaches this to the child.

    D)   a and b.

    The answer is B. The child goes back and corrects errors made in a running record. Self correction occurs when children begin to correct some of their own reading errors. Generally this behavior is accompanied by the re-reading of the previous phrase or sentence.

12. **Sometimes children can be asked to demonstrate their understanding of a text in a non-written format. This might include all of the following** *except* **(Easy) (Skill 1.2)**

    A)   a story map.

    B)   a Venn diagram.

    C)   storyboarding a part of the story with dialogue bubbles.

    D)   retelling or paraphrasing.

    The answer is D. Children are expected and encouraged to tell as much of a story as they can remember. Re-telling is far more extensive than just summarizing. Children should include the beginning, middle and end plot lines and should be able to tell about the book's characters.

13. **Mrs. Young is a first grade teacher trying to select a books that are "just right" for her students to read independently. She needs to consider which of the following: (Rigorous) (Skill 1.2)**

    A) Illustrations should support the meaning of the text.

    B) Content that relates to student interest and experiences

    C) Predictable text structures and language patterns

    D) All of the above

    The answer is D. It is important that all of the above factors be considered when selecting books for young children.

14. **Julia has been hired to work in a school that serves a local public housing project. She is working with kindergarten children and has been asked to focus on shared reading. She selects (Rigorous) (Skill 1.2)**

    A) chapter books.

    B) riddle books.

    C) alphabet books.

    D) wordless picture books.

    The answer is D. Wordless picture books allow students to derive the story events from the illustrations and prevent stumbling over words they are unable to indentify.

15. **Mr. Mandrake is subbing for Ms. Matley. He sees by the schedule that he is supposed to start the day after the morning meeting with a Read-Aloud. He notes a large picture on the easel and grabs the book just two minutes before the Read-Aloud is to start. He shouldn't heave a sigh of relief because (Rigorous) (Skill 1.2)**

A) he needs to be familiar with the book so that he can plan the read-aloud.

B) he does not know if the class has already heard this book.

C) he has not planned vocabulary, themes, or activities to go with the book.

D) All of the above.

The answer is D. Teachers should not only use wordless stories (books which tell their narratives through pictures alone), but can also make targeted use of big books for read-alouds, so that young children become habituated to the use of illustrations as an important component for constructing meaning. The teacher should model for the child how to reference an illustration for help in identifying a word in the text the child does not recognize.

16. **When taking a child's running record, the kinds of self corrections the child makes (Average Rigor) (Skill 1.3)**

A) are not important, but the percentage of accuracy is important.

B) may show something about which cueing systems the child relies on.

C) can be meaningful if analyzed over several records.

D) Both b and c

The answer is D. A running record provides the teacher with insight into what a child is thinking and how they are approaching a text as they read. Teachers are better able to understand a student's strengths and weaknesses.

17. **Ms. Rivers is preparing for a parent teacher conference. She does all of the following *except* (Average Rigor) (Skill 1.3)**

   A)   Collects individual child running records.

   B)   Puts away all the book bags and leveled pots so the classroom will be more spacious.

   C)   Puts out by each child's seat the child's weekly log and spelling folder.

   D)   Sets up work samples by each child's place.

   The answer is B. A parent conference is a time to share student progress with parents. While it may be necessary to tidy the room or move things around to provide additional space, it is not a necessary part of the conference.

18. **Ms. James is seated with a child by her side. The child is reading aloud from an open book. Ms. James is teaching in a school that has embraced the Balanced Literacy Approach. Therefore it is most likely that Ms. James is writing and recording (Rigorous) (Skill 1.3)**

   A)   the child's use of expression in reading aloud.

   B)   the child's errors and miscues.

   C)   her observations of the child's attitude toward reading.

   D)   the child's feelings about the particular passage being read.

   The answer is B. Running records taken of children help the teacher learn about the cueing systems that children use. It is important for the teacher to adjust reading instruction based on the pattern of miscues gathered from several successive reading records. When the teacher carefully reviews a given student's substitutions and self corrections, certain patterns begin to surface

19. **Once a teacher has carefully recorded and documented a running record (Rigorous) (Skill 1.3)**

    A) there is nothing further to do as long as the teacher keeps the running record for conferences and documentation of grades.

    B) The teacher should review the running record and other subsequent ones taken for growth over time.

    C) The teacher should differentiate instruction for that particular student as indicated by growth over time and evidence of other needs.

    D) Both b and c

    The answer is C. After the completion of a running record, the teacher should analyze the record to determine the next teaching step that should occur for the student.

20. **A delegation from the United Kingdom has come to the United States and since they are considering adapting the balanced literacy approach, they are very interested in seeing the small group demonstrated. Mr. Adams knows that he should bring them into Greg's room when Greg is doing which activity? (Average Rigor) (Skill 2.1)**

    A) A mini lesson.

    B) A conference with individual students.

    C) A time when children are divided into small and independent study groups.

    D) A read-aloud.

    The answer is C. In a balanced literacy approach, small group time is when small groups of students are pulled to work independently with focused direction from the teacher.

21. **Mr. Adams was pleased with Ms. Ramirez's reading lesson, but he realized that she would have visually represented the comparisons she was trying to get the children to make better, if she had used (Rigorous) (Skill 2.1)**

    A)   a big book.

    B)   more expressive language.

    C)   a better literary example.

    D)   a graphic organizer.

    The answer is A. Big books are very effective in demonstrating how to work with text and various reading strategies.

22. **A "decodable text" is (Rigorous) (Skill 2.1)**

    A)   a text that a child can read aloud with correct pronunciations.

    B)   a text that a child can answer questions about with a high percentage of accuracy.

    C)   text written to match the sequence of letter-sound relationships that have been taught.

    D)   None of the above.

    The answer is A. Decodable books are vocabulary-controlled using language from word families with high predictability. Thus we get sentences like "Nan has a tan fan." Reading is seen as skills-based, and the skills are taught one at a time.

23. **In terms of a balanced literacy classroom, a "leveled bin" indicates (Easy) (Skill 2.2)**

    A) a plant set at child's eye level for descriptive writing purposes.

    B) a bin with books the child has selected.

    C) a bin with books leveled by the teacher.

    D) a bin with all kinds of reading materials including magazines and packaging on a child's level.

    The answer is C. The classroom library in the context of the balanced literacy approach to reading instruction is focused on leveled books. These are books which have been leveled with the support of Fountas and Pinnell's Guided Reading: Good First Teaching for All Children and Matching Books to Readers: Using Leveled Reading in Guided Reading, K-3.

24. **In a balanced literacy classroom, new vocabulary would most likely appear on (Easy) (Skill 2.2)**

    A) an experiential chart.

    B) a class newspaper.

    C) the word wall.

    D) outside the room on a bulletin board.

    The answer is C. A word wall is a classroom display of high frequency and/or grade level specific words available for student reference.

25. **Among the literary strategies that teachers can use to activate prior knowledge are (Easy) (Skill 2.2)**

    A)   predicting and previewing a story.

    B)   story mapping.

    C)   Venn diagramming.

    D)   linear arrays.

The answer is A. By predicting the events or preview a story the teacher can help students connect with and not only activate prior knowledge, but build vocabulary as well.

26. **In Ms. Francine's class, dictionary use is a punishment. Her principal observes her class and is (Average Rigor) (Skill 2.2)**

    A)   pleased with the way that Ms. Francine approaches dictionary use.

    B)   unconcerned with this approach to the use of the dictionary

    C)   convinced that the teacher should model her own fascination and pleasure in using the dictionary for the children.

    D)   delighted by the fact that children are being forced to use the dictionary.

The answer is C. Skills such as using a dictionary or reading should never be used as punishment. This can inhibit student progress. A good teacher should model the use of all tools so that children may come to learn to use and enjoy using various tools.

27. **As part of a study for a unit on the history of Massachusetts, Mr. Gentry is using the early childhood book *26 Letters and 99 Cents* by Tina Hoban. He wants his readers to study it and create a more detailed guide to their state using its concept. This is a technique frequently used in (Rigorous) (Skill 2.2)**

   A)   reading and writing workshop.

   B)   writing process instruction.

   C)   readers workshop.

   D)   technical writing.

   The answer is C. In a reader's workshop the teacher begins by presenting a mini-lesson on a reading/writing skill or concept. Students are then given uninterrupted time to read their various texts. Afterward students respond to what they have read in a reader response journal or reading log. Many reading workshops also include time for sharing.

28. **Ability grouping means (Rigorous) (Skill 2.2)**

   A)   grouping of children according to the results of an IQ test.

   B)   grouping of children with similar test results for instructional purposes.

   C)   grouping of children according to their oral reading accuracy rate.

   D)   grouping of children with similar needs for instructional purposes.

   The answer is D. It is often difficult to meet each child's needs individually in a large classroom. Therefore, teachers often group students with similar needs to make the most efficient use of time and to provide students with others to work with.

29. **The major difference between phonemic and phonological awareness is (Average Rigor) (Skill 3.1)**

    A)   one deals with a series of discrete sounds and the other with sound-spelling relationships.

    B)   one is involved with teaching and learning alliteration and rhymes.

    C)   phonemic awareness is a specific type of phonological awareness that deals with separate phonemes within a given word.

    D)   phonological awareness is associated with printed words.

    The answer is C. Phonemic awareness is a specific type of phonological awareness which focuses on the ability to distinguish, manipulate and blend specific sounds or phonemes within an individual word.

30. **Phonological awareness includes all of the following skills *except* (Average Rigor) (Skill 3.1)**

    A)   rhyming and syllabification

    B)   blending sounds into words

    C)   understanding the meaning of the root word

    D.   removing initial sounds and substituting others

    The answer is C. Phonological awareness involves the recognition that spoken words are composed of a set of smaller units such as onsets and rimes, syllables, and sounds.

31. **All of the following are true about phonological awareness** *except* **(Average Rigor) (Skill 3.1)**

    A)   it may involve print.

    B)   it is a prerequisite for spelling and phonics.

    C)   activities can be done by the children with their eyes closed.

    D)   it starts before letter recognition is taught.

    The answer is A. Phonological Awareness is the ability to recognize the sounds of spoken language and how they can be blended together, segmented, and switched/manipulated to form new combinations and words.

32. **The theorist in early reading (emergent reading) who has identified five tasks for phonemic awareness is (Average Rigor) (Skill 3.1)**

    A)   John Munro

    B)   Brian Cambourne

    C)   Marilyn Jager Adams

    D)   Lucy Calkins

    The answer is C. Theorist Marilyn Jager Adams who researches early reading has outlined five basic types of phonemic awareness tasks. Task 1- Ability to hear rhymes and alliteration. Task 2- Ability to do oddity tasks (recognize the member of a set that is different.) Task 3 –The ability to orally blend words and split syllables. Task 4 –The ability to orally segment word. Task 5- The ability to do phonics manipulation tasks.

33. **A teacher is asking children to look at the beginning letters of words. She then asks the child to connect the beginning letter to the text and story and to think about what word would make sense there. This is an example of (Average Rigor) (Skill 3.1)**

    A) a balanced literacy approach.

    B) a phonemic approach.

    C) a phonic approach.

    D) an ELL-differentiated approach.

    The answer is C. Instruction begins with a strong phonics approach, learning letter-sound relationships and often using basal readers or decodable books.

34. **An oddity task is one in which children (Rigorous) (Skill 3.1)**

    A) identify the odd number in a mathematical series and talk about how they did it.

    B) perform a creative exercise designed for differentiated learning styles.

    C) recognize which sound is odd in a series of like sounds.

    D) design a different activity for themselves.

    The answer is C. The ability to detect an oddity is the ability to recognize the member of a set that is different [odd] among the group. For example, the children would look at the pictures of grass, a garden and a rose and then answer "Which one starts with a different sound?"

35. **By definition, which children in a classroom will have trouble with syntactic cues? (Average Rigor) (Skill 3.2)**

    A)   Those from families who do not have household libraries.

    B)   Those not in a top reading group.

    C)   Those from ELL backgrounds.

    D)   All of the above.

The answer is C. By definition a child from an ELL background does not have a strong accurate sense of what "sounds right" in English. Not all English phonemes are present in various ELL native languages; for example, the sound of /th/ does not appear in Spanish. Some native language phonemes may and do conflict with English phonemes.

36. **Ronald's parents are hearing impaired. He probably will need (Average Rigor) (Skill 3.2)**

    A)   extensive work with the use of picture cues

    B)   work with songs, rhymes and read alouds to promote phonemic awareness.

    C)   no extra work or support.

    D)   None of the above.

The answer is B. Because of his parent's impairment, Ronald may not have been exposed to normal auditory communication that would be necessary to have a strong sense of phonemic awareness. He may need additional work to strengthen those skills.

37. Gracie seems to be struggling with her reading, even in first grade, although her mother works at a publishing firm and her dad is an editor. Her speech is also full of mispronunciations, although her parents were born in the school neighborhood. Gracie should be checked by (Average Rigor) (Skill 3.2)

    A)   a reading specialist.

    B)   a speech therapist or an audiologist

    C)   a pediatrician.

    D)   a psychologist.

    The answer is B. A speech therapist or an audiologist works with students who show difficulties in pronouncing words to improve the quality of their speech.

38. Most of the children in first-year teacher Ms. James's class are really doing well in their phonemic awareness assessments. However, Ms. James is very concerned about three children who do not seem to be able to distinguish between spoken words that "sound alike" but are different. Since she is a first-year teacher, she feels her inexperience may be to blame. In truth, the reason these three children have not yet demonstrated phonemic awareness is most likely that (Rigorous) (Skill 3.2)

    A)   they are not capable of becoming good readers.

    B)   they are bored in class.

    C)   they may be from an ELL background.

    D)   Ms. James does not pronounce the different phonemes clearly enough.

    The answer is C. All children are capable of becoming good readers, and choices B and D, given Ms. James's dedication, are not the most likely reasons these three children (a small number of the class) are struggling. Children who have problems with phonics generally have not acquired or been exposed to phonemic awareness activities at home or in preschool-2. This includes extensive songs, rhymes and read-alouds.

39. **Four of Ms. Wolmark's students have lived in other countries. She is particularly pleased to be studying Sumerian proverbs with them as part of the sixth grade unit in analyzing the sayings of other cultures because (Rigorous) (Skill 3.2)**

   A) this gives her a break from teaching and the children can share sayings from other cultures they and their families have experienced.

   B) this validates the experiences and expertise of ELL learners in her classroom.

   C) This provides her children from the US with a lens on other cultural values.

   D) All of the above.

The answer is D. It is recommended that all teachers of reading and particularly those who are working with ELL students use meaningful, student centered, and culturally customized activities. These activities may include: language games, word walls, and poems. Some of these activities might, if possible, be initiated in the child's first language and then reiterated in English.

40. **"Beautiful Beth is the Best Girl in the Bradley Bay area." This sentence could be used to help children learn about (Easy) (Skill 3.3)**

   A) assonance.

   B) alliteration.

   C) rhyming pairs.

   D) None of the above

The answer is B. Alliteration is the term for a series of words that begin with the same sound as in "Beautiful Beth is the Best Girl in the Bradley Bay area."

41. **Andrew is just starting school, but it looks like he will be successful in reading because (Average Rigor) (Skill 3.3)**

    A)   he comes from a family which cares about his progress.

    B)   he is phonemically aware and knows his alphabet.

    C)   he has been in pre-school.

    D)   he is well behaved.

    The answer is B. Since the ability to distinguish between individual sounds, or phonemes, within words is a prerequisite to association of sounds with letters and manipulating sounds to blend words—a fancy way of saying "reading," the teaching of phonemic awareness is crucial to emergent literacy (early childhood K-2 reading instruction). Children need a strong background in phonemic awareness in order for phonics instruction (sound –spelling relationship-printed materials) to be effective.

42. **As a parent walked through the first grade floor of her school, she kept hearing repeated clapping. Most likely the children were (Average Rigor) (Skill 3.3)**

    A)   clapping to show respect for one another.

    B)   rehearsing for how they would clap at a play.

    C)   clapping out syllables of multi-syllabic words.

    D)   All of the above.

    The answer is C. The objective of this activity is for children to understand that there are every syllable in a polysyllabic word can be studied for its spelling patterns in the same way that monosyllabic words are studied for their spelling patterns. First the teacher reads the poem with the children. As they are reading it aloud, the children clap the beats of the poem and the teacher uses a colored marker to place a tic (/) above each syllable.

43. **The term graphophonemic awareness refers to (Easy) (Skill 4.1)**

    A)   handwriting skills.

    B)   letter to sound recognition.

    C)   alphabetic principle.

    D)   Phonemic awareness

The answer is C. Graphophonemic involves:
- Match all consonant and short vowel sounds.
- Read one's own name.
- Read one syllable words and high frequency words.
- Demonstrate ability to read and understand that as letters in words change, so do the sounds.
- Generate the sounds from all letters including consonant blends and long vowel patterns. Blend those different sounds into recognizable words.
- Read common sight words.
- Read common word families.

44. **The best way for a teacher to track a student's progress in demonstrating the alphabetic principal/ graphophonemic awareness is to (Rigorous) (Skill 4.1)**

    A)   provide group assessments

    B)   maintain individual records

    C)   assess with standardized tests

    D)   have the student assessed by a team of teachers

The answer is B. The teacher will want to maintain individual records of children's reading behaviors demonstrating alphabetic principle/graphophonemic awareness.

45. **Environmental print is available at all of the following *except* (Easy) (Skill 4.2)**

    A) within a newspaper.

    B) on the page of a library book.

    C) on a supermarket circular.

    D) in a commercial flyer.

    The answer is B. Environmental print involves print from items such as signs, boxes, etc. Magazines and catalogues are another source of environmental print that is accessible with ads for child centered products. Supermarket circulars and coupons from the newspaper are also excellent for engaging children in using environmental print as reading, especially when combined with dramatic play centers or prop boxes.

46. **Book handling skills include ALL of the following *except* (Easy) (Skill 4.2)**

    A) putting a cellophane or plastic cover on a book.

    B) identifying the back cover of the book.

    C) reading the book jacket.

    D) reading dedication page and the title page of the book.

    The answer is A. As a student learns book handling they are learning the correct way to hold and read a book. This can include identifying book parts and special pages.

47. **The best way for a primary grade teacher to model directionality and one to one word matching would be (Easy) (Skill 4.2)**

    A)   using a regular library or classroom text book.

    B)   using her own person reading book.

    C)   using a big book.

    D)   using a book dummy.

    The answer is C. Teachers often use big books to model reading skills for children. Teaching directionality and one-to-one word matching are just two of the skills that can be taught.

48. **An effective way to build vocabulary and to make connections with mandated science and mathematics material is to teach Greek and Latin roots using (Average Rigor) (Skill 4.2)**

    A)   semantic maps.

    B)   hierarchical arrays.

    C)   linear arrays.

    D)   word webs.

    The answer is D. For example, during readings on rodents (a favorite of first and second graders), the teacher draws her class's attention to the fact that beavers, gnaw at things with their teeth. She then connects the "dent" root or derivative to the children's lives, other words they are familiar with or experiences. The children then volunteer "dentist," "dental," "denture." The teacher begins to place these in a graphic organizer, or word web.

49. **A district observer notes that fifth graders are showing younger peers in the third grade how to hold a book and walk around with it, they assume (Average Rigor) (Skill 4.2)**

    A) that the fifth graders are particularly theatrical.

    B) that the fifth graders are proud of how they read stories aloud.

    C) that the fifth graders are training the younger children in book holding.

    D) that this has nothing to do with instruction.

    The answer is C. Students often learn better from other students. It is important to provide opportunities for students of various ages or levels to work together to learn from each other.

50. **Dictionary study (Average Rigor) (Skill 4.3)**

    A) can begin in grades 1 or 2.

    B) can begin in pre-K using the lush picture dictionaries.

    C) should start on grade three level.

    D) Both A and B.

    The answer is D, Dictionary skills should be taught at an early age to assist students in discovering meaning of words. The use of a dictionary is often used to support the reading of a particular text.

51. Greg Ball went to an author signing where Faith Ringgold gave a talk about one of her many books. He was so inspired by her presence and by his reading of her book *Tar Beach* that he used the book for his reading and writing workshop activities. His supervisor wrote in his plan book, that he was pleased that Greg had used the book as an/a _____ book. (Average Rigor) (Skill 4.3)

    A) basic book.

    B) feature book.

    C) anchor book.

    D) focus book.

    The answer is C. *Anchor book* is a balanced literacy term for a book that is purposely read repeatedly and used as part of both the reading and writing workshop.

52. The work of Chard and Osborn (1999) in establishing guidelines for children with reading disabilities has shown that it is essential for them to (Rigorous) (Skill 4.3)

    A) Read wordless picture books.

    B) Learn at least 10 sight words.

    C) Work intensely on the alphabetic principle.

    D) Focus on using syntactic clues.

    The answer is C. David J. Chard and Jean Osborn (1999) have reflected on the guidelines necessary for teachers to use in selecting supplemental phonics and word-recognition materials for addressing students with learning disabilities. They note that an important way to help children with reading disabilities figure out the system underlying the printed word is leading them to understand the alphabetic principle.

53. **To decode is to (Easy) (Skill 5.1)**

   A)   construct meaning.

   B)   sound out a printed sequence of letters.

   C)   use a special code to decipher a message.

   D)   None of the above.

   The answer is B. To decode means to change communication signals into messages. Reading comprehension requires that the reader learn the code within which a message is written and be able to decode it to get the message.

54. **A theorist who believes that there is a finite body of approved literature children should be taught on various grade levels and has produced books about what everyone needs to know to be literate on various grade levels is (Rigorous) (Skill 5.1)**

   A)   Rudolf Flesch

   B)   J. David Cooper

   C)   John Dewey

   D)   E. D. Hirsch

   The answer is B. J. David Cooper (2004) and other advocates of the Balanced Literacy Approach, feel that children become literate, effective communicators and able to comprehend, by learning phonics and other aspects of word identification through the use of engaging reading texts. Engaging text, as defined by the balanced literacy group, are those texts which contain highly predictable elements of rhyme, sound patterns, and plot.

55. The science fair is coming up and Ms. Gardner is trying to find time in her busy schedule to work on her class's earth worm diary project. With all of the mandated tests and assemblies, she has not found time to start her students on their earth worm research. Within the context of reading instruction, she can (Rigorous) (Skill 5.1)

A) begin a thematic study unit.

B) start with a read aloud of the *Diary of an Earth Worm* by Doreen Cronin.

C) scaffold the research process by going online with her children using an approved search engine to find matches for earthworm sites.

D) All of the above.

The answer is D. Ms. Gardner can integrate the topic into various curriculum areas in order to prepare her students for the upcoming project such as in an integrated unit. Literature studies or read alouds can be selected to enhance units. Technology can be utilized to share more current resources and interactive sites.

56. The first grade class is on a neighborhood walk. As the children approach the neighborhood Kentucky Fried Chicken chain, Danny reads from the store window "Kentucky Fried Chicken Hot and Crunchy." Danny has never read or been taught to read this before. The most likely explanation for Danny's being able to read this is that he is (Easy) (Skill 5.2)

A) an advanced reader who is self improving.

B) his parents have taught him to read the signs and materials at the Kentucky Fried Chicken store.

C) he is in the logographic phrase of phonics learning.

D) this was just a lucky guess on his part.

The answer is C. Children recognize whole words that have significance for them such as their own names or the names of stores they frequent or products that their parents buy. Examples are McDonald's, SuperValu, and the like. Strategies which nurture development in this phase include explicit labeling of class room objects, components, furniture and materials and showing the children's names in print as often as possible.

57. **An observer enters Julia's first grade classroom. Children are working with oak tag strips and placing the word letters on these strips on a sentence strip holder. Then they seem to be involved in some kind of counting. The observer is confused. This activity is taking place during the reading block. Julia explains that (Average Rigor) (Skill 5.2)**

   A) the children are counting letters.

   B) this is word sorting and the children are grouping words by length, common letters and sound.

   C) the children are combining mathematics counting and word study.

   D) the children are doing a strategy sheet based on a particular word family

The answer is B. This activity allows children to focus closely on the specific features of words and to begin to understand the basic elements of letter sound relationships. Start with one syllable (monosyllabic) words. Have the children group them by their length, common letters, sound, and/or spelling pattern.

58. **Randy is proud of how many new vocabulary words he has learned. He enjoys playing with a device his teacher has, since it helps him to show all the words he can create from various letters. The device is a (Average Rigor) (Skill 5.2)**

   A) word strip.

   B) letter holder for making words.

   C) word mask.

   D) None of the above.

The answer is B. Through use of this letter holder, children can experience how letters can be rearranged, added, or removed to make new words. They can use these cards also to focus as needed on letter sequences and to support them in recognizing spelling patterns in words.

59. A natural role for a highly proficient reader would be (Average Rigor) (Skill 5.2)

   A)   to assist the teacher with cleaning the classroom and organizing the student
       folders.

   B)   to develop charts for the teacher by copying needed poems for full class study.

   C)   tutor and support struggling readers.

   D)   work on personal own interests while the teacher works with the rest of the class.

The answer is C. Highly proficient readers can sometimes support early readers through a partner relationship. Some children, particularly the emergent and beginning early readers, benefit from reading books with partners. The partners sit side by side and each one takes turns reading the entire text.

60. Margaret is the winning PS 123 orator. She loves reciting poetry by Shel Silverstein. Who would guess that she is also a poet in her first language? Margaret's first language is definitely (Average Rigor) (Skill 5.2)

   A)   English.

   B)   French.

   C)   Spanish.

   D)   not English.

The answer is D. When speaking of a child's first language, it involves another language besides English.

61. **The sequence of learning phonics skills includes (Rigorous) (Skill 5.2)**

    A) letter naming.

    B) letter sounds.

    C) variant vowels and diphthongs.

    D) All of the above.

    The answer is D. Here is the sequence of phonics skills
    - Letter Naming
    - Letter Sounds
    - Short Vowels in CVC Words
    - Short Vowels with Digraphs and Trigraphs (/tch/
    - Short Vowels and Consonant Blends
    - Long Vowels
    - Variant Vowels and Diphthongs
    - R- and L- Controlled Vowels
    - Multisyllabic Words

62. **Asking a child if what he or she has read makes sense to him or her, is prompting the child to use (Easy) (Skill 5.4)**

    A) phonics cues.

    B) syntactic cues.

    C) semantic cues.

    D) prior knowledge.

    The answer is C. Semantic cues—children use their prior knowledge, sense of the story, and pictures to support their predicting and confirming the meaning of the text.

63. "Ballgame" is a _____word. Its meaning is derived from the combination of "Ball" and "Game." (Easy) (Skill 5.4)

A) contraction

B) compound

C) portmanteau

D) palindrome

The answer is B. Compound words occur when two or more base words are connected to form a new word. The meaning of the new word is in some way connected with that of the base word. Examples are firefighter, newspaper, and pigtail.

64. Cues in reading are (Easy) (Skill 5.4)

A) vowel sounds.

B) digraphs.

C) sources of information used by readers to help them construct meaning.

D) None of the above.

The answer is C. Cuing systems assist readers to construct meaning. These include syntactic and semantic.

65. The word "bat" is a _____word for "batter-up." (Easy) (Skill 5.4)

   A) suffix

   B) prefix

   C) root word

   D) inflectional ending

The answer is C. This is a word from which another word is developed. The second word can be said to have its "root" in the first, such as *vis*, to see, in visor or vision.

66. A bound morpheme is (Average Rigor) Skill 5.4

   A) a prefix.

   B) a contraction.

   C) an inflectional ending that can be added to a base word to change its case, gender, number, tense or form.

   D) a root word.

The answer is C. Morphemes—the smallest units of meaning in words. There are two types of morphemes: free morphemes, which can stand alone such as love; and bound morphemes, which must be attached to another morpheme to carry meaning such as *-ed* in loved.

67. **A key theorist who supports a phonics centered approach is (Average Rigor) (Skill 5.4)**

   A)   Marie Clay.

   B)   Sharon Taberski.

   C)   Shelley Harwayne.

   D)   Rudolf Flesch.

The answer is D. Researchers, such as Flesch (1981), support a phonics-centered foundation before the use of engaging reading texts. This is at the crux of the phonics versus whole language/ balanced literacy/ integrated language arts, teaching of reading controversy.

68. **Children "own" words when all of the following happen *except* (Average Rigor) (Skill 5.4)**

   A)   they find these words on their own.

   B)   the teacher provides a mandated word list.

   C)   they use the words in their own writings.

   D)   the words appear in literature that interests them.

The answer is B. When students take ownership of words this generally means that the words are of special significance to the child. This could mean that they use the words frequently in their writing, they appear in favorite books, or they discover the words on their own.

69. **In order to get children to compile specialized vocabulary, they can use (Average Rigor) (Skill 5.4)**

    A)   newspapers.

    B)   Internet resources and approved web-sites that focus on the special interest.

    C)   experts they can interview.

    D)   All of the above.

    The answer is D. Vocabulary lists can be compiled from just about any source possible.

70. **When you ask a child if what he or she has just read "sounds right" to him or her, you are trying to get that child to use (Average Rigor) (Skill 5.4)**

    A)   phonics cues.

    B)   syntactic cues.

    C)   semantic cues.

    D)   prior knowledge.

    The answer is B. Syntactic cues use the order of words and the student's knowledge of the oral English language to help determine if what was read could be accurate.

71. **If children are engaged in creating a museum within classroom project to exhibit their work, they are (Average Rigor) (Skill 5.4)**

    A)   not doing any reading or writing.

    B)   doing many authentic reading, writing, and researching tasks.

    C)   not likely to visit a real museum.

    D)   All of the above.

    The answer is B. By creating a museum within the classroom students take ownership in the creation of their project. The project would generally involve a topic meaningful to the student. The student would be more motivated to create a quality product.

72. **A discussion circle can convene (Average Rigor) (Skill 5.4)**

    A)   after the children have finished reading a text as a group.

    B)   before the children read a text as a group.

    C)   While the reading of the text is going on.

    D)   All of the above.

    The answer is A. A discussion circle is an activity which fits nicely into the balanced literacy lesson format. After the children conclude a particular text, Cooper suggests that respond to the book in discussion circles. Among the prompts, the teacher-coach might suggest that the children focus on words of interest they encountered in the text. These can also be words that they heard if the text was read aloud. Children can be asked to share something funny or upsetting or unusual about the words they have read. Through this focus on children's response to words as the center of the discussion circle, peers become more interested in word study.

73. While the supervisor is pleased overall with Barbara's first year of teaching, he feels that given the fact that two of her students are transfers from Mexico and one student has a hearing impairment, she has to plan for (Rigorous) (Skill 5.4)

    A)   extra homework for all of them.

    B)   extra time for the hearing impaired child.

    C)   a buddy to work with the two students from Mexico.

    D)   differentiated instruction to meet these students varied special needs.

    The answer is D. In order for all students to be successful it is necessary for a teacher to assess each student to determine their current needs and the design instruction to meet the needs of the individual student. This is known as differentiating instruction.

74. Based on individual conferences with many children, the teacher realizes that although they are all self-improving readers, they need help in better use of the context to define words. The teacher decided to try the use of (Rigorous) (Skill 5.4)

    A)   a dictionary to look up words.

    B)   a thesaurus to use with the dictionary.

    C)   contextual redefinition training.

    D)   instruction in how to effectively use a dictionary.

    The answer is C. This strategy encourages children to use the context more effectively by presenting them with sufficient context before they begin reading. it models for the children the use of contextual clues to make informed guesses about word meanings.

75. **As Ms. Wolmark looks at the mandated vocabulary curriculum for the 6th grade, she notes that she can opt to teach foreign words and abbreviations which have become part of the English language. She decides (Rigorous) (Skill 5.4)**

A) to forego that since she is not a teacher of foreign language.

B) to teach only foreign words from the native language of her four ELL students.

C) to use the ELL students' native languages as a start for an extensive study of foreign language words.

D) to teach 2-3 foreign language words that are now in English and let it go at that.

The answer is C. Incorporating the native language of ELL students into instruction helps to form a bond between their native language and English. It also serves as a point of confidence that connects that student with the other students in the class.

76. **Structural analysis is (Rigorous) (Skill 5.4)**

A) the "sounding out" a printed sequence of letters based on knowledge of letter sound correspondences

B) when the teacher keeps a detailed recording of the errors or inaccurate attempts of a child reader during a reading assessment

C) the process of hearing a spoken word and identifying its separate phonemes or syllables.

D) the process of examining the words in the text for meaningful word units (affixes, base words, inflected endings).

The answer is D. Structural analysis of words as defined by J. David Cooper (2004) involves the study of significant word parts. This analysis can help the child with pronunciation and constructed meaning.

77. **Tim is not in the same ability group as his best friend Alex. He starts to cry even though he is a second grader. The teacher comforts him by telling him the truth that (Rigorous) (Skill 5.5)**

    A) he is just as smart as Alex.

    B) he can play with Alex during recess.

    C) ability groups change as the children's needs in them change during the year.

    D) Tim is smarter than his best friend Alex.

    The answer is C. Ability grouping is the grouping of children with similar needs for instructional purposes. Ability groups do not remain constant throughout the year, but change as the children's needs within them change.

78. **Two consonants placed together in a word to make a unique sound is a (Easy) (Skill 5.6)**

    A) consonant digraph

    B) consonant blend

    C) morpheme

    D) phoneme

    The answer is A. Consonant digraphs are two consonants of the English language which, when placed together in a word, make a unique sound neither makes when alone. Examples: ch, th, sh, and wh.

79. **Young children often spell words they write according to the way the letters sound. This is called (Easy) (Skill 6.1)**

    A) spelling lists

    B) incorrect spelling

    C) developmental spelling

    D) invented spelling

    The answer is D. Spelling is of utmost importance in the writing process. At first young children will use invented spelling in which they write the words according to letter sounds.

80. **The thirty-seven dependable spelling patterns called "rimes" were identified by (Rigorous) (Skill 6.2)**

    A) Calkins

    B) Wylie and Durrell

    C) Clay and Flesch

    D) Flesch

    The answer is B. Wylie and Durrell have identified spelling patterns that are in their classic thirty-seven "dependable" rimes.

81. **The best ways to select words students need to learn to spell include all of the following** *except* **(Rigorous) (Skill 6.2)**

A) misspelled words from student writing

B) lists of theme words

C) lists from a spelling textbook

D) lists of words from content areas

The answer is C. Some of the techniques teachers use to determine the words students need to spell include lists of misspelled words from student writing, lists of theme words, lists of words from the content areas, and word banks.

82. **Direct teaching of a concept or strategy means (Average Rigor) (Skill 6.3)**

A) the teacher teaches the concept or strategy as part of a genre lesson.

B) the teacher teaches the concept as part of the writing workshop.

C) the teacher explicitly announces to the class that this strategy will be taught.

D) the teacher teaches the strategy to a small group of children or to an individual child.

The answer is D. Direct teaching occurs when the teacher specifically teaches or explains a skill to a student or group of students.

83. **There are two basic types of text structure: (Easy) (Skill 7.1)**

    A) Fiction and non-fiction.

    B) Primary and pre-K.

    C) Expository and narrative.

    D) Wordless and text rich.

The answer is C. Expository text is non-fiction that provides information and facts. This text type is what newspapers, science, mathematics and history texts use. Currently there is much focus, even in elementary schools, on teaching children how to comprehend and author expository texts. They must produce brochures, guides, recipes, and procedural accounts on most elementary grade levels. The teaching of reading of expository texts requires working with a particular vocabulary and concept structure that is very different from that of the narrative text. Therefore time must be taken to teach the reading of expository texts and contrast it with the reading of narrative texts.

Narrative text tells or communicates a story. Narrative texts are novels, short stories and plays. Some poems are narratives as well. The narrative text needs to be taught differently than the expository text because of its structure.

84. **Vocabulary should be introduced after reading if (Average Rigor) (Skill 7.2)**

    A) The children have identified words from their reading which were difficult and which they need explained.

    B) The text is appropriate for vocabulary building.

    C) The teacher would like to teach vocabulary after the reading.

    D) A and B

The answer is D. Introduce vocabulary after reading if the children themselves have shared words which they found difficult or interesting, the children need to expand their vocabulary, or the text itself is one that is particularly suited for vocabulary building.

85. **A teacher discovers after considering his class's prior knowledge of the story material that he would need to teach 12 words at least before he starts teaching the story to the whole group. This indicates (Rigorous) (Skill 7.2)**

   A)   the children will need a read-aloud.

   B)   the children will need independent reading.

   C)   the children will need guided reading.

   D)   the children will need shared reading.

   The answer is C. Stories that include so many words to be taught may prove difficult for a student to read independently. They would need assistance in attacking these words. The best way to complete this lesson is through guided reading.

86. **Factors that affect the level of comprehension a student demonstrates when reading a story include all of the following *except* (Rigorous) (Skill 7.2)**

   A)   lack of background knowledge

   B)   inability to spell words correctly

   C)   lack of word recognition skills

   D)   inability to determine the meanings of words through context clues.

   The answer is B. Although spelling is an important skill for students to learn, it does not affect a student's level of comprehension.

87. **Teachers should select at least _____words for pre-reading vocabulary discussion. (Rigorous) (Skill 7.2)**

    A)   12.

    B)   15.

    C)   2-3.

    D)   8-10.

The answer is C. The number of words that require explicit teaching should only be two or three. If the number is higher than that, the children need guided reading and the text needs to be broken down into smaller sections for teaching. When broken down into smaller sections, each text section should only have two to three words which need explicit teaching.

88. **Two steps a teacher might take before selecting words for study are (Rigorous) (Skill 7.2)**

    A)   reading the story and story mapping.

    B)   asking advice from a veteran teacher and the grade leader.

    C)   looking in a teacher's guide and copying out the words listed there.

    D)   All of the above are correct.

The answer is D. It may be beneficial for a teacher to use all of these resources when planning reading instruction.

89. A second grader is writing his first book review. He has conferred with his teacher several times while he was writing the book review. Now he is rehearsing it with the teacher before he reads it aloud to the class. The child's learning of how to compose and deliver a book review has been   (Rigorous) (Skill 7.2)

    A)   done independently.

    B)   assisted by family support.

    C)   done in a cooperative group setting.

    D)   scaffolded by the teacher.

The answer is D. Scaffolding refers to the teacher support necessary for the child to accomplish a task or to achieve a goal which the child could not accomplish on his/her own. Vygotsky termed this window of opportunity the "zone of proximal development." Ultimately as the child becomes more proficient or capable, the scaffold is withdrawn. The goal of scaffolding is to help the child to perform the reading task independently and internalize the behavior. During shared reading, the task is scaffolded by the teacher's reading to the children aloud. As the teacher reads, the teacher scaffolds the initial decoding and helps with the meaning making/construction.

90. The concerned parent whose child had a visual impairment wanted as much help for him as the teacher and the school district could give her. She begged: "Please, he didn't attend pre-school; he has no prior knowledge." Strictly speaking this is (Rigorous) (Skill 7.2)

    A)   correct, since he didn't get pre-school experiences.

    B)   incorrect, since prior knowledge covers everyone's experiences.

    C)   Incorrect, since he did have prior knowledge experiences but these didn't match those of many of his peers, so he would need to enhance his prior knowledge.

    D)   Both B and C

The answer is D. All students have prior knowledge, but that knowledge may differ from that of their peers.

91. **A strategy is (Average Rigor) (Skill 7.4)**

    A)   a practice or routine the teacher can continually refer to.

    B)   a practice or routine a child can continually refer to or use.

    C)   a sheet or template for a practice the child can continually fill out.

    D)   All of the above.

    The answer is D. All of the above are types of strategies.

92. **Making inferences from the text means that the reader (Average Rigor) (Skill 7.4)**

    A)   is making informed judgments based on available evidence.

    B)   is making a guess based on prior experiences.

    C)   is making a guess based on what the reader would like to be true of the text.

    D)   All of the above.

    The answer is A. Inferencing is a process that involves the reader making a reasonable judgment based on the information given and engages children to literally construct meaning.

93. **The Stop and Think Strategy means that the child reader will (Average Rigor) (Skill 7.4)**

   A) read through until the end of the story or text.

   B) ask himself or herself if what he or she has read makes sense to him or her.

   C) stop after reading some text and write down his/her concerns.

   D) All of the above

   The answer is B. When a student is reading, it is helpful for them to periodically stop and question themselves to see if what they have just read makes sense.

94. **To help children with "main idea" questions, the teacher should (Rigorous) (Skill 7.4)**

   A) Give out a strategy sheet on the main idea for children to place in their reader's notebooks.

   B) Model responding to such a question as part of guided reading.

   C) Have children create "main idea questions" to go with their writings.

   D) All of the above.

   The answer is D. Identifying main ideas can be improved when the children have an explicit strategy for identifying important information. All of the above strategies can be beneficial in identifying the main idea.

95. **The five key strategies for a child reading of informational/ expository texts include (Rigorous) (Skill 7.4)**

    A)   identifying key information from the pictures or illustrations

    B)   having a plan for making sensible meaning from the passage

    C)   Looking for points of trivia within the text.

    D)   None of the above

The answer is B. Monitoring means self-clarifying: As a child reads, the reader often realizes that what he or she is reading is not making sense. The reader then has to have a plan for making sensible meaning out of the excerpt. Cooper and other balanced literacy advocates have a stop and think strategy which they use with children. The child reflects, "Does this make sense to me?" When the child concludes that it does not, the child then either re-reads, reads ahead in the text, looks up unknown words or asks for help from the teacher.

96. **The strategy in which a graphic organizer is used to help identify what students know, what they want to know, and what they learned is referred to as   (Easy) (Skill 7.5)**

    A)   a bubble map

    B)   a reading log

    C)   a K-W-L- chart

    D)   a Venn diagram

The answer is C. A K-W-L chart is a graphic organizer strategy which activates children's prior knowledge and also helps them to target their reading of expository texts. This focus is achieved through having the children reflect on three key questions

97. **When they are in 6th grade, children should be able to independently go through an unfamiliar collection and** (Average Rigor) (Skill 7.5)

    A) use only the table of contents.

    B) use the first line indices, and find a poem by author and subject.

    C) use only the glossary.

    D) None of the above.

    The answer is B. Standards require that a 6th grade student be able to complete the above task.

98. **One of the many ways in which a child can demonstrate comprehension of a story is by** (Average Rigor) (Skill 7.5)

    A) filling in a strategy sheet.

    B) retelling the story orally.

    C) retelling the story in writing.

    D) All of the above.

    The answer is D. All are examples of ways a child can demonstrate that they understand what they have read.

99. **A fifth grade teacher has subscribed to an online version of a local newspaper. She can help the students examine this resource and how it compares to the print version by noting the following differences. (Rigorous) (Skill 7.5)**

    A) Use of video to document events

    B) Use of sound clips in addition to written text

    C) Links to other web resources

    D) All of the above

    The answer is D. Online resources contain other forms of media that go beyond the printed word. Audio and video clips can be used to enhance the experience of the learner.

100. **Mark is a brand new teacher who is not from the neighborhood where his school is located. He is a bit nervous as this is his first teaching assignment. He does not yet know how to relax enough to get his students to activate prior experience. He should (Rigorous) (Skill 8.2)**

    A) try a free recall question: "Tell us what you know about..."

    B) try an unstructured question: "Let's talk about..."

    C) use word association: "What do you associate X with?"

    D) All of the above.

    The answer is B. An unstructured question is open-ended and can lead to great discussion. This type of question can also provide the teacher with more insight into the student's thoughts.

101. **Ms. Angel has to be certain that her fourth graders know the characteristics of the historical fiction genre. She can best support them in becoming comfortable with this genre by (Easy) (Skill 8.3)**

A) providing sequel and prequel writing opportunities using that genre.

B) reading them many different works from that genre.

C) Both A and B.

D) having them look up the definition of that genre in a literary encyclopedia.

The answer is C. When introducing genres such as historical fiction the teacher may connect it to a point in history with writing activities or by reading other books focused upon the same period.

102. **An excellent research project that can combine dictionary study with science research would be (Average Rigor) (Skill 9.2)**

A) a student-authored dictionary terms and phrases about earthworms.

B) a teacher-developed specialized dictionary of words and phrases about earthworms.

C) a collection of articles on earthworms put together by the school librarian.

D) Both B and C.

The answer is A. It is always more meaningful to students if they can take ownership of any part of their learning. A student-authored dictionary would include terms of interest to the student.

103. **Factual book features children should learn include (Average Rigor) (Skill 9.3)**

    A)   captions.

    B)   glossaries.

    C)   diagrams.

    D)   All of the above.

    The answer is D. Factual books may contain the items listed above as well as others. In order for students to successfully read factual books it is important that they learn to utilize various features.

104. **Teaching students how to set goals, modeling how to take notes, and how to create an outline are all examples of   (Rigorous) (Skill 9.3)**

    A)   study skills.

    B)   comprehension strategies.

    C)   read aloud strategies.

    D)   discussion skills.

    The answer is A. One of the most important ways of helping students experience success in school, especially with reading and studying in the content areas, is to teach them how to study. This involves such skills as how to take notes, summarize, find information in reference materials, and use maps and graphics. A fundamental part of teaching study skills also involves teaching students to set goals, organize their material, and manage their time.

105. **Historical fiction, mythology, folklore, realistic fiction, mystery, and legends are known as (Easy) (Skill 10.1)**

    A)   reading styles.

    B)   young adult topics.

    C)   genres.

    D)   booklists.

    The answer is C. A genre is a particular category of literature.

106. **Nonfiction genres include all of the following *except* (Easy) (Skill 10.1)**

    A)   essays

    B)   poetry

    C)   speech

    D)   biography

    The answer is B. Nonfiction genres include essays, narrative nonfiction, biography, speech, and autobiographies

107. **The Developing Readers Assessment System for leveling books was developed by** (Rigorous) (Skill 10.1)

A) Calkins and Clay

B) Fountas and Pinnell

C) Wylie and Durrell

D) Flesch and Clay

The answer is B. Fountas and Pinnell created a leveling system for books. Knowing these levels will be helpful in meeting the instructional needs of the students in a more efficient manner.

108. **Monthly book clubs, book fairs, read-a-thons, and the class library are all examples of** (Rigorous) (Skill 10.2)

A) ways to foster reading outside class.

B) ways to raise money for the school library.

C) ways to raise money for the classroom library.

D) None of the above.

The answer is A. Providing students with opportunities to read outside of class is a key component of reading success. These events allow students to build their own home libraries or to spend time reading with friends and family.

109. As Ms. Maxwell enters a first grade class, the teacher is busily writing down what the children are saying. The teacher is probably doing this to (Easy) (Skill 11.1)

A) demonstrate how to copy down speech.

B) make a connection and promote awareness of the relationship between spoken and written language.

C) authenticate the children's comments.

D) raise the children's self esteem.

The answer is B. By writing down what the children are saying, the teacher promotes the awareness of the relationship between the spoken and written word. Other strategies include:
- Reading together big-print and oversized books to teach print conventions such as directionality.
- Practicing how to handle a book: How to turn pages, to find the top and bottom of pages, and how to tell the difference between the front and back covers.
- Discussing and comparing with children the length, appearance and boundaries of specific words.

110. To encode means that you (Average Rigor) (Skill 11.1)

A) decode a second time.

B) construct meaning from a code.

C) tell someone a message.

D) None of the above.

The answer is B. Encode is to change a message into symbols. For example, readers encode oral language into writing.

111. **Author's viewpoint questions stump Gary. His teacher can help him by asking him during their reading conferences   (Average Rigor) (Skill 11.1)**

   A)   if Gary feels the book he is reading is right for him.

   B)   what the author would say about what the character is doing in the story.

   C)   how the story can be changed to another genre.

   D)   if Gary wants to read more books by this author.

   The answer is B. Author's viewpoint refers to what the author was thinking or feeling as they wrote the book. Questions may include: What do you think the author meant by having the character say that statement? (mediated scaffolding)

112. **Ms. Clark is seen by outside observers from her district, seated in front of her class of sixth graders with a notebook in her lap and an easel. She reads aloud from a book and then writes down a series of questions. As she reads along, she sometimes writes down the answers to her own questions. This is most likely   (Average Rigor) (Skill 11.2)**

   A)   a sign that Ms. Clark is uncertain of her own comprehension capacity.

   B)   she is modeling self questioning for the children.

   C)   she is aware that she is being watched and wants to make a good impression.

   D)   All of the above.

   The answer is B. One of the most effective ways to teach students how to use various strategies is through modeling.

113. **The stage at which average four and five year old children write letters backwards, upside down or create their own letters is called (Rigorous) (Skill 11.3)**

    A)   making invented spellings

    B)   making mock letters and words

    C)   creating developmental spelling

    D)   language development

    The answer is B. In the beginning phases of writing, students are trying to make sense of the letters and how they work together. Young children begin the writing process by making up their own letters and words in an attempt to write like their older counterparts.

114. **At a faculty meeting Ms. Riley found out that she might have crisscrossers in her class and that Mr. Brown had them and he was happy about it.   (Rigorous) (Skill 11.4)**

    A)   Crisscrossers are students who have skipped a grade.

    B)   Crisscrossers are students with excellent skills in reading and in Math.

    C)   Crisscrossers are second language learners who have a positive attitude toward first and second language l earning.

    D)   Crisscrossers are second language learners who are only positive about English Language Learning.

    The answer is: C. Crisscrossers is an ELL term for second language learners who have a positive attitude toward both first language and second language learning. These second language learners, children from ELL backgrounds, are comfortable navigating back and forth between the two languages as they learn.

115. The teacher is working on a life science unit in grade five and using many print and electronic sources for information. Some of these words have a linear and some of them a hierarchical relationship to one another. The teacher has spent much time explaining how the words connect with one another. At this point, it would be a good idea to (Rigorous) (Skill 12.2)

    A) use a root family diagram or tree.

    B) work with the base words.

    C) use hierarchical and linear arrays.

    D) start semantic mapping for a particular concept.

    The answer is C. Hierarchical and linear array vocabulary development strategies lend themselves well to support the struggling learners or second language learners. The use of the arrays allows these learners to use a visual format to "see" and diagram word relationships. Furthermore the diagrams are easy to make, and they can be illustrated.

116. A technique used after a story has been read. It includes identifying the main elements and categorizing the main events in sequential order. A graphic representation is often used to illustrate the story structure and sequence of events is called (Rigorous) (Skill 12.2)

    A) story mapping

    B) hierarchy organizer

    C) K-W-L chart

    D) Venn diagram

    The answer is A. Story mapping is a technique used after a story has been read. It includes identifying the main elements and categorizing the main events in sequential order. A graphic representation is often used to illustrate the story structure and sequence of events.

117. **Taking responsibility for a child's own learning will usually involve the child in   (Average Rigor) (Skill 12.3)**

    A)   reading and writing on his/her own.

    B)   developing a personal literacy project which will later be shared with the teacher and peers and family.

    C)   putting away books and materials when directed.

    D)   Both A and B.

    The answer is D. While keeping one's area neat and tidy is important, it does not directly engage students in taking responsibility for their own learning. When students are involved in they are able to select meaningful projects and take and active role in planning their leaning.

118. **If a student has a poor vocabulary, the teacher should recommend first that (Skill 13.1, Average Rigor)**

    A.   the student read newspapers, magazines and books on a regular basis.

    B.   the student enroll in a Latin class.

    C.   the student write the words repetitively after looking them up in the dictionary.

    D.   the student use a thesaurus to locate synonyms and incorporate them into his/her vocabulary

    The answer is A. It is up to the teacher to help the student choose reading material, but the student must be able to choose where to search for the reading pleasure indispensable for enriching vocabulary.

119. **The synonyms *gyro*, *hero*, and *submarine* reflect which influence on language usage? (Skill13.1 Average Rigor)**

    A. Social

    B. Geographical

    C. Historical

    D. Personal

    The answer is B. They are interchangeable but their use depends on the region of the United States, not on the social class of the speaker. Nor is there any historical context around any of them. The usage can be personal, but will most often vary with the region.

120. **Which aspect of language is innate? (Skill 13.1 Rigorous)**

    A. Biological capability to articulate sounds understood by other humans

    B. Cognitive ability to create syntactical structures

    C. Capacity for using semantics to convey meaning in a social environment

    D. Ability to vary inflections and accents

    The answer is A. A. Language ability is innate and the biological capability to produce sounds lets children learn semantics and syntactical structures through trial and error. Linguists agree that language is first a vocal system of word symbols that enable a human to communicate his/her feelings, thoughts, and desires to other human beings.

121. **The arrangement and relationship of words in sentences or sentence structures best describes** **(Skill 13.1, Rigorous)**

  A.   style.

  B.   discourse.

  C.   thesis.

  D.   syntax.

The answer is D. Syntax is the grammatical structure of sentences. Style is the manner of expression of writing or speaking. Discourse is an extended expression of thought through either oral or written communication. A thesis is the unifying main idea that can be either explicit or implicit.

122. **The teacher should choose words for pre-story discussion and exploration based on   (Average Rigor) (Skill 13.2)**

  A)   the teacher's interest.

  B)   whether the teacher feels the children have prior knowledge of or experience with the words.

  C)   a pre-existing grade level required vocabulary list.

  D)   words that will impress his or her supervisor.

The answer is B. It is up to the teacher to determine when vocabulary needs to be introduced. If vocabulary is selected to by introduced prior to reading the story it is generally done to assist students in developing prior knowledge.

123. **"Sounds right" can sound wrong to** (Rigorous) (Skill 13.2)

    A)   any reader who is not a fluent or early reader.

    B)   an ELL reader.

    C)   a struggling reader.

    D)   None of the above.

    The answer is B. The English language contains sounds that are not found in other languages and some letters have more than one sound. Because ELL students are not native to English then many of the words will not sound right.

124. **Maria was an outstanding student in her elementary school in Brazil. Now she is nervous about starting fourth grade in the US, although she learned English as a second language in Brazil. She and her parents should be relieved to know that** (Rigorous) (Skill 13.3)

    A)   she will get extra help in the United States with her English.

    B)   there is a positive and strong correlation between a child's native language and his/her learning of English.

    C)   her classmates will help her.

    D)   she will have a few months to study for the reading test.

    The answer is B. Students who have demonstrated highly proficient reading levels in their native language often demonstrate that same level of proficiency in the learning of English.

125. **A very bright child in a grade one class came from a family which did not a have a strong oral story telling or story reading tradition in its native language. This child would need support in developing (Rigorous) (Skill 13.3)**

A) letter-sound correspondence skills.

B) schemata for generic concepts most children have in their memories and experiences based on family oral traditions and read a loud.

C) oral expressiveness.

D) Both B and C.

The answer is B. Teacher educators should not approach the needs of ELL learners in reading the same as they do native speakers. Those children whose families are not from a focused oral literacy and reading culture in the native language will need additional oral language rhymes, read-alouds, and singing as supports for reading skills development in both their native and the English language.

Constructed Response Questions

Constructed Response Question One

Jean is a first-year teacher who is taking over the classroom of a thirty-year veteran teacher who is retiring. Jean goes in to meet with the teacher. The teacher, Ms. Banks, talks about the importance of teaching the young first graders the concepts of print.

She gives Jean a list of these concepts and suggests that Jean create some assessment format so that she can be certain that all of her first graders learn these concepts. She also tells Jean that she will be volunteering her time in a neighborhood preschool program close to her home and so she will be taking her private books and materials with her. She suggests that Jean go over the list of concepts of print and consider the needs of her class as she prepares for teaching this crucial set of skills. Before Jean leaves the classroom, Ms. Banks tells her that the kindergarten teacher has let her know that three children who will be in her class next year are from ELL backgrounds where their families are not involved in oral story telling or reading from native language texts.

Ms. Banks' concepts of print list:

- STARTS ON LEFT

- GOES FROM LEFT TO RIGHT

- RETURN SWEEP

- MATCHES WORDS BY POINTING

- POINTS TO JUST ONE WORD

- POINTS TO FIRST AND LAST WORD

- POINTS TO 1 LETTER

- POINTS TO FIRST AND LAST LETTER

- PARTS of the BOOK: Cover, Title Page, Dedication page, Author and Illustrator

Jean thanks Ms. Banks for all of this help and asks if she can send Ms. Banks some of her teaching ideas for Concepts of Print and the ways she plans to differentiate instruction for her ELL students before the end of the year. Ms. Banks smiles and says she feels good to know that her classroom will be taken over by Jean. She promises to review Jean's response.

Constructed Response Answer One

First, as far as assessment for the key skills of concepts of print, I have decided that it is very important that I have a record of when and how well each of my students masters these concepts. After much thought, I realized that I will be keeping assessment notebooks for all of my students as part of my general reading and teaching. Therefore, I plan to print out all the key concepts of print on an 8½" x 11" piece of paper in a grid format. This sheet will be included with other assessment grids for each individual child.

After conferencing with the child, I will determine the child has demonstrated mastery of a particular concept and check it off on the grid and date that mastery. If I have other comments to make about the child's level of mastery or fluency, I will make an anecdotal notation about the child as well. I think that this will guarantee that I have a detailed checklist record and anecdotal record of all my children's individual progress on concepts of print.

I plan to use big books and many of the latest picture books, including Caldecott-award winners in demonstrating and sharing with children many of the concepts of print. I will do much of my instruction mini-lessons. In fact I intend to use some of my own favorite alphabet books to introduce these conventions. With a book like Clare Beaton's *Zoe and her Zebra*, I can easily and naturally cover the title page, cover, illustrator, and also manage to engage the children in the use of repetitive language.

Once I have shared that delightful book with the children as a read-aloud, we will be able to return to it again and use the repetitive language of it in its big book format to demonstrate for the children how they can point under each word as if there is a button to push. I can also demonstrate for the children how they should start at the top of the text and move from left to right. I will model going back to the left and under the previous line in a return sweep.

After modeling this as part of the mini-lesson, the children can be divided in small groups or pairs and take other big book and practice the "point under each word" and the "return sweep" as part of "shared reading" or buddy reading. I should be able to identify some highly proficient readers who will be happy to serve as 'buddy" reader/tutors for the ELL children. I will ask that these buddies take time in small groups to work on another book from the alphabet book collection to share with the class as a whole. The use of the alphabet books also helps me to get some time in on the alphabetic principle.

I will also do a classroom writing workshop using the original alphabet book I use for the read-aloud, say *Zoe and Her Zebra* as a model for creating our own story. Perhaps we will call it *Barry and His Boxer*. In this way we will have a concrete literary product that demonstrates the children's mastery of and fluency in the concepts of print as they create an "in style of" story about a peer using illustrations, title page, dedication page, numbering of pages, back and front cover and other concepts of print.

I think that using individualized assessments, a group/class collaborative writing project, and an anchor alphabet book will help me successfully teach the concepts of print and address the needs of my ELL learners as well.

Constructed Response Question Two

Marianne has been selected as one of a team of teachers who will start teaching in a brand new school building that has been under construction for several years. While Marianne, a grade three teacher, is thrilled to be moving into new facilities, she is a bit overwhelmed to have to "set up her room" all over again at the new site. Her administrator Mr. Adams tells her that there are five new teachers with no previous experience teaching primary school age children who will be on staff. He tells her that these educators could really use help setting up their classrooms.

Marianne smiles and decides that she would very much like to use her set-up of her own grade three classroom as a workshop and demonstration for setting up a literacy teaching environment for these new staff members. Mr. Adams thinks that is a great idea and asks Marianne for an agenda and for a general description of what she will cover in her three-hour workshop so that he can give it to the district office.

Marianne is happy to comply because she realizes that she will be assisting new colleagues and getting ten helping hands to help her set up all the materials she has accumulated over a twenty-year career.

Constructed Response Answer Two

The concept of sharing with new colleagues how to set up a classroom is very exciting to me. I know, based on my experiences, how crucial a well-planned and conceptualized space is for young learners' literacy learning. Therefore this is an agenda for what I will cover in my three-hour in-service session for my new colleagues.

First, I will discuss how, whatever the size of the classroom space, it must be sectioned off into the following areas: a meeting area, with a sofa or "soft" setting; a chair, easel and basket to store book bags; a conference table; children's tables; and bin/basket main area for trade books; and another space for computers.

I may even give out a diagram of my classroom from my old school and some pictures. We will discuss collaboratively how I will set up my own new space as well as how they will want to set up their own spaces to allow for different uses of space within their own classrooms.

I will get into the issue of whether or not they want to have a traditional desk or use smaller tables for everyone. I think that they will need time to consider their own teaching styles in this regard. All teachers need to set up a space where they can easily confer with children and have access to individual assessment notebooks, reading folders (plus poetry/spelling, reading response, and handwriting notebooks) for all their students. I intend to show them how to prepare these folders for each child and how to store them so they can get to them when they need to make additional annotations for each child. Given the fact that I am working with new colleagues, I suspect that this will take at least an hour and a half of our time. I am also going to model for them a weekly reading log.

Most important of all, I am going to spend the major amount of time talking to them about the book bins as I place mine around the classroom. I will show them how to label the books using the Fountas and Pinnell levels and how to arrange the book bins with the spines out so that the children can see the books. Together we will examine how the bookcases should be close to the walls and the expository books should be separated from the narrative texts. I will also get together my audio-cassettes and book sets so that they can see how I set up my read-along center for all my children. I will share some dual language tapes I use with ELL students as well. I have some extra "author's hats" and author's chair slipcovers I will share with them.

I also intend to show them how to select big books for the easel display and anchor books to be shown there as well. By the way, I will also coach them how to write away for supplies and how to store supplies in common areas so that some children are not missing necessary materials for class activities.

Even though we are focusing on literacy, I am going to show them where to store mathematics materials, other texts, and art supplies. I will end the session by making sure that they know where to place their chart wall and the word wall. If I have time, I will sit down with each of them and start them on the word wall and some key charts for their first day. They will leave my room with an actual experience of setting up a literacy environment, plus viable teaching and reading suggestions for the first day. Most importantly, I will be available for an in-school classroom consultation, if necessary.

Tips and Reflections
for Tackling the Constructed Response Questions:

- Use as many phrases and words from the question as possible in your response.

- Be specific. Mention specific books, authors, theorists, and strategies you have studied. Even though this is a test about the teaching of reading, make specific use of children's trade books and literature if appropriate.

- Use as many details as you are given in the question to make your response. Write no more than 5-7 moderately brief paragraphs. The more you write, the larger the margin for error. Check your spelling and grammar, and check to see that you answered everything that was asked, but no more than what was asked. Be positive and proactive about your ability to respond to whichever situation is presented.

- Stick with strategies, teaching ideas, and methods that are tried and true.

- Reread your writing at least twice for spelling and grammatical errors.

XAMonline, INC. 21 Orient Ave. Melrose, MA 02176

Toll Free number 800-509-4128

TO ORDER Fax 781-662-9268 OR www.XAMonline.com

CALIFORNIA SUBJECT EXAMINATIONS - CSET - 2008

PO#   Store/School:

Address 1:

Address 2 (Ship to other):

City, State Zip

Credit card number_____-_____-_____-_____   expiration_____

EMAIL _____

PHONE   **FAX**

ISBN	TITLE	Qty	Retail	Total
978-1-58197-595-6	RICA Reading Instruction Competence Assessment			
978-1-58197-596-3	CBEST CA Basic Educational Skills			
978-1-58197-901-5	CSET French Sample Test 149, 150			
978-1-58197-622-9	CSET Spanish 145, 146, 147			
978-1-58197-803-2	CSET MSAT Multiple Subject 101, 102, 103			
978-1-58197-261-0	CSET English 105, 106, 107			
978-1-58197-608-3	CSET Foundational-Level Mathematics 110, 111			
978-1-58197-285-6	CSET Mathematics 110, 111, 112			
978-1-58197-340-2	CSET Social Science 114, 115			
978-1-58197-342-6	CSET General Science 118, 119			
978-1-58197-809-4	CSET Biology-Life Science 120, 124			
978-1-58197-395-2	CSET Chemistry 121, 125			
978-1-58197-571-0	CSET Earth and Planetary Science 122, 126			
978-1-58197-817-9	CSET Physics 123, 127			
978-1-58197-299-3	CSET Physical Education, 129, 130, 131			
978-1-58197-813-1	CSET Art Sample Subtest 140			
			SUBTOTAL	
			Ship	$8.70
			TOTAL	